Editors' Corner

Constance M. Arzigian, Katherine P. Stevenson, and Vicki L. Twinde-Javner

This issue reflects the diversity of our archaeological discipline. Two articles report on experimental projects to help understand the manufacture of special items, including native copper artifacts, and pendants made by Native Americans from European trade beads. The long history of our discipline in Wisconsin is reflected in the documentation of a beautiful birdstone that was first reported in 1909, the description of 1960s fieldwork at Preston Rockshelter, and the publication of a report first drafted in the 1980s on rice rats and climate change. We are pleased to be making this information more widely available. Reflecting current research, we have a new synthesis on the occurrence and significance of mounds in Oneota contexts. Last, but certainly not least, a number of Wisconsin archaeologists received awards in 2016 for their contributions, and we share their accomplishments.

We received a number of comments from people concerning an article in the last issue on culturally modified trees, and we would like to continue this dialogue. See the "Proposal for a Forum" to learn how to share your ideas.

We want to thank those who have served as peer reviewers for the journal, providing invaluable specialized expertise and critical review of the contents. If you are willing to add your name to our list of potential peer reviewers, just let the editors know. Also, let us know if there is a book you'd like to see reviewed (or send us your review).

Finally, we are pleased to remind you that the digital archives collection of *The Wisconsin Archeologist* from 1901 to 2010 (110 years!) is available for purchase from the Wisconsin Archeological Society website. The collection is fully searchable, with PDFs of each article. It is available on a USB drive at a cost of $100 for the archives, plus $10 for the USB drive and postage. If you just want to purchase an update to the first archives (which extended to 1981), the cost is only $30 plus $10 for USB drive and shipping.

As always, we welcome your input and support!

*Connie Arzigian, Kathy Stevenson, and Vicki
   Twinde-Javner*
Mississippi Valley Archaeology Center
University of Wisconsin–La Crosse

---

*Constance M. Arzigian, Katherine P. Stevenson, and Vicki L. Twinde-Javner, Mississippi Valley Archaeology Center,
University of Wisconsin–La Crosse*

The Wisconsin Archeologist, 2016, 97(2):3

Culturally Modified Trees—Questions, Data, and Ideas: A Proposal for a Forum

Robert Sasso

Proposal

The recent publication of "History and Analysis of Wisconsin Culturally Modified Trees" by Wisconsin Archeological Society (WAS) member David J. Tovar in *The Wisconsin Archeologist* (Volume 97[1]:53–83) has generated a great response from the WAS membership. In light of this, the Society wishes to provide an opportunity for further discussion of this topic through an informal poster-style forum to be held at the Fall 2017 WAS meeting, scheduled for Saturday, September 30 at Beloit College.

We hope that Society members will bring images of potentially culturally modified trees of which they are aware, as well as any pertinent information they wish to share about them (location, age and/or size, nature of modification, etc.) and any ideas regarding their interpretation. Likewise, we hope that anyone interested in the structure and form of trees, how they grow under variable conditions of physical stress, natural and human sources of modification, or related topics also will wish to participate. For those wishing to contribute but unable to attend, we encourage you to submit any information and/or materials to the forum session organizer, below. We plan to assemble selected contributions for publication in an upcoming volume of *The Wisconsin Archeologist*.

If you are interested in participating in the poster forum or submitting materials or information, or syou imply wish to be kept informed about the topic, please email me at sasso@uwp.edu or contact me at the following address:

Dr. Robert Sasso
Department of Sociology and Anthropology
University of Wisconsin-Parkside
900 Wood Road, Box 2000
Kenosha, WI 53141-2000

Images: Mid-nineteenth century drawings of two culturally modified trees, one older (top), the other a sapling (left), included in Increase Lapham's unpublished field notes and dated May 30, 1850. These were drawn during a visit to the Burlington area on the Fox River in western Racine County (redrafted by Sasso, 2017).

The Catfish Creek Birdstone, Dane County, Wisconsin

James Beer

Charles E. Brown, Secretary of the Wisconsin Archeological Society, published his "Birdstone Ceremonials of Wisconsin" in *The Wisconsin Archeologist* in January of 1909. The front cover of his report had three Wisconsin hardstone birds on it: the Ozaukee County Birdstone (JRB 2) (Beer 2003); the Dane County Birdstone made of steatite (JRB 27); and a Menominee, Waukesha County, birdstone made of porphyry and with several inclusions or tally marks at the back of its neck. The current location of this third birdstone is unknown to the author of this article.

The Dane County Birdstone (JRB 27) arrived in Monroe, Wisconsin, on January 8, 2016, and is the fourteenth Wisconsin birdstone in the Beer Collection, and the twenty-seventh birdstone overall (Beer 2003, 2012, 2014, 2015). It is shown in Figure 1. When it was in the Joseph F. Ringeisen Jr. collection, it was his Number 4 birdstone, and he described it in his records as follows:

> Round button eyes, found by a farmer on Catfish Creek, in Dunkirk Township, Dane County, Wisconsin and sold to G.R. Moore, a dealer in antiquities who sold it to William H. Ellsworth, a prominent collector of Indian Relics of Milwaukee, Wisconsin from whom I bought it from him in 1906.

This shiny black steatite birdstone has an upturned beak that is squared off at its end, and has a deep undercut jaw with rounded eyes mounted on short stalks. The tip of the tail turns upwards and has an attachment groove located on it. The birdstone sits

Figure 1. The Catfish Creek Birdstone.

James Beer, Green County, Wisconsin

on two bars, one fore and one aft; they are square on the bottom, but are unperforated. The stone is only $2\,{}^{5}/_{8}$ inches long.

Brown (1909:9, Figure 22) shows a birdstone almost identical in shape to this Dane County birdstone. That one was made of porphyry and was once in the Smithsonian Institution; it then traveled to the Earl Townsend Jr. Collection and is considered to be the finest birdstone in private hands. Brown (1909:19) describes the other birdstone and compares it to the current specimen:

> The curious little bird stone captured in Fig. 22 (Plate 9) comes from Vernon County, and is in the U.S. National Museum. It is reported to be made of granite. In the Ringeisen cabinet is a specimen of almost identical form. It is shown in our frontispiece.

Joseph F. Ringeisen Jr. (Koup 1995) sold his entire collection to Dr. T. Hugh Young of Nashville, Tennessee (Young 1949; more examples of birdstones are in Young 1982–1983). Young then passed the Dane County birdstone on to J. Clemens Caldwell of Danville, Kentucky (Caldwell No. B:23). The Dane County Bird was the last birdstone sold from the J. Clemens Caldwell collection; Phillip Foley acquired it, and shortly thereafter sold it to Attorney Oliver Skrivanie of Fish Creek, Wisconsin (Skrivanie 1990). It is reported that when the birdstone was found, it was covered with red ocher (see Ritzenthaler and Quimby 1962 for discussion on the Red Ocher culture). However upon examination, it is impossible to see any red ocher now, as the birdstone has been handled by humans since its recovery over one hundred years ago.

This birdstone was previously published in:

- 1909: The Birdstone Ceremonials of Wisconsin, *The Wisconsin Archeologist*, Brown (1909), Vol. 8(1):Frontispiece; Plate 9, drawing #22

- 1959: *Birdstones of the North American Indian*, Earl C. Townsend, Jr. (1959:678–679)

- 1985: *The Fluted Axe*, Highsmith (1985:72)

- 2000: *Legends of Prehistoric Art*, Vol. 1, Bobby Onken (2000:245)

- 2009: *Prehistoric American*, Vol. 43(4), Ringeisen Chart on pg. 60-61, No. 13 on chart

References Cited

Beer, James R.
2003   Ozaukee County Birdstone Stays Home in Wisconsin. *Central States Archaeological Journal* 50(1):39.
2012   The Birdstone Collection of James R. Beer. *The Wisconsin Archeologist* 93(2):108–111.
2014   A Black Porphyry Birdstone from Winnebago County, Wisconsin. *The Wisconsin Archeologist* 95(1):4.
2015   Two Elongated Slate Wisconsin Birdstones. *The Wisconsin Archeologist* 96(1):73–77.

Brown, Charles E.
1909   The Bird-Stone Ceremonials of Wisconsin. *The Wisconsin Archeologist* (o.s.) 8(1):1–21.

Highsmith, Gale V.
1985   *The Fluted Axe*. G. V. Highsmith, Milwaukee.

Koup, Bill
1995   The Joseph Ringeisen, Jr. Birdstone Collection, Part II. *Prehistoric American* 29:9.

Onken, Bobby
2000   *Legends of Prehistoric Art*, Vol. 1. Hynek Printing, Richland Center, Wisconsin.

Prehistoric American
2009   Ringeisen Birdstone Chart No. 4. *Prehistoric American* 43(4):60–61.

Ritzenthaler, Robert E., and George I. Quimby
1962   The Red Ocher Culture of the Upper Great Lakes and Adjacent Areas. *Fieldiana Anthropology* 36(11):243–275.

Skrivanie, Oliver
1990   Photos of Skrivanie Visit to J. Clemens Caldwell Collection.

Townsend, Earl C., Jr.
1959   *Birdstones of the North American Indian: A Study of These Most Interesting Stone Forms, the Area of Their Distribution, Their Cultural Provenience, Possible Uses, and Antiquity*. Duke University Press, Durham, North Carolina.

Young, T. Hugh, M.D.
1949   Birds Go South in Winter. *Journal of the Illinois State Archeological Society* 6(4):11.
1982–1983 *Prehistoric Art-Archaeology* 1983, 17(4) and 19(1), Birdstone Specialized Issue.

Experimental Archaeology and Native Copper: Metallographic Analysis of Cold Forging Versus Hot Forging

Sara Crook

Abstract

Native copper has been used for millennia in the Midwest, but specific manufacturing methods are not well known. Experiments and metallographic analysis of native copper were undertaken, which documented consistent differences in the grain structure of cold forged versus hot forged specimens. These differences can only be observed in specimens left in a worked state. Once specimens of cold or hot forging are re-annealed, the grain structures become too similar to distinguish a specific type of manufacturing process. The reference set created through these experiments may be used for comparative analysis of copper artifacts from the Old Copper Complex, in order to make inferences regarding what types of manufacturing techniques were employed by ancient coppersmiths of the Archaic period in the Midwestern United States.

Introduction

The significance of native copper deposits in the Lake Superior region of North America has long been established. These large copper deposits have been used for approximately the last 7,000 years (Levine 2007), beginning at least by the Middle Archaic period around 5000 B.P. (Theler and Boszhardt 2003). Copper was mainly manufactured into a variety of utilitarian tools and was used by many different groups living in and around the region (Vernon 1990:499). For this reason, copper artifacts from the Middle Archaic period are not usually attributed to a single culture. Instead, the term Old Copper Complex is used to describe the mining, manufacturing, trading, and use of copper that thrived until the beginning of the Late Archaic period around 3000 B.P. (Vernon 1990).

Existing literature on native copper artifacts from the Old Copper Complex has often addressed the question of whether or not hot forging techniques were being employed by ancient coppersmiths (Clark and Purdy 1982; Ehrhardt 2009; LaRonge 2001; Martin 1999; Peterson 2003, 2004; Schroeder and Ruhl 1968; Vernon 1990; Wilson and Sayre 1935). This question inspired me to design and carry out an experimental archaeology and metallographic analysis project; the methods, results, and conclusions are described in this paper. The research goal was to create a reference set of native copper forged with a variety of techniques to be used in the comparative analysis of copper artifacts from the Old Copper Complex.

The creation and analysis of the reference set has shown a consistent difference in the grain structure of cold forged, hot forged, and combination forged specimens. These differences can only be observed in specimens left in a worked state. Once specimens were re-annealed, the grain structures became too similar to distinguish a specific type of manufacturing process. The reference set created through these experiments may be used to make inferences regarding the types of manufacturing techniques employed by ancient coppersmiths.

Background

Old Copper Complex Sites and Mining Techniques

The Middle Archaic bands in the Great Lakes region were the first people to quarry and use native copper to make utilitarian objects. Quarries existed mainly in the Lake Superior region, with particularly

Sara Crook, La Crosse, Wisconsin

The Wisconsin Archeologist, 2016, 97(2):9–27

important large copper mines on the Keweenaw Peninsula and Isle Royale; these quarries provided large quantities of raw material for ancient coppersmiths. Another source of native copper is known as "float copper," which can be found in the form of nuggets carried from their original sources by glacial ice sheets (Gibbon 1998). Some scholars argue that float copper may have been the earliest source used by Archaic peoples (Ehrhardt 2009; Pleger 2000).

Archaeological sites of the Old Copper Complex have not been found in abundance, and only a handful of excavated sites have been researched and published. The Osceola, Oconto, and Reigh sites are primarily cemeteries and have been essential to the study of the Old Copper Complex because of the existence of copper objects as burial goods (Wittry and Ritzenthaler 1956). However, the vast majority of Old Copper Complex artifacts have been surface finds and therefore have little to no archaeological context (Fregni 2009).

The Osceola site (47GT24) is located along the banks of the Mississippi River where it converges with the Grant River in Grant County, Wisconsin. The site was discovered in 1945 (Wittry and Ritzenthaler 1956). Radiocarbon dates from the site range from around 4130 to 3500 B.P. (Theler and Boszhardt 2003). When occupied, the site was not located directly on the bank of the river; however, the building of a dam in Dubuque, Iowa, changed the flow of the river and exposed the site by erosion (Wittry and Ritzenthaler 1956). Archaeologists cannot be sure how many burials originally existed at the site because a portion of it was washed away by the river, but they have estimated that there might have been five hundred burials (Wittry and Ritzenthaler 1956:244). Robert Ritzenthaler excavated the remaining burials in 1945 to recover as many as possible before the site was entirely destroyed. Burials were predominantly secondary bundles, some of which also had evidence of cremation. They had been placed either individually or in groups of two or three. As excavation proceeded, it became apparent that remains had not all been buried at once; instead, evidence suggested that the cemetery had been used for a period of time (Wittry and Ritzenthaler 1956:244). Most copper and stone artifacts did not appear to have been directly associated with specific burials, but were found concentrated in the center of the burial area (Wittry and Ritzenthaler 1956:245). Three burials had been covered with a layer of small stones at the time of burial (Wittry and Ritzenthaler 1956:244), an unusual burial practice for the Old Copper Complex.

Copper artifacts found at Osceola consisted of a variety of implements such as "awls (most common), socketed spuds, socketed projectile points, a knife, and ornamental forms" (Wittry and Ritzenthaler 1956:245). The ornamental objects included a variety of rolled copper beads, finger rings, a bracelet, a small clasp, and an ornamental hook (Wittry and Ritzenthaler 1956:245).

The Oconto site (47OC45) in Oconto County, Wisconsin, was excavated by Ritzenthaler and Warren Wittry in 1952. More recent AMS radiocarbon dates place the site between 4000 and 3000 B.C. (Pleger 2000:174). Quarrying had destroyed a portion of this site before excavation. Pleger (2000) wrote that the excavators estimated the cemetery may have contained up to two hundred burials prior to the damages; 53 burials were excavated. Only 12 of these individuals were buried with grave goods, and the age and sex of these individuals varied, leading archaeologists to believe that the inhabitants of this site lived in an egalitarian society (Pleger 2000). A variety of burial styles were used, including primary, primary flexed, and secondary bundle burials, some of which were cremated (Pleger 2000:175).

Burial goods from the Oconto site consisted of stone, copper, and bone artifacts. Copper artifacts included projectile points, awls, fish hooks, one spiral piece of copper, spatulas, crescent knives, and a bracelet. Other artifacts found in association with burials included chert scrapers, projectile points, and a whistle made from a swan bone (Pleger 2000).

Unlike the Osceola site, Oconto did have some signs of possible habitation, based on five to eight post holes that were identified and thought to have been part of an oval structure around thirteen feet in width (Wittry and Ritzenthaler 1956:245). It is hard to say how often this structure had been used or inhabited, or to discern its purpose.

The third burial site, Reigh (47WN1), is located on Lake Butte des Morts in Winnebago County, Wisconsin. The site dates to approximately 1700 B.C., overlapping the transition from the Archaic to the Early Woodland period (Fregni 2009:123), thus providing information on cultural changes over time. The Reigh site produced more copper objects than Osceola or Oconto. The "ace of spades" point type was discovered here, along with beads, and a headdress made of copper strips (Fregni 2009). The discovery of more elaborate ornamental objects may represent the beginning of a transition in copper use.

Binford (1962) discussed this transition from utilitarian to nonutilitarian usage and attributed it to the early use of ornamental objects as status markers. Populations were growing during the transition from the Archaic to the Woodland periods, and Binford (1962) argued that people started using status markers because the larger populations made it impossible

to know everyone personally. These utilitarian and ornamental copper objects would have allowed anyone to know the status an individual had achieved simply by looking at them. Another important factor to consider is the time commitment required to create copper objects, whether for tool or ornamental use. Stone tools could be made more quickly than copper and were just as, if not more, effective (Binford 1962). Over time people started to make copper predominantly into ornamental objects and returned to making most tools out of stone because of time commitments and effectiveness. The creation of ornamental objects appears to have become common practice by the Early to Middle Woodland periods (Binford 1962).

Archaeometallurgy technologies have allowed archaeologists to track the source of copper used to create tools from the Old Copper Complex. This method, known as Trace Elemental Analysis, can indicate the exact elemental composition of a copper artifact. With this information one can compare the elemental composition of an artifact with that of copper from known mining sites, and in some cases can confirm where the raw copper was originally mined (Fregni 2009). The mining sites that appear to be associated with the Old Copper Complex include surface quarries on Isle Royale and the Keweenaw Peninsula in Michigan, and the Brule River in northeast Wisconsin (Fregni 2009). Copper from Isle Royale and the Keweenaw Peninsula are identifiable by the inclusions of "silver and a distinct parallel grain on the long axis" (Fregni 2009:123). Mining sites are very important for understanding the ways in which copper was removed from the bedrock. Unfortunately, many of them have been destroyed by modern mining industries, leaving few opportunities to learn more about the process.

Mining techniques were discussed by William H. Holmes (1901) in a publication written shortly after excavations of the ancient mines on Isle Royale. The large number of hammerstones scattered around the ancient mines was an indication of their importance as mining tools. A polished band around the center of many hammerstones was interpreted by Holmes (1901:694) to be evidence of hafting. These stones were described by Holmes (1901:692) as "varying from three to twelve inches in length and from an inch to eight inches in diameter, a few specimens reaching a weight of perhaps sixty pounds." Copper could not be broken or cut from the bedrock. Instead, people would have crushed the rock with hammerstones until it broke free (Holmes 1901). It is likely that wood and bone tools were also used at the mines, and could have been formed into ideal wedges to be hit with hammerstones, allowing stone and copper to be removed at a faster pace. Fires were built beside the bedrock to weaken the rock and make it easier to break away. Ancient miners also used water to douse the hot rocks, causing cracking in the bedrock due to rapid temperature change (Fregni 2009; Holmes 1901). Fires have also proved important because the resulting charcoal can be used for radiocarbon dating. Without this organic material it would be very hard to establish dates for these ancient mines.

Holmes (1901) was able to determine that very little tunneling took place at the mines of Isle Royale. Instead, large pits were formed as the copper was removed; one that Holmes excavated (1901:690) was about ten feet deep and twenty feet in diameter. Pits appeared to have been worked until they no longer produced copper. Once exhausted of copper, the pits appear to have been used as dumping grounds for unwanted rock and broken hammerstones (Holmes 1901). Holmes also observed that there was no evidence for copper shaping on the island. Instead he concluded that "it seems … more likely that the pieces of metal obtained were carried away to distant centers of population to be worked up by skilled local artisans, and we may fairly assume that a considerable trade existed in the raw material" (Holmes 1901:695).

Thus, there is considerable evidence of the use of native copper by Archaic and Woodland populations, and some information on how the raw copper was obtained. Metalworking methods, however, have been harder to reconstruct from the archaeological record alone. Experimental archaeology has been undertaken to help fill this gap.

Copper Structure and Terminology

Forging was defined by LaRonge (2001:373) as "the percussive movement of metal by a hammer as it compresses metal against an anvil face… to move material in a controlled direction without the removal of material," so as to, for example, spread or taper a piece of copper. Hammering, on the other hand, is a term that indicates reoccurring blows in the same location, often to remove material, as done with lithic technologies (La Ronge 2001). For the purposes of this paper, cold forging is the term used to describe copper that has only been forged at ambient temperatures, and the term hot forging indicates copper forged while in a red-hot state.

Annealing is the process of heating metal to a temperature that accelerates the "movement of atoms and the subsequent recrystallization" (McCreight 2004:3). As stated by Wilson and Sayre (1935:111), annealing "causes the crystal units to group themselves once more into equiaxed grains, and further annealing produces the phenomenon of absorption of one grain by another, resulting in grain growth." The extent

of annealing is dependent upon two main variables, temperature and time. Vernon (1990:502) notes that recrystallization is also affected by "the degree of prior cold working . . . and impurities in the metal." While recrystallization of copper can occur at any temperature, the time required decreases as temperature increases. Clark and Purdy (1982:54) concluded that 99.98 percent pure copper would require a recrystallization period of "greater than 100,000 years at 25°C." Their work has shown that copper artifacts from the Old Copper Complex would not have been deposited in the archaeological record for a long enough time for substantial recrystallization to occur. For this reason we can conclude that any artifacts exhibiting evidence of annealing processes were most likely intentionally heat treated by their creators.

Copper is composed of face-centered cubic crystal units (Vernon 1990:500). During the process of solidification, crystal units align, forming grains. While crystal units within each individual grain are oriented in the same direction, crystal units in adjacent grains are not, creating irregularities known as vacancies or dislocations along grain boundaries (McCreight 2004; Vernon 1990). These vacancies, as well as shearing along one or more of the 12 slip systems within crystal units, contribute to malleability and allow plastic deformation to occur during the forging process (Vernon 1990). As the metal is worked, grains are broken up into smaller grains, creating more grain boundaries and vacancies. Plastic deformation of individual grains minimizes the size of vacancies and reduces malleability, resulting in a work-hardened metal (McCreight 2004). Continuing to forge copper in a work-hardened state will cause the metal to fracture. Archaic coppersmiths must have been aware that heat treating, or annealing, would increase malleability and, in return, allow for further manipulation.

To analyze the grain structure of native copper one must have a basic understanding of the structural phenomenon of twins. According to Maddin et al. (1980:216) twins are

> Metallographic features which appear as parallel bands within a single grain [and] are perhaps the most distinctive indication of native copper. Although twins are always present in cold hammered and recrystallized copper . . . the twins in unworked native copper are generally longer and thinner.

Primary growth twins are those that are formed during recrystallization, and mechanical twins are those formed by cold deformation through the application of physical stress (Rostoker and Dvorak 1965; Vernon 1990). The shape, size, and level of plastic

deformation exhibited in twins can be used to infer the physical alterations to which native copper has been subjected. Figure 1 is an example of twins and grain boundaries without the presence of the plastic deformation characteristic of annealed specimens. Figure 2 exhibits plastic deformation among twins and grain boundaries, which was found to be characteristic of cold forged specimens left in a work-hardened state.

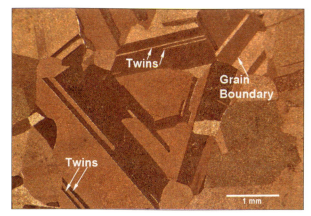

Figure 1. Photo showing twins and grain boundaries with crisp and relatively straight edges as a result of annealing. Plastic deformation is not present. Specimen CF.1, originally photographed at 40x.

Figure 2. Photo showing plastic deformation of twins and grain boundaries as a result of cold forging. Note the curved edges on both the twins and grain boundaries. Specimen CF.3, originally photographed at 40x.

Possibility of Hot Forging

Thus far, the archaeological record has not provided any evidence for the smelting or casting of copper in the Great Lakes region prior to European contact. The manipulation of copper during the Old Copper

Complex appears to have been accomplished through a series of forging and annealing cycles. The apparent absence of smelting and casting technologies should in no way imply that these early coppersmiths did not possess an extensive knowledge of copper and its working properties. The wide variety of copper artifacts found to date would have required comprehensive knowledge of both fire and copper manipulation.

As mentioned above, the question of whether or not hot forging techniques were used by Old Copper Complex coppersmiths has been raised by many scholars. Ehrhardt (2009), LaRonge (2001), Peterson (2003 and 2004), and Wilson and Sayre (1935) have all written that some hot forging techniques were likely employed during this time period. Forging metal in a red-hot state allows for a quick reduction in the thickness of a specimen (LaRonge 2001; Peterson 2003, 2004). LaRonge (2001:373) states that care must be applied when using hot forging techniques because "if copper is rigorously struck after it has lost a red heat, micro-fractures can occur. . . Once fractures have developed further forging will cause them to increase in size, reducing the piece to scrap."

While hot forging can be beneficial when applied correctly, there is always the issue of handling red hot metal. Vernon (1990:502) notes that the archaeological record has not provided evidence for tools that would have been appropriate for handling hot metals. On the other hand, Peterson (2004:58) suggests that "hot ingots can be pushed out of a fire with green sticks, and picked up while hot with a scoop, tube, lever or two copper spikes used like chop-sticks." If organic materials were used as tools it is unlikely that these artifacts would have preserved in the archaeological record.

Clark and Purdy (1982), Schroeder and Ruhl (1968), and Vernon (1990) have concluded that distinguishing the microstructure of cold forged specimens from hot forged specimens is not easily accomplished. In response to these arguments, Martin (1999:137) suggests that "Systematic investigations of changes in copper subjected to experimental hot working may be a valid source of new inferences about the prehistoric feasibility of such techniques and their changing applications over time." The experiment discussed in this paper was conducted with the hope of shedding some new light upon a persistently debated subject.

Methods

Many steps were required for the successful completion of this experiment. The equipment and methods used are described in detail with the hope

that they will be helpful to others carrying out similar experiments in the future, and to clarify each step to the reader.

Cutting, Polishing, and Etching

The first step was to acquire a native copper specimen for the experiments. It was determined that a single raw native copper nugget would be sectioned and forged. This was done to ensure that each specimen had a consistent elemental composition, because native copper, while known for its extreme purity, can be included with other elements (Coghlana and Willows 1962:61). Therefore, a single nugget is much more likely to have a consistent elemental composition than a variety of native copper nuggets. The copper nugget used in this experiment was purchased from Gary's Rock Shop in Viroqua, Wisconsin and originated from a source in Calumet, Michigan (Figure 3).

Figure 3. Native copper nugget used for the experiment.

The next step was to section the copper nugget into slabs using a diamond wet saw in a lapidary shop. The average thickness of each slab was 8.1 mm. While much of the copper nugget was very solid, some areas had a variety of other included minerals. To be consistent and to allow for a successful forging process, the solid slabs were cut up into a total of 12 pieces. Four of these were selected for cold forging, four for hot forging, and four for a combination of hot and cold forging. One slab with inclusions was sectioned into

four pieces, two of which were selected for cold forging and two for hot forging. This was done to see if inclusions would have any effect on the grain structure of the finished specimens in comparison to those without inclusions. (An example of the section of the copper nugget with inclusions can be seen in Figure 4; the slabs prior to sectioning are shown in Figure 5.) It is very likely that ancient coppersmiths were also selective when choosing copper to work. While creating artifact replications, Joe Neubauer discovered

that "the copper nugget's original characteristics prior to manufacturing lead to the end result" (Peterson 2003:103), a phenomenon that was also observed during this experiment. While the dimensions of each specimen changed as a result of forging, the overall shape retained similarities to that of the original sample. Table 1 lists the forging technique used on each specimen and whether it was annealed after forging or left in a work-hardened state. Table 2 has the dimensions of each specimen; as each has a natural and

Figure 4. Photo showing the inclusions in one section of the copper nugget.

Figure 5. Solid copper slabs to be sectioned (along the black line); the slab with inclusions is on the far right.

TABLE 1. FORGING TECHNIQUE AND FINAL STATE OF EACH SPECIMEN.

Specimen	Cold Forged	Hot Forged	Hot and Cold Forged	Annealed	Worked as Final Stage
CF.1	X			X	
CF.2	X			X	
CF.3	X				X
CF.4	X				X
HF.1		X		X	
HF.2		X		X	
HF.3		X			X
HF.4		X			X
BF.1			X	X	
BF.2			X	X	
BF.3			X		X
BF.4			X		X
IC.1	X			X	
IC.2	X				X
IH.3		X		X	
IH.4		X			X

TABLE 2. DIMENSIONS AT COMPLETION.

Specimen	Length (mm)	Width (mm)	Thickness (mm)
CF.1	44.4	21.4	2.1
CF.2	43.8	26.1	2.3
CF.3	42.7	24.3	2.3
CF.4	38.1	22.1	1.9
HF.1	41.3	27.4	2.1
HF.2	45.9	25.3	2.2
HF.3	42.6	27.1	2.4
HF.4	41.2	33.3	2.1
BF.1	49.4	25.2	1.6
BF.2	43.5	26.3	2.2
BF.3	37.7	29.1	1.8
BF.4	39.8	31.2	2.1
IC.1	35.6	20.3	2.0
IC.2	33.2	26.9	2.2
IH.3	35.7	25.0	1.7
IH.4	39.3	22.9	1.7

irregular shape, the length and width were measured at the longest and widest points.

Next each specimen was given a designation, and one surface of each was polished to a mirror finish to allow examination of grain. The polishing was accomplished using a variety of lapidary grinding wheels in sequence. The first two were diamond wheels of 80 and 100 grit. The next three were silicon carbide and diamond grit belts of 150, 220, and 400 grit. From there each specimen was hand polished with 600 and 1500 grit wet/dry sandpaper and finished with polishing paper. The four specimens intended for cold forging were labeled CF.1, CF.2, CF.3, and CF.4. The hot forging specimens were labeled HF.1, HF.2, HF.3, and HF.4. Those specimens that were to be forged with both hot and cold techniques were labeled BF.1, BF.2, BF.3, and BF.4. Lastly, the four pieces with inclusions were labeled IC.1, IC.2, IH.3, and IH.4.

Etching and Microstructure Analysis

After polishing was complete, the next step was to etch each specimen to reveal grain structure. According to the Copper Development Association (2015), "Etching is a controlled corrosion process resulting from electrolytic action between surface areas of different potential. Etching reveals the microstructure of a material by selective dissolution of the structure." A copper etching mordant of greater than 30 percent ferric chloride and 5 percent hydrochloric acid was purchased for the etching process.

Before etching, each specimen was cleaned in a hot Sparex acid compound solution and an ultrasonic cleaner. It was then rinsed in distilled water, and the surface to be etched was cleaned with acetone on a cotton swab. The copper specimens were placed on the bottom of a glass container with the polished sides facing upward, and the etching mordant was poured in so that the solution was about 3 cm deep. Etching solution will weaken with use, so an exact time frame for the specimens to be left in the solution cannot be given. Also, the inclusions and oxidized edges of the copper slabs are believed to have caused other chemical reactions within the solution, which likely had an effect on the strength of the mordant as well. A bright flashlight was used to check the metal surface periodically to see if the grain structure had begun to appear. One should also note that the extent of etching could not be observed until the specimen was rinsed, cleaned with denatured alcohol, and immersed in a hot Sparex solution to remove oxides that had accumulated on the surface. Therefore, some specimens were taken in and out of the etching solution multiple times to achieve the desired result. On average each specimen was submersed in the etching mordant for approximately 2½ to 3 hours.

Once all specimens were etched, they were brought to the Mississippi Valley Archaeology Center at the University of Wisconsin–La Crosse, where the crystalline structures were examined under an Olympus SZX7 microscope with a Nikon D5000 digital camera attachment. Photographs were taken at magnifications of 8x, 10x, 20x, and 40x. The crystalline structure of the raw native copper consisted of large grains that were visible with the naked eye. Figure 6 is an example of the large grain structure and inclusions present in the native copper nugget prior to any forging. This particular specimen was 4.9 cm tall and 2.6 cm wide at the midpoint. While this slab was not used in the experiment, it did originate from the same copper nugget and portrays a similar grain structure to the specimens used.

Figure 6. Natural crystalline structure of native copper. (Photo by Lee Harwell.)

Hafting Hammerstones

Evidence from the archaeological record has indicated that hammerstones were sometimes hafted onto wooden handles. Hafting hammerstones allowed

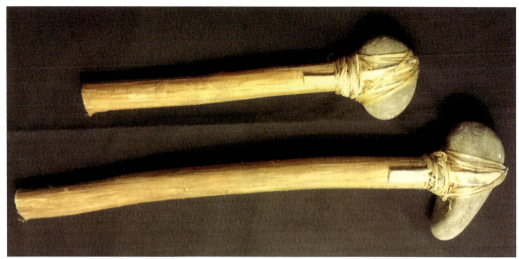

Figure 7. Hafted hammerstones.

coppersmiths to exert more force with each hammer strike, increasing efficiency of the manufacturing process and decreasing the amount of energy expended. For this experiment, two hammerstones were hafted and used in the forging process, along with a large hand-held hammerstone and a stone anvil. The finished hammerstones are shown in Figure 7.

Any experienced artisan knows the importance of having the right tool for the job at hand. For this reason, it is safe to assume ancient coppersmiths were also selective when choosing which raw materials would be used for the fabrication tools. Great care was taken when picking through many river-tumbled rocks to find those with ideal proportions for hafting. The important attributes were shape, balance, and hardness. The shape of the striking face will affect the way in which the metal spreads. For example, a stone that comes to a point will create indents, while a flat stone will spread the metal evenly and leave a flat surface. Specific shapes would have been used to accomplish distinctive tasks. Balance was found to be important when deciding where to grind a groove into the stone. If the groove is not placed properly, the rawhide strips and leather strap wrapped around the stone can slide out of place, resulting in an insecure haft. One must also consider the balance of weight, because excess on either side of the haft will cause the stone to come loose after some use. Lastly, the stone needs to be hard enough not to break apart during the forging process.

Once appropriate stones were collected, grooves were ground around the stones with an industrial grinder. For efficiency, this step was not carried out using the traditional process of grinding with another stone, nor would machine grinding have an effect on the results of this experiment. Branches were collected,

cut, and stripped to be used as handles. The width and length of the handles was determined by the shape and weight of the stone to be hafted.

A combination of sinew, animal hide glue, leather, copper "nails," and rawhide strips were used to attach the stones to the wooden handles. Ligaments from a deer leg were dried and pounded to create thin strips of sinew, as shown in Figure 8. Animal hide glue (purchased commercially) was added to a small amount of water, heated, and occasionally stirred until all the water was absorbed, resulting in a consistency similar to that of household craft glue. The end of the handle was then carved to fit the shape of the stone and its groove. A leather strip was secured to one side of the handle with a copper nail. Next a mixture of sinew and animal hide glue was placed between the stone and the handle. Animal hide glue was also spread along the entire groove where the leather strap would be placed. Then the leather was pulled tight around the stone and attached to the other side of the handle

Figure 8. Deer ligament, or sinew at bottom; pounded into strips at top.

with another copper nail. From there the rawhide strips were soaked in hot water until they became soft and stretchable. These were then tied around the handle and woven around the stone and handle in a crisscrossing pattern. When one strip was near its end, another was knotted onto it and the wrapping continued. It was important to pull hard so the rawhide was wrapped tightly but not so hard that the rawhide strip would break. Once the wrapping was finished, the hammers were left to dry for 48 hours. As the rawhide, sinew, and glue dried, shrinkage occurred, allowing the haft to tighten.

Fire Maintenance, Annealing, and Forging

A fire pit was dug approximately 50 cm in diameter and 20 cm deep. The pit was then lined with river-tumbled metamorphic rocks to act as heat insulators. Caution should be used during the first fire in such a pit because moisture trapped inside of the rocks will expand when exposed to heat, which can cause the rocks to shatter, creating a safety hazard. For this reason, and the possibility that shifting of coals could have buried the copper specimens, no copper was heated in the first fire.

For the actual forging process, white oak was burned in the pit until a bed of hot coals was created. At this point the rocks lining the pit were no longer visible. Two logs placed parallel to each other on opposite sides of the bed of coals acted as a foundation upon which other logs could be stacked perpendicularly to create a wood "oven." As a result, a space of about 5 cm between the coals and the base of the top layer of logs was created. This technique worked well to maintain heat and created a perfect space in which to place the copper. A photo of the wood "oven" is shown in Figure 9. Copper specimens were placed on top of a steel mesh sheet that was set directly onto the hot coals. This technique was used because the copper quickly turns the same color as the coals. The mesh stopped copper from being misplaced and ensured that specimens were not mixed up. An example of this can be seen in Figure 10. As soon as the top logs were replaced, the coals returned to the bright red color observable in the upper portion of Figure 10.

The time required to anneal, or prepare for hot forging, varied depending on the temperature of the fire, which increased as a larger bed of coals built up throughout the day. Maintenance was required to keep the fire from diminishing. Logs had to be regularly added and maneuvered to ensure that the oven would not collapse in upon itself. As tending the fire was a full-time job, having an assistant was extremely helpful. This observation supports LaRonge's (2001) argument that copper smithing was likely a group effort during the Old Copper Complex. Not only would it have been more difficult to do with a single person, it also would have been inefficient in terms of resources and the amount of energy exerted. Peterson (2003:102) states that Joe Neubauer often had three white oak fires burning at once for the efficient annealing of multiple pieces of copper.

Due to the lack of funding for a pyrometer that would read high enough temperatures, the temperature of the fire was not recorded during these experiments. However, LaRonge did record the temperatures during his experiments and, because he was also heating copper on a bed of oak embers, the temperature ranges are likely to have been similar. He states that "the average temperature of the fire was easily maintained at around 865–920°C and eventually climbed to approximately 1073°C over a four hour period" (LaRonge 2001:379). A pyrometer with a reading limit of 538°C was used in this experiment and got an error reading around the edges of the fire, indicating that the center was at a temperature much higher than 538°C. Joe Neubauer also used white oak for his experiments and found that high enough temperatures were reached to sweat or melt silver inclusions out of the copper (Peterson 2003:103). The melt point of silver is approximately 961°C, which is also within the temperature range reported by LaRonge. The fire temperatures of this experiment should have been within the same ranges observed by LaRonge and Neubauer.

Coppersmiths of the Archaic period likely used color as a temperature indicator. As stated by LaRonge (2001:374) "All ferrous metals go through three visible stages during heating. The first change is called 'gloss-off' during which iridescent colors appear to run across the metal's surface" (shown in Figure 11). The second stage is referred to as "black heat" and is reached once the metal loses its reflectivity and turns black due to the presence of surface oxides, as seen in Figure 12 (LaRonge 2001). Lastly, "the metal reaches a 'red heat' that is the broadest visible range appearing at around 200–225°C and building in intensity until the melting temperatures around 1080°C are reached" (LaRonge 2001:374). Because of its convenience, metalsmiths today continue to use this method to know when a metal has reached annealing temperatures. McCreight (2004) states that copper has reached an accelerated annealing temperature when it turns a dull red color. For this experiment the copper was allowed to climb to a bright red color and was held in that state for approximately 20 minutes, after which it was removed to be cooled or forged in a hot state. Figure 13 shows the average color of the copper in the "red heat" stage.

Figure 9. Wood "oven" made from white oak logs.

Figure 10. Copper placed into coals on top of steel mesh.

Figure 11. Copper pieces in the "gloss-off" stage. (Photo by Taylor Thingvold.)

Figure 12. Copper pieces in the "black-heat" stage. (Photo by Taylor Thingvold.)

Figure 13. Copper pieces in the "red-heat" stage.

Forging of the copper was done in four rounds so that the copper pieces in the fire all required the same forging technique, another precaution taken to ensure that specimens were not mixed up. Each group of four was also placed into the fire in numerical order to further ensure accuracy. Specimens CF.1, CF.2, CF.3, and CF.4 were placed into the fire first and allowed to stay at annealing temperatures for approximately 20 minutes. At that point they were removed from the fire with copper tongs and allowed to air cool for about two minutes and were then quenched in water. Next they were each forged on a stone anvil with a large hand-held hammerstone until they reached a work-hardened state, as shown in Figure 14. The hafted hammerstones were also used in the forging process to further work any raised surfaces. Cold forged specimens were struck approximately 30 times before reaching a work-hardened state.

One knows when to stop forging because the auditory tone of the metal changes. LaRonge has described these auditory clues as changing from a "dull metallic clank" to a "high pitched tinny ring" (LaRonge 2001:375). When this "high pitched tinny ring" becomes audible, one should cease forging because the metal has reached a work-hardened state. The sense of touch can also be used, because an experienced metalsmith can feel when the metal has stopped spreading as readily. Once in a work-hardened state, the cold forging specimens were placed back into the fire and held at annealing temperatures for another 20 minutes. They were then removed from the fire, cooled, and forged as before. When they had once again reached a work-hardened state, CF.1 and CF.2 were placed back in the fire to be re-annealed, and CF.3 and CF.4 were left alone.

The next set to go into the fire was HF.1, HF.2, HF.3, and HF.4. These specimens were also held at annealing temperatures for approximately 20 minutes, after which they were removed one at a time and forged while in a red-hot state. There was a noticeable difference in the malleability of the metal, for they were reduced in thickness much faster than the cold forging specimens. The hot specimens were only struck between seven and ten times before being placed directly back into the fire. This was done to ensure that they were truly only worked in a hot state and to avoid fractures as discussed by LaRonge (2001). Each specimen went through this process twice. After the forging was complete, HF.1 and HF.2 were re-annealed and HF.3 and HF.4 were left in a worked state.

The third set to go in the fire was BF.1, BF.2, BF.3, and BF.4. These were brought to and held at annealing temperatures in the same way. The specimens were removed from the fire one at a time, worked in a red-hot state, and continued to be worked until they reached the same level of work hardness as the cold forged specimens. They were then placed back into the fire, and this process was repeated. When the forging was complete, BF.1 and BF.2 were re-annealed and BF.3 and BF.4 were left in a work hardened state.

Lastly, the four specimens with inclusions were forged. IC.1 went through the same process as CF.1 and CF.2, while IC.2 was treated the same way as CF.3 and CF.4. IH.3 went through the same forging and annealing process as HF.1 and HF.2, and IH.4 was created the same way as HF.3 and HF.4. After all the forging was complete, it was interesting to note the changes in the stone anvil and hammerstone. Figure 15 shows the copper residue that built up on the stones during the forging process. It also shows damage to the hammerstone, which increased throughout the experiment. These attributes could assist in the identification of hammerstones and stone anvils found in the archaeological record, but it should be noted that the copper residue would be very unlikely to survive in situ. Copper residue on the tools used for this experiment weathered away within a year and a half. The result of all the forging was 16 small sheets of native copper. The next step was to clean, polish, and etch the specimens in preparation for analysis. This was accomplished in the same manner as discussed in the previous etching section.

When the second stage of etching was complete, the specimens were once again analyzed and photographed with the same microscope and camera. The results of the metallographic analysis are discussed in the next section.

Results

Elemental Analysis

A scanning electron microscope (SEM) in the Physics Department at the University of Wisconsin–La Crosse was used to perform energy dispersive spectroscopy (EDS) on the native copper to evaluate the elemental composition of the samples. SEM is used to produce topographic images by scanning the sample with a focused beam of electrons. As the electron beam penetrates the sample, secondary electrons are released from the outer shell of atoms in the sample, producing a signal that is transformed into an image. In addition to secondary electrons, the sample also releases X-rays. The energy of these X-rays is specific to the element that emitted them, allowing EDS to be used for the determination of the elemental composition of a sample (Goldstein et al. 2003).

Figure 14. Showing forging process with stone anvil and large hammerstone.(Photo by Taylor Thingvold.)

Figure 15. Stone anvil and large hammerstone after forging. Note the copper residue on working surfaces and damage to the hammerstone.

EDS results show that the copper nugget used in this experiment is composed of relatively pure copper in areas without inclusions. Traces of carbon were also detected but are likely due to the presence of fine dust particles on the surface of the metal. It is also possible that the carbon is present from the annealing and forging process. This is further confirmed by looking at the relative carbon and copper content, identified as 90.2 percent copper and 9.8 percent carbon. Figure 16 is an EDS image showing the copper and carbon content. The copper is represented in pink, while the carbon is represented in yellow. Note how the traces of carbon are concentrated around the edges of grains and recessed areas of the surface. This pattern of carbon dispersal further suggests the presence of dust particles on the sample surface. This image also shows that copper was detected universally throughout the sample section. A higher carbon content is observable in the lower left corner, which was near the edge of the sample, and is likely due to the carbon tape used to adhere the sample to the platform. No other elements were detected above a 5 percent relative concentration,

leading to the conclusion that the native copper used in this experiment is considered to be pure. The sample shown in Figure 16 is CF.1 after forging and annealing had taken place.

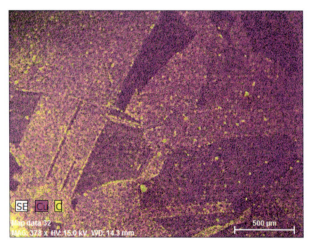

Figure 16. EDS image showing both copper (pink) and carbon. (yellow)

Metallographic Analysis

As stated above, the metallographic analysis of the 16 copper sheets resulting from this experiment shows consistent differences in grain structures depending on the type of forging techniques applied. While the majority of the analysis was done under a microscope at 8x, 10x, 20x, and 40x, the grain structure was also visible to the naked eye. For clarity purposes, photographs of full specimens (Figures 17–20) have been included, as well as photographs taken with the microscope (Figures 21–30). To enhance the visibility of the grain structure, full specimen photographs were adjusted in contrast, saturation, and brightness using Adobe Photoshop. No alterations were made that would affect the shape or size of the grain structure.

Metallographic analysis of the native copper used for these experiments has indicated that all forged specimens exhibit a grain structure smaller than that of raw native copper. It should also be noted that the occurrence of twins in each specimen increased substantially after the application of forging and annealing. This result is consistent with observations made by Maddin et al. (1980) and Clark and Purdy (1982).

All specimens that were annealed after the working process display a very similar grain structure regardless of which forging techniques were applied. Each specimen was annealed under similar conditions and time frames; therefore, the grain size exhibited in annealed specimens is analogous. For this reason the use of this reference set for comparative analysis is limited to copper objects left in a work-hardened state. All further discussion of results will fall under the category of work-hardened specimens. Similarities of annealed specimens can be observed in Figures 21, 22, 25, 27, and 28. Characteristics of annealing are also present in the grain structure of the specimens with inclusions. This is important because it shows a consistency in grain structure with specimens with no inclusions, indicating that the presence of inclusions did not change the results, regardless of the forging process used.

The most distinct difference can be observed between work-hardened specimens created with cold forging versus those created with hot forging. The grain structures of cold forged specimens are more homogeneous than those of hot forging and consist of relatively larger grains. Compression during forging caused plastic deformation along slip systems and reduced the size of vacancies, resulting in a curved appearance along grain boundaries and twins. Hot forged specimens are composed of a heterogeneous mixture of small grains surrounding larger grains. Larger grains in hot forged specimens tend to be smaller than those of cold forged specimens and show few signs of plastic deformation, with straight edges along grain boundaries and twins. It is believed that the smaller grains were produced during the first few hammer strikes when the metal was red hot and the copper was quickly reduced in thickness. This reduction broke larger grains into smaller ones, and the rapid decrease of heat did not allow time for crystals to grow into an equiaxed structure (McCreight 2004). These differences can be seen in Figures 24 and 30.

Figure 17. Cold forged samples; from left to right: CF.1, CF.2, CF.3, CF.4. Dimensions of CF.1: 44.4 mm long x 21.4 mm wide. (Photo by Lee Harwell.)

Figure 18. Hot forged samples; from left to right: HF.1, HF.2, HF.3, HF.4. Dimensions of HF.1: 41.3 mm long x 27.4 mm wide. (Photo by Lee Harwell.)

Figure 19. Hot and cold forged samples; from left to right: BF.1, BF.2, BF.3, BF.4. Dimensions of BF.1: 49.4 mm long x 25.2 mm wide. (Photo by Lee Harwell.)

Figure 20. Samples with inclusions; from left to right: cold forged IC.1, IC.2; hot forged IH.3, IH.4. Dimensions of IC.1: 35.6 mm long x 20.3 mm wide. (Photo by Lee Harwell.)

Specimens forged in both hot and cold state exhibit characteristics from each technique. While the heterogeneous mixture of small and large grains is present, consistent with hot forging, the larger grain boundaries and twins also show the same plastic deformation present in the cold forged specimens. This is significant because it shows that the evidence of hot forging still exists after the specimens were cold forged as well. Figure 26 is a photograph of BF.4 where this grain structure can be observed. The same similarities were present in the annealed specimens as seen in Figure 25.

Figure 21. CF.1 Cold Forged and Annealed. Note crisp grain boundaries and straight twins.

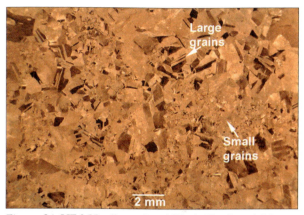

Figure 24. HF.3 Hot Forged and Work-Hardened. Note clusters of large and small grains, and the relatively straight edges of larger grain boundaries and twins.

Figure 22. HF.1 Hot Forged and Annealed. Note similar grain structure to CF.1.

Figure 25. BF.1 Hot/Cold Forged and Annealed. Note similarities to CF.1 and HF.1.

Figure 23. CF.3 Cold Forged and Work-Hardened. Note plastic deformation of grain boundaries and twins, examples of which are indicated with arrows.

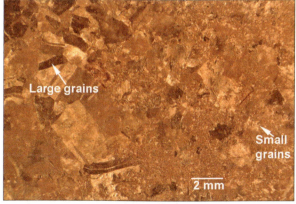

Figure 26. BF.4 Hot/Cold Forged and Work-Hardened. Note characteristics of both hot and cold forging: mixture of large and small grains resulting from hot forging; plastic deformation of grain boundaries and twins characteristic of cold forging.

Copper specimens with inclusions showed consistent results in the grain structure. This is also significant because it shows that the grain structure of native copper with inclusions responded to forging in the same manner as solid native copper. The grain structures of these specimens can be seen in Figures 27, 28, 29, and 30.

Figure 27. IC.1 Cold Forged and Annealed. Note similarities to other annealed specimens.

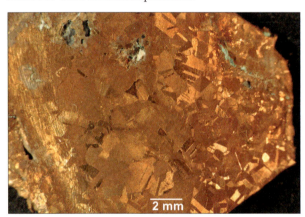

Figure 28. IH.3 Hot Forged and Annealed. Note similarities to other annealed specimens.

Figure 29. IC.2 Cold Forged and Work-Hardened. Note similarities to CF.3. Plastic deformation of twins and grain boundaries present.

Figure 30. IH.4 Hot Forged and Work-Hardened. Note similarities to HF.3.

Conclusions

Metallographic analysis of native copper forged with a variety of techniques has shown that consistent differences in grain structure can be observed in cold forged, hot forged, and combination forged specimens. The visual indicators of hot forging continued to exist after further cold forging had taken place in specimens forged with a combination of these techniques. For these reasons, it has been concluded that with careful comparative metallographic analysis of copper artifacts from the Old Copper Complex, one may be able to make inferences regarding whether or not hot forging techniques were being exploited by looking for the hot forging characteristics exhibited in this reference set. All specimens that were re-annealed after working exhibit a grain structure with enough similarities that metallographic analysis cannot be used to determine a specific type of manufacturing process. Therefore, it is unlikely that specific forging processes can be determined in artifacts that show evidence of annealing as the final stage of manufacturing.

One problem with metallographic analysis is that it requires the partial destruction of artifacts. As of today, we do not possess the technology to observe grain structures without polishing and etching. In order to carry out this analysis one must grind a section of an artifact's surface, causing irreversible damage. As archaeologists are charged with preserving the past, the decision of whether or not to do destructive analysis on an artifact should never be taken lightly. It is important for one to weigh the extent of damage alongside the benefits before coming to a decision. Unfortunately, this dilemma is one from which archaeologists will never be freed. It is in the

very nature of our discipline to deconstruct in order to reconstruct the past. Every time a site is excavated the archaeological record is dismantled in the process. While technological advances are ever increasing our ability to observe aspects of the past without digging, there are some questions that just cannot be answered without excavation, just as grain structure cannot be observed without polishing and etching. One should always use careful consideration and keep meticulous records when carrying out destructive analysis of any kind. As the saying goes, "what is done is done"; once you get there, there is no turning back.

The first step of future research should be to repeat this experiment multiple times with native copper from different regions to see if consistent results can be observed. A reference set made of copper from multiple regions could render itself useful anywhere early copper manufacturing was pursued. Also, the reference set created through this experiment, and those of future experiments, should be compared to existing literature in which metallographic analysis of Old Copper Complex artifacts has been carried out and discussed. The partial destruction of these artifacts has already taken place, and the opportunity to learn more from them should not be ignored.

One way in which further research could be conducted without destructive analysis of artifacts would be to carry out metallographic analysis of artifact recreations made by experimental archaeologist and metalsmith Joe Neubauer. The "Neubauer Process" "reproduced over three hundred finished ancient tool and ornament duplicates" (Peterson 2003:102). This process was recorded by David H. Peterson while he spent four years observing Joe Neubauer at work (2003, 2004). As Neubauer was known to use some hot forging techniques, metallographic analysis of his work could provide priceless insight to the hot forging debate. If hot forging characteristics could be identified in the grain structure of his recreations, destructive analysis of artifacts may be further justified.

Another avenue for future research would be to make more artifact recreations with detailed records of the working process. Analysis of those recreations could also provide a great deal of insight for understanding what metallographic characteristics are consistent with particular manufacturing processes. It would also be interesting to create another reference set where the number of anneal-forge cycles is increased to see what changes may be observable.

In no way was this experiment and analysis meant to definitively solve the debate over the possibility of hot forging. Instead it should be considered a stepping stone for future research. Further experiments and analyses are required to answer the question of whether or not hot forging techniques were employed by Archaic coppersmiths. If this question is answered in the future, it could allow us to better understand the preferred technological practices of Archaic copper manufacturing societies of the Old Copper Complex.

The original samples from this project are curated at the Mississippi Valley Archaeology Center at the University of Wisconsin–La Crosse.

Acknowledgments

This research was done as a Senior Thesis for a Bachelor of Science degree in the Archaeology and Anthropology Department of the University of Wisconsin–La Crosse. There are many people I wish to thank for their assistance and support through this project. First of all I would like to thank my family for their unwavering moral and financial support, without which this experiment would not have been possible. A huge thank you to my readers Dr. Katherine Grillo and Dr. Constance Arzigian for all their help and professional assistance, and to the members of my reading group, April Rothenbach, Sarah Schultz, and Alexandra Welsh, for their support, helpful revisions, and suggestions. Thanks to Dr. Seth King and Dr. Sarah Lantvit for their assistance with the elemental analysis of the native copper used in this experiment. For allowing me to build a fire pit and occupy their backyard for multiple days, a big thank you to TJ DiCiaula and Heather Henry, and their daughters Jophi and Xia DiCiaula and Holly Henry for their assistance, their smiles, and their love. I would like to thank David Mindel for the use of his lapidary shop and for being an open ear to bounce ideas off of. I was blessed to have two photographers willing to donate their time and effort to this project: thank you, Taylor Thingvold and Lee Harwell. A huge thank you to John, Peg, and Hans Pieper for the supply of white oak, good food, moral support, and assistance around the fire. Thanks to my dear friend Lance Red Hawk for his assistance in hafting hammerstones and moral support. I owe a great deal of gratitude to the metalsmithing masters who have taught me so much over the years: Bill Howard, Missy Howard, Aaron Howard, Glenn Prescott, Dimitri Pavlov, and Terri Garcia. A big thank you to the Mississippi Valley Archaeology Center for the use of the microscope and digital camera. I would also like to thank my good friends David Brown and Emily Zilke for their moral support and for allowing me to talk about and polish copper at their home for hours on end.

References Cited

Binford, Lewis R.
  1962   Archaeology as Anthropology. *American Antiquity* 28(2):217–225.

Clark, David E., and Barbara A. Purdy
  1982   Early Metallurgy in North America. In *Early Pyrotechnology: The Evolution of the First Fire-Using Industries*, edited by Theodore A. Wertime and Steven F. Wertime, pp. 45–58. Smithsonian Institution Press, Washington, D.C.

Coghlana, H. H., and R. Willows
  1962   A Note upon Native Copper: Its Occurrence and Properties. *Proceedings of the Prehistoric Society* 28:58–67.

Copper Development Association
  2015   *Microstructures of Copper and Copper Alloys.* Electronic document, www.copper.org, accessed April 12, 2015.

Cushing, Frank H.
  1894   Primitive Copper Working: An Experimental Study. *American Anthropologist* 7:93–117.

Ehrhardt, Kathleen L.
  2009   Copper Working Technologies, Contexts of Use, and Social Complexity in the Eastern Woodlands of Native North America. *Journal of World Prehistory* 22:213–235.

Fregni, Giovanna
  2009   A Study of the Manufacture of Copper Spearheads in the Old Copper Complex. *The Minnesota Archaeologist* 68:121–131.

Gibbon, Guy
  1998   Old Copper in Minnesota: A Review. *Plains Anthropologist* 43(136):27–50.

Goldstein, Joseph, Dale Newbury, David Joy, Charles Lyman, Patrick Echlin, Eric Lifshin, Linda Sawyer, and Joseph Michael
  2003   *Scanning Electron Microscopy and X-Ray Microanalysis.* 3rd ed. Springer Science and Business Media, New York.

Holmes, William H.
  1901   Aboriginal Copper Mines of Isle Royale, Lake Superior. *American Anthropologist* 3:684–696.

LaRonge, Michael
  2001   An Experimental Analysis of Great Lakes Archaic Copper Smithing. *North American Archaeologist* 22(4):371–385.

Levine, Mary Ann
  2007   Overcoming Disciplinary Solitude: The Archaeology and Geology of Native Copper in Eastern North America. *Geoarchaeology: An International Journal* 22(1):49–66.

Maddin, R., T. Stech Wheeler, and J.D. Muhly
  1980   Distinguishing Artifacts Made of Native Copper. *Journal of Archaeological Science* 7:211–225.

Martin, Susan R.
  1999   *Wonderful Power: The Story of Ancient Copper Working in the Lake Superior Basin.* Wayne State University Press, Detroit.

McCreight, Tim
  2004   *Complete Metalsmith: Professional Edition.* Brynmorgen Press, Portland, Maine.

Peterson, David H.
  2003   Red Metal Poundings and the "Neubauer Process": Copper Culture Metallurgical Technology. *Central States Archaeological Journal* 50(2):102–107.

Peterson, David H.
  2004   The Neubauer Process: 1999–2003 Observations. *Central States Archaeological Journal* 51(1):56–59.

Pleger, Thomas C.
  2000   Old Copper and Red Ochre Social Complexity. *Midcontinental Journal of Archaeology* 25(2):169–190.

Rostoker, William, and James R. Dvorak
  1965   *Interpretation of Metallographic Structures.* Academic Press, New York.

Schroeder, David L., and Katharine C. Ruhl
  1968   Metallurgical Characteristics of North American Prehistoric Copper Work. *American Antiquity* 33(2):162–169.

Theler, James L., and Robert F. Boszhardt
  2003   *Twelve Millennia: Archaeology of the Upper Mississippi River Valley.* University of Iowa Press, Iowa City.

Vernon, William W.
  1990   New Archaeometallurgical Perspectives on the Old Copper Industry of North America. In *Archaeological Geology of North America*, edited by Norman P. Lasca and Jack Donahue, pp. 499–512. Geological Society of America, Boulder, Colorado.

Wilson, Curtis L., and Melville Sayre
  1935   A Brief Metallographic Study of Primitive Copper Work. *American Antiquity* 1(2):109–112.

Wittry, Warren L., and Robert E. Ritzenthaler
  1956   The Old Copper Complex: An Archaic Manifestation in Wisconsin. *American Antiquity* 21(3):244–254.

Technologies of Refired Glass Pendant Production: Experimental Replication Results

Sarah Schultz and Heather Walder

Abstract

This article examines the archaeological evidence for the re-forming of glass trade beads into larger glass pendants, which have been recovered from seventeenth- and eighteenth-century sites across the Plains and Midwest regions of North America. Drawing on ethnohistoric sources and material properties of artifacts, we investigate the pendant production process using experimental archaeology, the process of recreating ancient technologies in an effort to better understand them. Prior attempts to replicate this process have produced conclusions that are inconsistent with the material properties of glass and metal components involved in the process. Through documenting the physical properties of glass pendants from archaeological contexts and experimenting with replicating this technology, a probable production sequence for making refired glass pendants is proposed.

Introduction

During the seventeenth and early eighteenth centuries in the North American Upper Great Lakes region, interactions among diverse peoples occurred through the exchange of European-made items such as copper and brass kettles, glass trade beads, cloth, firearms, and other commodities. Indigenous people often treated these items as "raw materials" that could be transformed by applying existing and innovative technological practices (Bradley 1987; Ehrhardt 2005; Turgeon 1997). Glass trade beads, which were produced in European workshops in Venice, Amsterdam, Paris, London, and perhaps other locales as well (Bradley 2007; Dussubieux 2009; Dussubieux and Karklins 2016; Janssens et al. 2013; Tyler and Willmott 2005;

Van der Linden et al. 2005), also sometimes served as raw materials for ornament production (Walder 2013). Archaeologists have identified small glass pendants apparently made of reworked European trade beads in historic-era assemblages from archaeological sites across the Plains and Midwest regions of North America (Brown 1972; Ubelaker and Bass 1970). Most of the complete pendants from the Upper Great Lakes region are trapezoidal in shape, opaque, and either solid turquoise blue or striped blue and white.

The origin of the glass reworking technology has been a point of debate (Brown 1972; Ubelaker and Bass 1970). With available evidence, it is not possible to determine if Indigenous people developed the knowledge of reworking glass beads independently, or if Europeans introduced the idea along with the beads. Ethnohistoric and archaeological evidence identifies glass pendant production in the Plains region of North America at least as early as 1730 (Brown 1972). Refired glass fragments from the Zimmerman site, dated to the mid- to late seventeenth century in Illinois (Brown 1961), and the roughly contemporary Gillette Grove site in northwest Iowa (Shott et al. 2002), show that this technology was present across the greater Midwest earlier than Margaret K. Brown's estimate, but this does not clarify whether the technology developed in the Plains and spread eastward or vice versa.

In a previous ethnohistoric and archaeological study, it was suggested that Plains peoples, particularly the Arikara who lived along the Missouri River, specialized in a process of powdering, reshaping, and heating re-formed glass on metal pans to make trapezoidal blue glass pendants (Ubelaker and Bass 1970). Archaeologists argued that peoples on the Plains then traded the finished pendants eastward into the Midwest through down-the-line exchanges along the Mississippi River and its tributaries (Brown

Sarah Schultz, University of Wisconsin–La Crosse; Heather Walder, Michigan State University

The Wisconsin Archeologist, 2016, 97(2):29–47

1972; Howard 1972). Local production in the Great Lakes was not proposed. However, some evidence of on-site pendant production at locations in Wisconsin and Michigan has been identified on the basis of compositional similarity between the glass beads and pendants found at Upper Great Lakes sites (Walder 2013, 2015:281–313). Further evidence has emerged in the form of possible tools or waste from pendant production, such as probable glass residue adhering to several metal fragments in assemblages of copper-base metal from archaeological sites where glass pendants have also been recovered. Based on findings of similarities in chemical composition between glass beads and refired glass artifacts, Walder has previously argued that on-site glass pendant production took place in the Upper Great Lakes region in at least one location, the Rock Island site (Walder 2013).

The production process used to fashion the glass pendants remains unclear. However, the evidence of blue glass residue on copper plates indicates that heating the pendants on metal sheets was part of the process in some instances. A prior attempt to recreate glass pendants stated that the optimum temperature to achieve glass fusion is 1500°C (Ubelaker and Bass 1970:473). However, the melting point of copper is 1082°C (Bentor 1996), much lower than the melting point of the glass. This means that the copper plates underneath the glass would have melted before the glass would have fully fused. We considered the possibility that the 1500°C recorded by Ubelaker and Bass might simply be a confusion between Celsius and Fahrenheit, and that the authors meant to write 1500°F (815°C), a temperature achievable in a hot campfire. However, our study demonstrates that this is too low a temperature for fusing powdered glass particles. If mis-reporting was not the case, since Native North Americans did not independently develop technological knowledge of copper smelting, achieving such high temperatures as 1500°C is unlikely to have occurred in pendant production processes. In this paper, we demonstrate that firing at lower heat, at temperatures approaching 1000°C, would have been sufficient to fuse glass powder into pendant shapes, and that the products of experimental refiring are comparable in their material properties to glass pendants recovered in the archaeological record. Therefore, Indigenous peoples in both the Plains and the Midwest may have developed glass refiring technology, or exchanged knowledge of this process, as well as finished pendants, across these regions. It remains unclear if the technique of refiring glass beads to produce pendants was first developed locally in North America, if it was introduced by Europeans, or if collaboration and sharing of technological know-how took place.

Background

Both ethnohistory and recently conducted chemical compositional analyses provide insight into the processes that could have been used to produce glass pendants. This section reviews the archaeological and historical contexts of glass pendants in the Midwest and provides an overview of existing understandings of the pendant production process, as documented historically.

Archaeological Contexts of Pendants

Refired glass pendants have been identified at late seventeenth and eighteenth century archaeological sites across the Midwest (Brown 1972), and Walder has examined pendants in collections from sites ranging from Western Iowa to the Straits of Mackinac, in Michigan. Pendants and fragments of refired glass are recovered from sites attributed to diverse ethnic groups. East of the Mississippi River, pendants have been found in the Odawa-affiliated levels of Rock Island, Wisconsin (Mason 1986:203–204); the colonial trading contexts of Fort Michilimackinac, Michigan (Stone 1974:138), and Madeline Island, Wisconsin (Al Galazen collection at the Madeline Island Museum, personal observation by Walder, see Birmingham and Salzer 1984 for general discussion of colonial Madeline Island); a predominantly Tionontate-Wendat (Petun-Huron) village at the Marquette Mission site (Branstner 1992:190) and nearby cemetery area at Gros Cap near the Straits of Mackinac at St. Ignace, Michigan (Martin 1979:27); the Illinois Grand Village of the Kaskaskia at Zimmerman, near Starved Rock, Illinois (Brown 1975:33–34); and a single broken fragment from the Meskwaki-affiliated Mahler portion of the Doty Island site (personal observation of fragment by Walder, site report Mason and Mason 1997) at the north end of Lake Winnebago in Wisconsin (Figure 1). Other glass pendants from the Midwest have been noted but not observed by the authors. They come from sites ranging from 21SL80, a site in Voyageurs National Park, Northern Minnesota, (Erik Drake, personal communication to Walder 2015), and from Grand Island, Michigan (Erik Drake, personal communication to Walder 2015) to as far south as the French River L'Abbe Mission on Monk's Mound at Cahokia (Walthall and Benchley 1987). This geographic distribution may indicate that pendants were traded freely among different Native and European peoples present in North America, and also that interaction among groups led to loss and deposition of pendant fragments at sites across the region.

In the cases of the Rock Island site component dated to c. 1760, Marquette Mission, and Michilimackinac,

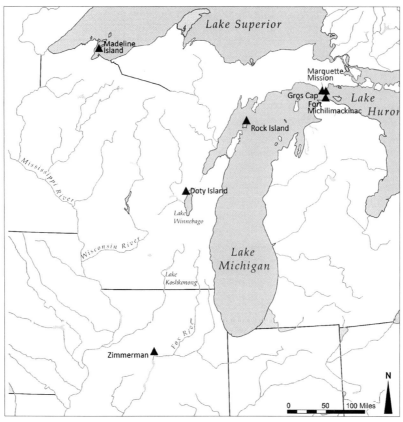

Figure 1. Map of locations where refired glass pendants have been recovered and subjected to compositional analysis for comparison with glass beads from the same sites. (Map by Walder.)

there was a direct and sustained European presence in various forms such as trading outposts, missionary activity, and French colonial fortifications. Since pendants come from historically documented French, British, and Métis (persons of mixed European and American Indian ancestry) contexts within the fortifications of Michilimackinac, European production of the refired glass pendants cannot be ruled out, though these artifacts are generally considered "Native-made" by archaeologists no matter the social context of their deposition (e.g., Brown 1972, 1975; Evans 2001:24; Walthall and Benchley 1987:44). It is possible, then, that in the Upper Great Lakes region, refired glass pendants might have been produced predominantly at sites where there were significant European populations and influences. This contrasts with the social context of limited direct interaction documented at the protohistoric Arikara occupations at the Leavenworth and Sully sites, where pendants were produced in the Plains region (Ubelaker and Bass 1970). Even if production of glass pendants in the Midwest was restricted to certain locales like the Straits of Mackinac and Rock Island, which served as key trading hubs with evidence of significant European interaction, it

would be unsurprising to find glass pendants widely distributed in this region. Without more information about the meanings of these adornments in their use-contexts, it is difficult to determine if wearing a refired glass pendant was a mark of ethnicity, social status, or some other aspect of social identity.

Compositional Analyses of Pendants

Glass beads from four archaeological sites in the Midwest have been identified as compositionally similar to the pendants from those same sites, providing indirect evidence that pendant production may have taken place there (Walder 2015:311–312). These sites are Rock Island (47DR128), Fort Michilimackinac (20EM52), Marquette Mission (20MK82 and 20MK99), and Gillett Grove (13CY2). Significant behavioral and cultural differences have been described at each of these sites. Gillette Grove is a protohistoric Oneota or ancestral Ioway settlement in Western Iowa with no evidence of direct or sustained European contact, dated to c. A.D. 1500 to 1700 (Shott et al. 2002). Conversely, Rock Island was a trading hub for many Native groups as well as Europeans (Mason 1986). The pendants from Rock Island come

from levels associated with later seventeenth- and eighteenth-century occupations at that site, c. A.D. 1670–1760. At least one pendant from Rock Island is confidently associated with an Odawa village context there, dated to c. 1760. The Marquette Mission site has been attributed to French Jesuit habitations and a closely affiliated Tionontate-Wendat (Petun-Huron) community occupied from c. 1671 to 1670 (Branstner 1992). Finally, Fort Michilimackinac was a French and British military outpost with known Métis residents (Stone 1974). Pendants come from both French and British-associated contexts within the fort. Therefore, the process of pendant production does not appear to have been limited to a particular ethnic group or community in the Midwest.

The technological knowledge of producing glass pendants could have been exchanged widely, perhaps along the same routes as the artifacts themselves, or knowledge could have been restricted to local specialists at sites across the region. Based on compositional similarity between beads and pendants, some pendants possibly produced at Marquette Mission may have been traded to communities identified in archaeological contexts on Madeline Island in northern Wisconsin, and at Doty Island in Lake Winnebago, highlighting the exchange networks connecting the Upper Great Lakes region (Walder 2015:325–327). Recipients of pendants obtained through trade would not necessarily have known how they were made, or their meaning to the original community producing them; traded finished objects could have sparked technological experimentation in places where the process of making pendants was otherwise unknown.

Based on the compositional similarity between beads and pendants, pendant production seems to have been more limited than trade in these objects. Although sites of probable pendant production in the Midwest were occupied by diverse ethnic groups, the Meskwaki, as relative newcomers to the region, are conspicuously absent from any significant historical or archaeological presence at possible pendant-production sites. The small pendant fragment from the Doty Island site Mahler portion, which possibly was inhabited by a Meskwaki group c. 1680–1710 (Mason and Mason 1997), is an anomaly. There is no indication that glass pendants were produced or widely used at the Doty Island site during its occupation, nor have glass pendants or refired glass fragments been recovered on any other Meskwaki-affiliated sites, including the thoroughly investigated Bell site (47WN9) (Behm 2008). Compositionally, the Doty Island fragment is most similar to pendants produced at Marquette Mission and those recovered on Madeline Island (Walder 2013:388). The pendant

could have been obtained by a Doty Island resident through trade, or worn by someone not of Meskwaki ethnicity, perhaps a visitor or trader, and broken or chipped at the Doty Island site.

Cross-Cultural Comparison and Ethnohistory

In other parts of the world, generally similar glass reworking practices have been documented. For example, at 1500 B.C. in Egypt and A.D. 1700 in West Africa, powdered glass was refired in clay molds to make beads and vases respectively. There are similarities between these examples and the remelted glass pendants in North American in that they rely on the general properties of working with and remelting glass, but not necessarily the techniques used for reheating and shaping the glass itself. In West Africa people were using clay molds, kilns, and crucibles to remelt this glass (Gott 2014). The remelted glass in West Africa kilns has a high lime and alumina content, making the properties of the glass different from what is found archaeologically in North America. This high lime and alumina glass was found to melt optimally at around 1200°C (Lankton et al. 2006), a temperature higher than Native Americans would have been able to replicate. Similarly, studies of early glass technology in ancient Egypt demonstrate that people also were melting the powdered glass using clay molds and also using kilns and doing so in a very controlled manner and on a more industrial scale (Nicholson and Shaw 2000). Furthermore, although glass and metal do not necessarily have the same properties, in Egypt and West Africa copper and bronze casting technology had already been developed when people began working with glass. This is not the case among the Native American groups refiring glass pendants. Studying the process of powdering and refiring glass cross-culturally is informative because it might shed light on how glassworking and metalworking technologies are related and might have influenced each other. Because ancient Egyptian and West African processes of melting glass and casting metal are so similar, it may be that in those instances, the invention of sophisticated metal casting helped bring about the development and refinement of glassworking technology. Without such parallel development in North America, it is unsurprising that Native Americans innovated different ways of working with and refiring glass.

Although cross-cultural comparisons of refired glassworking techniques reveal no close technological similarities to the North American refired glass pendants, ethnohistoric evidence from North American contexts provides important insight into this process. Ubelaker and Bass (1970) extensively investigated

ethnohistoric records, including an account from Meriwether Lewis dated to c. A.D. 1805. Through their research, they demonstrated that the glass pendant production process used by Plains peoples required grinding beads to a powder, re-shaping the powder mixed with water into the appropriate shape, and heating the pendants in an open fire on metal or clay pans until fused (Gilmore 1924; Maximilian 1843 [as cited in Ubelaker and Bass 1970:472]; Thwaites 1905:272–274). For the sake of completeness, we review and provide additional commentary on the accounts investigated by Ubelaker and Bass below. We highlight commonalities and differences among recorded production practices.

One document suggests that the making of blue pendants was not an Indigenous invention at all, but rather that the process of crushing glass was taught to the Arikara. An account by Tabeau (Abel 1939:149) states that "a Spanish prisoner taught them (Arikara) how to melt our glass beads and to mold them into a shape that pleases them" (Ubelaker and Bass 1970:472). This reference highlights the possibility that the technology of pendant production may have been introduced by Europeans, and it is possible that the idea of producing refired glass pendants came from people of European origin. However, colonial biases regarding the technological sophistication of Indigenous people also may have influenced Tabeau's assertion. Regardless of the origin of this technology, refired pendants became an integral part of burial rituals and ideological practices of Plains communities (Howard 1972). The original source of technological knowledge for pendant-making in the Upper Great Lakes region is unknown, but recreating the process of pendant production may help clarify the cultural origins of this technology by highlighting similarities and differences in processes used across North America through time.

Although most of the historic accounts describe using clay molds as part of the process, perhaps similar in form to those used in Egyptian and West African contexts, Ubelaker and Bass (1970) argued that metal "firing pans," documented in fewer ethnohistoric references, also may have been used. Our experimental research supports this assertion. However, the account of Tabeau, mentioned above, describes a process of "molding" the glass as part of the production sequence, and indeed, molding is frequently mentioned in the ethnohistoric accounts. It is important to distinguish between the verb "molding," or shaping, and the use of clay molds themselves. Maximilian (1843:348) gives an account of a pendant production method observed while visiting Upper Missouri in 1833. He claimed that:

> Among the Mandans, Manitaries, and Arikkaras, the women, as Lewis and Clarke relate, manufacture beads from coloured glass. They powder those which they have obtained from the traders, and *mold* them into different shapes. This custom is, however, no longer common (Maximilian 1843:348, as cited in Ubelaker and Bass 1970:472; emphasis ours).

Powdering the glass beads seems to be a common first step in most production sequences. According to Maximilian, molding took place, but this verb may be synonymous with shaping the powdered glass, which could be done on a firing pan, not necessarily requiring a "mold" of clay or other material.

Another account of pendant production, this one discussing the blue and white coloration of the ornaments, came from the fur trader Denig (1930) in Missouri, and makes a specific reference to clay molds, stating:

> They (the Arikara) also have the art of melting beads of different colors and casting them in *molds of clay* for ear and other ornaments of various shapes, some of which are very ingeniously done. We have seen some in shape and size as drawn in plate 65, the groundwork blue, the Figure white, the whole about one-eighth inch thick, and *presenting a uniform glazed surface* (Denig 1930:413, as cited in Ubelaker and Bass 1970:472; emphasis ours).

The surface uniformity described reflects a relatively high-temperature method of reheating the glass. Unlike in Maximilian's and Tabeau's accounts, Denig's version of the process involves actual "molds of clay" as the method of shaping the pendants. Likewise, clay molds are involved in the description provided by George Bird Grinnell (1924:223), who describes the practice of the Cheyenne:

> they melted the glass, with which to make the beads, in the ladles used in melting lead for their bullets. These ornaments or charms were made in various shapes, often in the form of a lizard, as said, *or flat on one side and round on the other*. Sometimes they had a perforation through which a string might be passed; at other times merely a constriction between two ends about which a string was tied. *The mold was made of clay* (Grinnell 1924:223, as cited in Ubelaker and Bass 1970:472; emphasis ours).

Grinnell's account references the flat reverse and rounded obverse of an artifact that might be fired on a flat firing pan, but notes that a clay mold was used. If it were, it would have to have been relatively shallow

to allow for the rounding of the edges of one side of the pendant, an effect produced by the surface tension of fusing glass. To date, no archaeological evidence of clay molds of these types has been identified in published literature, or in the authors' examinations of artifact collections from sites where pendants have been recovered in the Midwest.

Of greatest interest to the present study is an account by Gilmore (1924:21), again cited in Ubelaker and Bass. This account mentions not clay molds, but rather the shaping of powdered glass paste on "firing pans" made from copper-base metal, including the butt-plates of firearms:

> Then they prepared a *firing pan from the brass rim or binding of the butt of an old musket* on which was laid a bed of sand. The powdered glass was moistened with water; then with a fine wooden tool this glass paste *was shaped* into the forms desired on the prepared bed of sand. The firing pan was carefully placed in a hot fire of dry elm wood, this wood being used because it would burn quietly without snapping or crackling. When heated to the proper temperature the glass paste became fused (Gilmore 1924:21 as cited in Ubelaker and Bass 1970:473; emphasis ours).

Ubelaker and Bass (1970: 473) agreed that firing pans, rather than clay molds, were more likely used to produce the Arikara pendants they studied, since such metal pans had been identified in burials they examined at the Leavenworth site. Some pans even had glass residue adhering to them. Placing the firing pan on a bed of sand or perhaps ash may be an important part of the process; it is possible that sand grains or ash prevent the glass pendants from sticking to the metal during heating.

Past Efforts at Pendant Process Replication

When replicating the pendant production process, Ubelaker and Bass stated that they completely fused a re-formed powdered glass paste at a temperature of about 1500°C by using a modern kiln (1970:472–473). However, their study does not take into account the range of temperature and heating conditions of an open fire, which might result in only partial glass melting. Glass ingredients such as finely ground silica and fluxes will sinter or partially fuse at approximately 650 to 800°C in a process known as fritting (Miller 2007:137); this could be achieved in an open fire without the need for a kiln or glass furnace. No matter what firing temperature was used to fuse glass pendants, the initial step of powdering the glass beads and reforming them into pendants would effectively homogenize the original glass recipes of whatever European bead types were used as raw material.

This is an important consideration in compositional analyses of glass pendants (Walder 2013).

Physical Attributes of Refired Pendants

Evidence from visual examination of refired glass artifacts supports the production method of low-temperature fusion of powdered glass on metal firing-pans rather than complete remelting of glass. Walder (2013, 2015) has documented pendants from archaeological contexts across the Midwest, photographing the obverse, reverse, and close-up using a Dinolite digital microscope. When pendants are magnified, grains of ground glass appear to be incompletely fritted together rather than fully melted; this is especially visible at the interface of different colors of glass in striped pendants (Figure 2). Also, some pendant fragments appear to have metal adhering to their surfaces (Figure 3).

Several physical characteristics of the pendants themselves provide indications of their production methods. The pendants are generally very flat on one side; when adhering metal is present, it is generally found on the flat side, which is considered the reverse side. Bubbles or other imperfections are also sometimes present on the reverse of the pendant (Figure 4, top) where it would have been in contact with the pan, but none appear on the obverse surface. Many pendants have rounded edges on the obverse (see Figure 4 bottom). This shape would result from the heating of a glass paste, which would hold together with the surface tension of the glass on the side not in contact with the metal pan, producing the rounded edge of the obverse side. Not all refired glass fragments have such a distinctive edge shape, and different craftspeople may have had multiple methods to heat and solidify the glass paste.

Figure 2. Interface between blue and white glass stripes of a glass pendant, showing grains of glass, heated until it fritted or sintered until it fused but did not fully melt. Scale bar = 1 mm. (Image by Walder.)

Figure 3. Pendant fragment from the Gros Cap site (Martin 1979) with possible metal adhering: top, plan view of reverse side; bottom, profile view. Scale in mm. (Image by Walder.)

Figure 4. Pendant: top, reverse side, flat smooth surface with small bubbles visible in plan view; bottom, profile view showing rounded edges on the obverse side and flattened edges on the reverse. (Image by Walder.)

A possible metal "firing pan" and several pieces of metal with a blue substance adhering were identified during Walder's analysis of reworked copper-based metals analyses of materials from the Rock Island site (Walder 2015:283) (Figure 5). These metal artifacts with blue residue are associated with an Odawa house structure dated to about 1760, from which context two refired glass pendant fragments also were recovered. The blue residue has sand grains stuck to it (see Gilmore 1924:21), and there is a trapezoidal discoloration that might have resulted from differential cooling of a hot pendant on the metal surface.

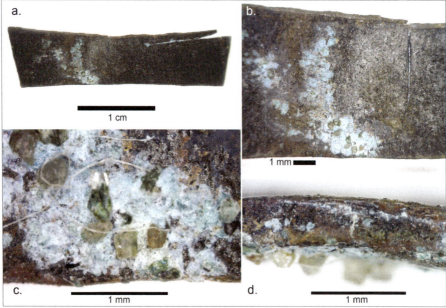

Figure 5. (a) Metal artifact with blue glass adhering to the surface, possibly a "firing pan" for pendant production; (b) trapezoidal discoloration, possibly resulting from glass heating on the metal surface; (c) sand grains, possibly part of the production process, adhering to the glass; (d) glass residue on the cut basal edge of the artifact. (Image by Walder.)

As described above, ethnographically documented production processes for refired glass pendants included both metal plates and glass beads, but few researchers have addressed both of these material types in the same assemblages. This may be one reason why the process is not well understood, since metals researchers may not recognize adhering glass material, while glass specialists are not looking through non-glass assemblages for glass pendant production waste. In addition, corrosion products of copper tend to be a similar blue-green hue as blue glass residue, and archaeologists not specifically looking for glass residue, a relatively rare form of production waste, may easily and understandably misidentify glass reside as corrosion products.

Chaîne Opératoire

A schematic diagram of a possible chaine opéra-toire or production process for refired glass pendants (Figure 6) illustrates the technological processes and materials needed to transform glass beads into pendants. This schematic summarizes existing under-standings of production processes specific to glass beads and refired glass pendants (drawn from Kidd and Kidd 1970; Miller 2007; Ubelaker and Bass 1970).

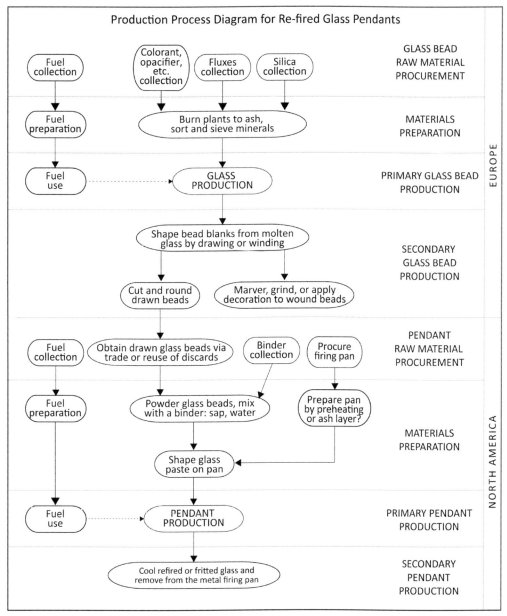

Figure 6. Chaîne Opératoire flow chart for making refired glass pendants, including both the glass bead production process in Europe and the refiring process as proposed for North America. (Image by Walder.)

Experimental Replication Methods

The replication of the pendant production processes demonstrated that soda-lime glass, the primary material used for historic-era trade beads, can fuse at a temperature below the melting point of copper, and that the physical characteristics of pendants from the archaeological record can be reproduced. Replication attempts took place both in a controlled setting, an enameling kiln, as well as in a less controlled campfire trial. Schultz designed and implemented the enameling kiln experimental method and procedure, which took place in the University of Wisconsin–La Crosse Art Department, while Walder conducted the informal campfire trial by collaborating with glass artisan Stephanie Aust. Modern soda lime glass was used in the experimental replications, since this material is very similar in composition to the historic soda lime glass used for beads, and because today it would be considered unethical to destroy historic glass trade beads for the purpose of this experiment. The differences between the modern glass used in the experimental replication and historic glass beads are the presence of colorants in glass beads, such as copper or cobalt to give the glass its blue hue, as well as trace amounts of impurities not found in modern glass. Soda lime glass is used in many of the commercial glasses available today, and it is primarily used to create windows and tablewear (Martin 2001).

Controlled Enameling Kiln Replication

For the kiln experimental replication, a clear drinking glass was used as raw material, and a frit grinder was constructed to crush the glass in a controlled and contained manner (Figure 7). The frit grinder was made

Figure 7. Frit grinder constructed to crush glass to a consistent size. (Image by Schultz.)

by welding steel tubing and a steel plate together. This also allowed for the glass to be easily crushed into pieces no larger than 2 mm. In the past, glass beads could have been crushed using a mortar and pestle, or simply between two stones; the frit grinder was used to effectively produce glass powder or frit of a consistent size. Note that some pendants from archaeological contexts have discolored "blotches" on their surface, such as the pendants from the Marquette Mission site (Figure 8). Such blotches may be a result of larger individual glass pieces of perhaps 2–5 mm in size fusing and partially melting into each other. These blotches occur in some but not all archaeological examples of pendants.

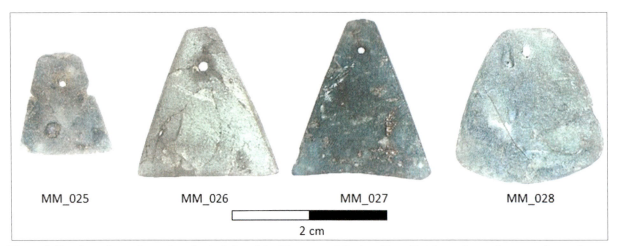

MM_025   MM_026   MM_027   MM_028

2 cm

Figure 8. Pendants from the archaeological site of the Marquette Mission. Note blotchy or inconsistent surface coloration, and smoothly rounded apertures of the pendants, especially visible on sample MM_026. (Image by Walder.)

After the frit was crushed into small and relatively uniform pieces, water was added to create a grainy paste. This paste was then placed on a 6mm thick copper sheet and formed into a trapezoidal shape. This copper sheet was somewhat thicker than many kettle fragments recovered from archaeological sites, but not out of the range of available metal scraps, such as those that could be obtained by modifying firearm parts, as documented ethnohistorically. The thicker metal sheet in this experiment helped reduce the stress on the glass after removal from the heat source and to prevent the glass from shattering. In a few of the experiments a thinner piece of copper was used to test this concept. This copper was 1.3 mm thick, slightly thicker than some copper-base metal kettle fragments identified archaeologically, and glass cracked and broke as it cooled on the thinner sheets.

After the glass was formed into a trapezoidal shape on the copper plate, it was then placed into an enameling kiln. An enameling kiln was used for this experiment rather than an open-air fire because it offered greater heat control, heated slowly and uniformly, and had a built-in thermometer for exact temperature readings. This kiln was heated to a final temperature of 1,000°C in intervals of 50°C, starting from 700°C. The glass was left at each interval for 15 minutes. At every interval the glass was photographed, and a copper rod was poked into the surface to test the malleability of the glass. Soda-lime glass has a softening point of about 724°C (Nixton 2014); therefore, the glass was checked at intervals below this point to confirm that no softening had occurred. The temperature of 1,000°C was not exceeded since the melting point of copper is 1083°C (Bentor 1996).

Testing the softness of the glass served multiple purposes. As illustrated above, many pendants from archaeological contexts have a distinctive, rounded or bulb shape on their edges. They have a mostly flat surface on top, with the corners of the pendant rounding towards the back. These corners come to a sharper edge on the back or reverse side, and the backs of these pendants are completely flat. This can only be achieved through a substantial melt during which the surface tension of the individual glass pieces gives way to the larger whole.

Furthermore, the apertures for stringing at the top of the pendants were not drilled, and they may have been formed while the glass was still in a semi-molten state. If these had been made using a drill, they would have much sharper edges, and cut marks would be present on the glass. Historic records mention that the holes were formed as part of the clay mold process (Thwaites 1904:272–274); however, this method was not formally tested in this experiment. Some

pendants found archaeologically have apertures that have rounded edges, which are identical in form to the edges of the pendants themselves. At the end of the experiment the glass was allowed to cool slowly in the kiln overnight to prevent cracking. The glass was then examined to see if the desired fusion had taken place, and the results compared to what has been found archaeologically.

Open-Air Uncontrolled Experiment

An informal attempt to produce a glass pendant in a campfire was also conducted as a proof-of-concept trial, once the results from the firing kiln trials were known. For this open-air firing experiment, Walder collaborated with a modern glass artisan, Stephanie Aust, to solve the particular problem of the glass pendant adhering to metal firing pans. Aust suggested that an ash layer between the metal pan and the glass powder would be sufficient to prevent sticking. In this trial, modern soda-lime glass beads were roughly crushed to particles sized approximately 2 to 6 mm, and placed on an ash layer approximately 2 mm thick, on an iron scrap, simulating the thickness of a firearm buttplate in this trial (Figure 9a). Note that glass particle size was an uncontrolled variable in this test, and additional trials of more finely crushed glass particles would likely produce some different results. The iron scrap plate was placed in a campfire, which was burning at a temperature of approximately 800 to 900°Celsius, visually estimated by the orange-red colors of the flames and coals (Figure 9b). Over the course of approximately three hours, the glass pieces could be seen smoothing and beginning to melt amid the coals (Figure 9c and 9d). The pan was left in the fire overnight, and Aust removed the firing pan from the firepit the next morning.

Results

In both of the experimental setups, it was possible to recreate some aspects of glass pendants that are found archaeologically. In the experiments that used the enameling kiln, the glass fragments began to adhere to one another around 800°C. At this temperature the surface of the glass remained mostly unchanged; however, the large individual glass granules started to round out into spheres, though they remained separate and did not pool together (Figure 10). The smaller glass granules began to adhere to one another, and the glass in contact with the copper began to stick to the surface of the plates. The glass visually remained the same until 950°C was reached and the surface tension of the glass began to give way. The surface of the glass

Figure 9. Open-air firing method using an ash layer between the glass fragments and metal pan: (a) crushed beads on ash layer on iron scrap; (b) iron scrap in campfire; (c) glass beginning to melt; (d) glass among ashes. (Images by Walder.)

began to smooth over (Figures 11 and 12), and it began developing liquid-like properties. Note the shiny texture present at this point that was absent from previous, lower-temperature attempts. Although the glass was somewhat malleable near 1,000°C, it is important to note the glass is nowhere near a molten state at that temperature, and that it was not viscous enough to roll off the copper sheet.

The blue flecks that can be seen in the experimental glass pendants are caused by the glass absorbing some of the copper from the plates and oxidizing. Oxidized copper turns a blue green color, and considering that copper was originally used as one of the coloring agents for the historic glass beads (Chafe et al. 1986), it is not surprising that the copper from the

plate contaminated the surface of the glass. In archaeological examples of pendants, blue staining from the oxidization of copper firing pans would be less visible on glass powder obtained from blue glass beads, since these would already contain copper as a colorant in the glass. In some trials of the replication experiment, copper dust was sprinkled over the surface of the clear glass pendants prior to firing, resulting in blue coloring of the glass (e.g., Figure 13). Note that the process of using copper dust was not documented archaeologically or ethnohistorically, but rather was part of Schultz's initial experimentation. Since copper was already present as a colorant in glass beads used to make pendants in the past, the addition of copper here

Figure 10. Photograph of the glass inside the kiln at 800°C. Note the uneven texture and that the individual glass chunks are still visible. Copper plate 3 x 7 inches. (Image by Schultz.)

Figure 11. Photograph of the glass at 950°C. Note that the surface texture has smoothed and become more homogenous. (Image by Schultz.)

Figure 12. Photograph of the cooled glass that was heated to 950°C. Note the lackluster surface and smooth appearance. (Image by Schultz.)

Figure 13. Left, copper sheet with glass residue adhering; right, experimental pendant sprinkled with copper dust and heated to 950°C. Note the bright blue coloring. (Image by Schultz.)

should not have affected the outcomes of the replication experiment.

The replication experiment shows that soda-lime glass in powdered form will fuse at approximately 1000°C, a temperature achievable in a hot, sustained campfire. Glass must be heated to this extreme temperature for an extended period of time. Since soda-lime glass will crack under drastic temperature changes, it is unlikely that past pendant producers would have quickly heated and removed their pendants from a fire. Leaving the glass overnight in the kiln allowed the temperature of the glass to come down at a steady rate to avoid cracking. In one of the preliminary experiments, within minutes after the glass had been removed from a 800°C kiln, it cracked into four large pieces, and micro-cracks were also visible under the surface of the glass (Figure 14).

These experiments also produced large individual granules, and discoloration that is also present in the archaeological glass pendants. Although the fritted glass particles did fuse at 1000°C, somewhat separate glass particles are still visible, as in archaeological examples (e.g., Figures 2 and 8). In addition, experimentally replicated pendants also had a rounded obverse edge and a flat reverse side, the same attributes observed in archaeological examples (e.g., Figure 4).

Throughout the experimental replication process using the kiln, several important observations were made. First, it proved extremely difficult to remove the refired glass from the copper sheets. In the few cases where the glass was successfully removed, it

was because the glass was heated on the 1.3 mm sheet of copper. The thinner piece of copper warped while cooling, causing a large crack to develop in between the copper sheet and the glass itself, allowing the glass to be removed from the sheet. Although the glass was able to be removed, it left a thin glass residue on the copper sheets (Figure 13).

The glass adhering to the surface of the copper could also explain why so many of the samples in the experimental replication cracked. When the copper plates were heated they would have expanded slightly. This would have taken place at a lower temperature than the melting point of the glass. The glass would have begun to melt onto the expanded copper sheets, and as the plates began to cool, the glass began to solidify before the copper plates could finish contracting. This shrinking caused the glass to crack. The thinner plates might have also allowed the copper itself to give more as the glass was pulling on the surface, while the thicker plates would have been too thick to warp with the glass. Similar cracked, fragmentary pieces of refired glass were identified by Walder in the archaeological assemblage of the Zimmerman Site in Illinois (Figure 15) and provide indirect evidence of pendant production at this site.

Ubelaker and Bass stated that in their experiments that a thin layer of firescale developed between the glass and the copper, making removal of the glass from the plate relatively easy. Firescale is a layer of oxides that form on the surface of a piece of metal when it is heated. When copper is heated it produces cuprous

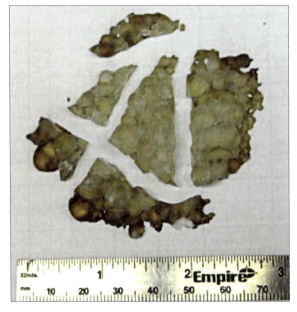

Figure 14. Photograph of cooled glass heated only to 800°C. Note the uneven texture and that the individual glass chunks are still visible. Also notice the cloudy appearance of the glass. (Photo by Schultz.)

Figure 15. Examples of incompletely fused, cracked, and otherwise unsuccessful attempts at pendant production. Artifacts are from the Zimmerman site. ZM_03 has possible copper oxide or "firescale" adhering to one surface, and ZM_06 is cracked as if it cooled too quickly. (Image by Walder.)

oxide and then cupric oxide (Zhang and Richardson 2016). This oxide forms a thin, hard black layer that can be broken off or removed with acid. In all of the present replication experiments, the firescale formed after the glass had already adhered to the surface of the copper plates. Firescale develops on copper at around 760°C, so the glass used in these experiments was at least softening somewhat before this temperature was reached. This is also shown by the copper coloring contamination visible on some of the clear glass experimental samples. Since the glass used in the experimental experiments was clear, it is possible to see that the copper and the glass fused before the black firescale present on the rest of the plate appeared (Figure 16).

Although brass could have been used as a firing pan in the past, it was not used in these experiments for various reasons. Brass has a melting point of between 900 and 940°C, depending on the ratio of copper to zinc (Callcut 2000). Using copper in these experiments meant that the glass could be tested at higher temperatures without the risk of the firing pan melting. The accumulation of firescale on the metal was also taken into consideration in these experiments, since the layer of oxides could explain how the glass was cleanly removed from the firing pans. Using brass would not produce as thick a layer of firescale, due to the lower concentration of copper in the alloy.

To address the problem of sticking and cracking, the ash layer trial in the campfire was conducted. The trial successfully produced a partially re-fired glass pendant that could easily be removed from the ash layer, which kept it from sticking to the metal firing pan. The obverse of the pendant shows the same smoothing and partial remelting observed in the kiln trials heated to 850–900°C (Figure 17).

Results of both experimental set-ups show that the ideal temperature for successfully fusing soda-lime glass is around 1,000°C. Below this temperature the glass only partially fuses, leaving a nonuniform and lackluster surface, which can be pitted or blotchy in appearance. This result is inconsistent with the previous attempt to recreate this process by Ubelaker and Bass (1970). They reported that the optimal temperature for the fusion of refired glass is 1,500°C. This would not be possible with the copper plate method because the plates would have melted long before this temperature was reached. It is possible that they could have confused Fahrenheit and Celsius in their publication. If so, then this would have meant that the glass optimally melted at 815°C (1,500°F) in their study. These results were not replicated in these experiments. Rather, our current experimental study demonstrated that this temperature was too low for glass fusion to take place. It is possible that a slight compositional difference between modern and historic glass could have

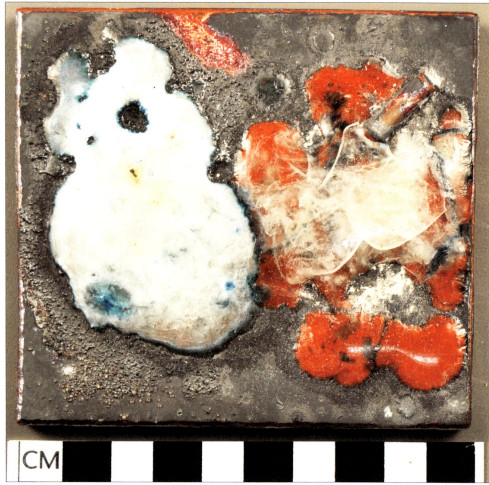

Figure 16. Experimental glass pendants heated to 950°C. Note that the pendant on the right appears to be a deep red because of copper contamination. The rest of the plate is covered in black firescale. (Image by Schultz.)

Figure 17. Experimental pendant with rounded edges produced by heating on an ash layer in a campfire with overnight cooling: left, obverse, showing partially fused glass fragments; right, reverse, showing ashy material still present, but no metal adhering to the flatter, back of the pendant. (Photos by Stephanie Aust, composite image by Walder.)

contributed to this difference, since modern soda-lime glass was used in the present study, while Ubelaker and Bass ground up archaeological glass beads for their experiment. However, in her previous chemical analysis research, Walder recorded no inconsistencies in the compositions of archaeological glass beads, such as extremely high levels of flux, that could explain the difference in melting temperatures. Ubelaker and Bass also mention (1970:474) that if the glass is left in the fire for too long, it will become so hot that it will run off of the copper plates. In this series of experiments, even at 1,000°C the glass was not nearly viscous enough to roll off the copper plates in this manner.

Conclusions and Future Directions

Although we identified the optimal temperature for the fusion of the powdered glass to produce refired glass pendants similar to those recovered archaeologically, there are still more questions that need to be answered. Throughout these experiments the trapezoidal shape was never able to be replicated; pendants generally did not hold their form well. It has been suggested that a finer crush of glass would help retain the desired shape after melting (William Billeck, personal communication to Schultz and Walder 2016). Although this might help with form, it is unclear if this would produce the same blotchy and irregular color pattern visible in some archaeological pendants. The hole in the top for stringing was also not replicated, despite attempts to poke or form such a hole when the glass was malleable. Since some historic accounts state the Arikara used wet clay molds (Grinnell 1924:223), it is possible that the hole could have been made as part of the mold. Clay molds were not tested in this experiment, since it is unclear what kind of clay would have been used, and because wet clay can explode when heated too quickly, due to the water in the clay evaporating and becoming trapped within the clay. Since the temperature trials of the experiment were done in an indoor environment with special equipment, attempting trials with wet clay molds would have been too risky.

The largest question left unanswered is how the pendants were removed cleanly from the copper plates. A firescale layer may have been created on the firing pans before the glass began to fuse; however, this was not replicated in these experiments. This could be explained by slight compositional differences between historic and modern soda-lime glass, causing the glass to begin to fuse above the temperature that firescale develops, around 760°C; however, further

research would have to be done to confirm this. Conversely, perhaps the copper plates or firing pans were preheated, allowing the firescale to form first. After the plate was preheated, the glass paste could have been placed on the plate, either while still warm or after cooling. Sand or an ashy layer could also have been used as a release or buffer between the glass and metal, since the campfire trial demonstrates that such a method is a viable way of preventing the pendants from sticking to the firing pan.

Future scientific examinations of artifacts associated with the production process would also be informative. The composition of the presumed glass material adhering to the metal "firing pan" from the Rock Island site and a metallic substance adhering to a pendant fragment (GC_05) from the Gros Cap site (Figure 3, above) could be verified using SEM-EDS, or Scanning Electron Microscopy with Energy Dispersive Spectroscopy. This nondestructive method allows both the visualization and compositional characterization of materials including both glass and copper-base metal. Metal artifacts with possible glass residue and pendants with adhering metal will be prioritized for future archaeometric research.

This experiment in replicating refired glass pendants changes our understanding of how Indigenous peoples could have formed these objects in the past. We have confirmed that the process of transforming glass beads into larger pendants is completely possible with technologies and materials that Native Americans had in the Midwest in the seventeenth and eighteenth centuries. Possible differences in refiring techniques, as well as differences in composition of the historic glass trade beads, leading to slightly different melting temperatures that in turn would affect firescale development, could also explain why some pendants appear to have adhered to the copper plates, while others appear to have been removed cleanly. Nevertheless, glass fusion to produce pendants is possible at temperatures obtainable in an outdoor wood fire. Although this does not necessarily make it an independently discovered skill, it is possible that glass re-forming is something the Native Americans developed without European influence. Since the process Native Americans used to create these pendants is so different than what is seen in ancient Egypt and West Africa, this might point to a completely independent discovery of how to work with glass. Although a complete understanding of the glass re-forming production sequence for North American refired glass pendants remains elusive, these experiments contribute to our knowledge of this unique technological process.

Acknowledgments

We thank the University of Wisconsin–La Crosse College of Liberal Studies (CLS) for a Spring 2016 Small Grant, obtained with the assistance of Dr. Constance Arzigian, who also provided significant editorial guidance. The CLS grant facilitated the preparation and revision of this article while both authors were at UW–La Crosse. Two reviewers, Dr. Laure Dussubieux and Dr. William T. Billeck, provided substantial technical and content-based critiques that were used to improve the quality of this article. Schultz thanks the UW–La Crosse Undergraduate Research Office for funding her initial grant, Dr. Brad Nichols and the Art Department for allowing her to use the enameling kiln, and Dr. Kate Grillo of the Department of Archaeology and Anthropology for help in developing the project for her thesis. Walder thanks the many curating institutions that provided her access to collections including refired glass pendants as part of her dissertation research undertaken in 2012 and 2013. The compositional analyses of the glass pendants took place at the Chicago Field Museum's Elemental Analysis Facility, under the direction of Dussubieux. Funding for travel to collections as well as compositional analyses was obtained from a National Science Foundation Doctoral Dissertation Improvement Grant (BCS-1321751, PI Sissel Schroeder). Ms. Stephanie Aust was generous with her materials, time, and talents in facilitating the outdoor replication experiment.

References Cited

Abel, A. H.
1939   *Tabeau's Narrative of Loisel's Expedition to the Upper Missouri*. University of Oklahoma Press, Norman.

Behm, Jeffery A.
2008   The Meskwaki in Eastern Wisconsin: Ethnohistory and Archaeology. *The Wisconsin Archeologist* 89(1&2):7–85.

Bentor, Yinon
1996   *Periodic Table: Copper*. Electronic document, http://www.chemicalelements.com/elements/cu.html, accessed February 15 2015.

Birmingham, Robert A., and Robert J. Salzer
1984   The Marina Site Excavations. Unpublished Monograph Number 1 of the Wisconsin Archeological Society. Manuscript on file at the Wisconsin Historical Society.

Bradley, James W.
1987   *Evolution of the Onondaga Iroquois: Accommodating Change, 1500–1655*. Syracuse University Press, Syracuse, New York.
2007   *Before Albany: An Archaeology of Native-Dutch Relations in the Capital Region, 1600–1664*. University of the State of New York, State Education Department, Albany.

Branstner, Susan M.
1992   Tionontate Huron Occupation at the Marquette Mission. In *Calumet and Fleur-de-Lys: Archaeology of Indian and French Contact in the Midcontinent*, edited by J. A. Walthall and T. E. Emerson, pp. 177–201. Smithsonian Institution Press, Washington D. C.

Brown, James A. (editor)
1961   *The Zimmerman Site*. Reports of Investigations Volume 9. Illinois State Museum, Springfield.

Brown, Margaret Kimball
1972   Native Made Glass Pendants from East of the Mississippi. *American Antiquity* 37(3):432–439.
1975   *The Zimmerman Site: Further Excavations at the Grand Village of Kaskaskia*. State of Illinois, Department of Registration and Education, Illinois State Museum, Springfield.

Callcut, Vin
2000   *Innovations. Newsletter of the Copper Development Association. Introduction to Brasses (Part II)*. Electronic document, https://www.copper.org/publications/newsletters/innovations/2000/01/brasses02.html#duplex, accessed November 8, 2016.

Chafe, Anne, Ronald G. V. Hancock, and Ian Kenyon
1986   A Note on the Neutron Activation Analysis of 16th and 17th Century Blue Glass Trade Beads from the Eastern Great Lakes. *Beads Journal of the Society of Bead Researchers* 1986(9):13–18.

Denig, E. T.
1930   *Indian Tribes of the Upper Missouri*. Forty Sixth Annual Report of the Bureau of American Ethnology 1928-1929, pp. 375–628. Washington, D. C.

Dussubieux, Laure
2009   Chemical Investigation of Some 17th Century French Glass Personal Ornaments. *Journal of Glass Studies* 51:95–110.

Dussubieux, Laure, and Karlis Karklins
2016   Glass Bead Production in Europe During the 17th Century: Elemental Analysis of Glass Material Found in London and Amsterdam. *Journal of Archaeological Science*: Reports 5:574–589.

Ehrhardt, Kathleen
2005   *European Metals in Native Hands*. University of Alabama Press, Tuscaloosa.

Evans, Lynn L. M.
2001   *House D of the Southeast Rowhouse: Excavations of Fort Michilimackinac, 1989–1997*. Mackinac State Historic Parks, Mackinac Island, Michigan.

Grinnell, George Bird
1924   *The Cheyenne Indians: Their History and Ways of Life*. 2 vols. Yale University Press, New Haven.

Gilmore, Melvin R.
1924   *Glass Bead Making by the Arikara*. Museum of the American Indian, Heye Foundation Indian Notes 2(1):20–21.

Gott, Suzanne
2014   Ghana's Glass Beadmaking Arts in Transcultural Dialogues. *African Arts* 47:110–129.

Howard, James H.
1972   Arikara Native-Made Glass Pendants: Their Probable Function. *American Antiquity* 37(1):93–97.

Janssens, K., S. Cagno, I. De Raedt, and P. Degryse
2013   Transfer of Glass Manufacturing Technology in the Sixteenth and Seventeenth Centuries from Southern to Northern Europe: Using Trace Element Patterns to Reveal the Spread from Venice via Antwerp to London. In *Modern Methods for Analysing Archaeological and Historical Glass*, edited by Koen Janssens, pp. 537–562. John Wiley & Sons, Oxford, United Kingdom.

Kidd, Kenneth E. and Martha A. Kidd
1970   *A Classification System for Glass Beads for the Use of Field Archaeologists*. Canadian Historic Sites: Occasional Papers in Archaeology and History No. 1. Department of Indian Affairs and Northern Development, Ottawa.

Lankton, James W., O Akin Ige, and Thilo Rehren
2006   Early Primary Glass Production in Southern Nigeria. *Journal of African Archaeology* 4(1):111–138.

Martin, Steve W.
2001   Glass Facts. Electronic document, http://www.texasglass.com/glass_facts/composition_of_Glass.htm, accessed February 15th, 2016.

Martin, Susan R.
1979   *Final Report: Phase II Archaeological Site Examination of the Gros Cap Cemetery Area, Mackinac County, Michigan*. Cultural Resource Management Reports No. 6. Michigan Technological University, Houghton.

Mason, Richard P., and Carol L. Mason
1997   A Brief Report on the Mahler Portion of the Doty Island Village Site. *The Wisconsin Archeologist* 79(1):208–231.

Mason, Ronald J.
1986   *Rock Island Historical Indian Archaeology in the Northern Lake Michigan Basin*. MCJA Special Paper No. 6. Kent State University Press, Kent, Ohio.

Maximilian, Prince of Wied
1843   *Travels in the Interior of North America*. Ackermann and Co., London.

Miller, Heather M. L.
2007   *Archaeological Approaches to Technology*. Elsevier/Academic Press, New York.

Nicholson, Paul T., and Ian Shaw
2000   *Ancient Egyptian Materials and Technology*. Cambridge University Press, New York.

Nixton, Doug
2014   *Physical Properties*. Electronic document. http://www.udel.edu/chem/GlassShop/PhysicalProperties.htm, accessed February 16 2015.

Shott, Michael J., Joseph A. Tiffany, John F. Doershuk, and Jason Titcomb.
2002   The Reliability of Surface Assemblages: Recent Results from the Gillett Grove Site, Clay County, Iowa. *Plains Anthropologist* 47(181):165–182.

Stone, Lyle M.
1974   *Fort Michilimackinac, 1715–1781: An Archaeological Perspective on the Revolutionary Frontier*. The Museum, Michigan State University, East Lansing.

Thwaites, Reuben Gold (editor)
1904–1905   *Original Journals of the Lewis and Clark Expedition, 1804–1806*. 7 vols. Dodd, Mead & Company, New York.

Turgeon, Laurier
1997   The Tale of the Kettle, Odyssey of an Intercultural Object. *Ethnohistory* 44(1):1–29.

Tyler, K., and H. B. Willmott
2005   *John Baker's Late 17th-Century Glasshouse at Vauxhall*. Museum of London Archaeology Service.

Ubelaker, Douglas H., and William Bass
1970   Arikara Glassworking Techniques at the Leavenworth and Sully Sites. *American Antiquity* 35(4):467–475.

Van der Linden, V., E. Bultinck, J. De Ruyter, O. Schalm, K. Janssens, W. Devos, and W. Tiri
2005   Compositional Analysis of 17–18th Century Archaeological Glass Fragments Excavated in Mechelen, Belgium: Comparison with Data from Neighboring Cities in the Low Countries. *Nuclear Instruments and Methods in Physics Research Section B: Beam Interactions with Materials and Atoms* 239(1–2):100–106.

Walder, Heather
2013   Laser Ablation–Inductively Coupled Plasma–Mass Spectrometry (LA-ICP-MS) Analysis of Refired Glass Pendants from the North American Upper Great Lakes. *Archaeological Chemistry* 8:365–395.

2015   *"...A Thousand Beads to Each Nation:" Exchange, Interactions, and Technological Practices in the Upper Great Lakes c. 1630–1730.* Ph.D. dissertation. Department of Anthropology, University of Wisconsin–Madison.

Walthall, John A., and Elizabeth D. Benchley

1987   *The River L'Abbe Mission: A French Colonial Church for the Cahokia Illini on Monks Mound.* Studies in Illinois Archaeology No. 2. Illinois Historic Preservation Agency, Springfield.

Zhang, J., and Richardson, H. W.

2016   Copper Compounds. *Ullmann's Encyclopedia of Industrial Chemistry.* 1–31.

Archaeological Remains of the Rice Rat (*Oryzomys*) as a Climatic Proxy in the American Midwest

Kent D. Vickery, James L. Theler, and Orrin C. Shane III

Abstract

The rice rat (Oryzomys) is found today south of a line that runs through southern Illinois, Missouri, and Kentucky. Yet, there are abundant records of rice rats found in archaeological and paleontological sites throughout the Ohio, Missouri, and Illinois River valleys, well north of the modern range. These occurrences along the rice rat's northern range are summarized for each of four pre-modern cultural periods, and hypotheses concerning their former presence in this area are evaluated, with particular attention to climatic explanations. By correlating the rice rat's former range limits with present-day mean minimum January isotherms, the following climatic reconstructions are proposed: the late Middle Woodland period (A.D. 150–450) was characterized by mild winters averaging ca. 4.2°C (7°F) warmer; Late Woodland (A.D. 450–950) winters were ca. 0.6°C (1°F) cooler; a return to milder winters approximating those of the late Middle Woodland occurred in Early Mississippian times (A.D. 1000–1400), and colder winters during the Late Mississippian–Historic period (A.D. 1500–1650) are evidenced by a 2.4°C (4°F) decrease, corresponding with the initial phase of the Neo-Boreal climatic episode.

Introduction

What was this creature doing in the forest primeval of yesterday, some 200–300 miles north of its present range? And why has its range shrunk so dramatically? This was more than just a local phenomenon. Archaeologists, in a broad belt of country from West-Central Illinois to Western Pennsylvania, have been unearthing rice rat bones where there are none living today! [Guilday 1961b:24]

Over the past 80 years, various hypotheses concerning the occurrence of rice rat (*Oryzomys palustris*) elements in archaeological sites north of the species' modern range have been presented in the literature. This study documents rice rat remains in archaeological and paleontological contexts in the American Midwest and assesses these hypotheses. We use the species' past occurrences north of its modern range as a proxy to reconstruct one parameter of climate (mean minimum January temperature) for selected prehistoric and early historic time periods.

This paper was written and revised several times between 1979 and 1986. The objective was to assess the numerous hypotheses regarding the appearance and disappearance of the rice rat, the bones of which had been recovered at many late prehistoric archaeological sites up to 500 km (300+ miles) north of its modern range limit. The paper's three authors each had their interest in this species piqued by the identification of rice rat remains from various late prehistoric contexts in southern Ohio. Vickery had been corresponding with Shane as early as 1969 regarding rice rat occurrences. Theler, an undergraduate student of Vickery's at the University of Cincinnati, assisted in excavations of sites in the Little Miami River valley in Hamilton County, Ohio, with abundant fauna, including rice rat remains, that formed the basis for his Master's thesis (Theler 1978) at the University of Wisconsin–Madison.

Our efforts combined, we reviewed the literature and contacted numerous colleagues, attempting to document all known occurrences of rice rat remains north of their modern range, and to assess hypotheses regarding the prehistoric presence of this regionally extirpated species. In the end, we favored a hypothesis that viewed a climatic shift to warmer cool-season conditions as the likely explanation for the range extension(s) of this rodent, spreading northward

Kent Vickery, 1942-2011; James L. Theler, Mississippi Valley Archaeology Center, University of Wisconsin–La Crosse; Orrin C. Shane III, Downeast Museum Services, Portland, Maine

The Wisconsin Archeologist, 2016, 97(2):49–80

along river valleys to find a commensal home in the middens of later prehistoric peoples.

Though a draft was completed by 1986, competing professional obligations and publication challenges left the paper in limbo. When Vickery retired from the University of Cincinnati in 2004, he sent Theler a box with the accumulated data, manuscript, correspondence, and illustrations. A recent review of the manuscript by Theler and Shane led to the conclusion that the paper had merit in its documentation of archaeological occurrences of rice rats, their ecology, and hypotheses regarding their range shifts in prehistory and could serve as a starting point for future research. This paper seems all the more relevant today as we face a world where climate change will surely shift animal populations again, as it has in the past.

We have not attempted to undertake a major revision of this paper; it stands largely where it was 30 years ago, with clarifications and endnotes. We commend the great efforts by the FAUNMAP Working Group (1996) and the Illinois State Museum (Graham et al. 1994) as they have recorded and plotted many rice rat remains in a temporal framework. A brief discussion of this paper and additional rice rat remains in late prehistoric context in southwestern Ohio is found in Theler and Harris (1988:9–10, 22). We note that one researcher in particular, Dr. Holmes A. Semken, Jr., has continued his interest in the occurrence of rice rats in archaeological contexts (Semken 1983), and he generously wrote the response (Semken 2016, this volume) for this paper.

Rice Rat Biology, Habitat, and Behavior

Rice rats (*Oryzomys palustris*) are small mammals weighing up to 80 grams (3 ounces), with a body length of 12 to 15 cm (4.7 to 5.9 inches); with the tail they range from 23 to 31 cm (9 to 12 inches) long (Figure 1). This makes them similar in size, though lighter in weight, compared to the eastern chipmunk (*Tamias striatus*). Rice rats are primarily nocturnal creatures and are considered semi-aquatic, preferring marshy areas and wet meadows, where they have above-ground runways in thick vegetation cover. They will occupy uplands with dense cover, where they dig borrows. They do not hibernate, but are active throughout the year, and must forage for food daily. They are omnivorous, but appear to prefer a wide range of animal tissue when available, and are not known to store food. Rice rats can reproduce rapidly. In Missouri, the breeding period spans February to November, and is perhaps year-round. Females can have two to six litters per year, with an average of four to five pups per litter.

They can reproduce at 50 to 60 days, and are adults at 120 days. Few individuals are believed to survive more than one year in the wild (Golley 1966:94; Negus et al. 1961:120; Schwartz and Schwartz 1981:172–173; Sharp 1967:2–4; Wolfe 1982:1–5).

Figure 1. A rice rat in marshy vegetation (CDC; https://commons.wikimedia.org/w/index. phpA?curid=9442206).

Distribution

Present

Uncertainties about the modern range of the rice rat (Hall and Kelson, 1959:555) (see Endnote 1) initiated our review of the relevant zoological literature to ascertain which of the archaeological sites with remains of this species are located north of its modern range. The occurrence of the rice rat throughout the southeastern United States has been documented by Goldman (1918) and others, and only literature relevant to establishing the modern northern margin was consulted (see Table 1 for references). Based on a county-by-county plotting of documented sightings or captures, this line (Figure 2) modifies Hall's (1981) Map 358 of the rice rat's distribution (see Endnote 1 for details). The modern distribution is predominantly south of the Ohio River, and south of the junction of the Missouri and Illinois Rivers with the Mississippi River.

It is likely that most specimens in this zone are of the subspecies *Oryzomys palustris palustris*. If present in the zone of northern occurrence, *O. p. texensis* (now *O. texensis*) would occur only at the western portion of its range (see Endnote 2).

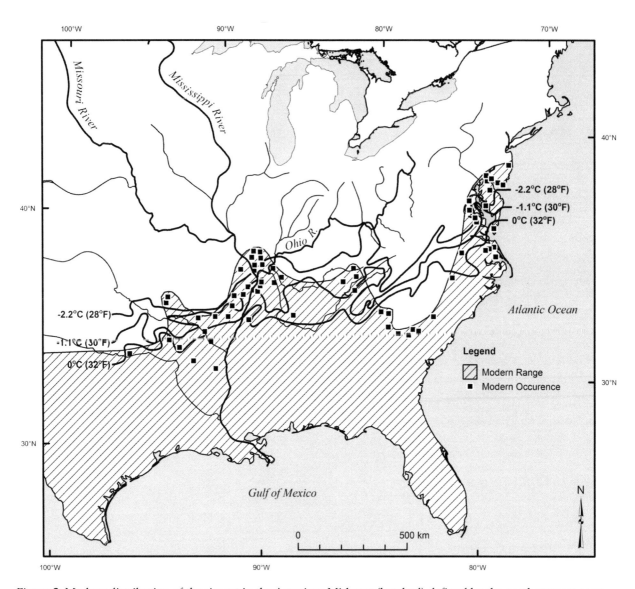

Figure 2. Modern distribution of the rice rat in the American Midwest (hatched) defined by the northernmost counties of occurrence (see Table 1) in relation to isotherms of mean minimum January temperature. Habitats may have been unsuitable for the rice rat in some areas north of this line (e.g., the Appalachians). Based on Barbour and Davis' (1974:167) distribution map, the Interior Low Plateau of Tennessee is included in the modern range.

Past

A "zone of northern occurrence" is defined as existing between the modern northern margin of the rice rat's range, as revised in this paper, and the northernmost extent of pre-modern occurrences. We surveyed the pertinent literature for reference to pre-modern occurrences of rice rats, and solicited unpublished information from faunal analysts who might have made such identifications north of the modern range. Within this area, more than 1,816 bones representing at least 389 individuals have been documented at 60 archaeological sites or site clusters in 10 states. Three of these sites have rice rat remains in more than one distinct component. The locations of all sites with rice rat remains are plotted in Figure 3, along with five paleontological occurrences (see Endnote 3).

Three additional paleontological occurrences are reported from Indiana: from Anderson Pit Cave in Monroe County, and Passenger Pigeon Cave and Raptor Roost in Harrison County (Holman and Richards 1981; Richards 1980). The Indiana specimens are regarded as pre-modern by Richards, including an innominate acetabulum with embedded shredded grass or root tendrils previously believed to have been hair (Ronald L. Richards, personal communication 1981). Due to the scarcity of cultural materials, it is

TABLE 1: MODERN OCCURANCES OF *ORYZOMYS*.

State	County	Reference	State	County	Reference
New Jersey	Ocean	Goldman 1918:24	Tennessee	Campbell	Goldman 1918:24
	Cape May	Ulmer 1951:121		Knox	Conaway 1954:263
	Cumberland	Goldman 1918:24		Lake	Goodpaster and Hoffmeister 1952:369
	Salem	Harlan 1837:385		Lawrence	Goldman 1918:24
Pennsylvania	Delaware	Ulmer 1951:122		Obion	Goodpaster and Hoffmeister 1952:369
Delaware	Kent	Schantz 1943:104		Shelby	Goldman 1918:24
	New Castle	Ulmer 1944:411	Illinois	Alexander	Klimstra and Scott 1956:3
Maryland	Charles	Howell 1927:312		Franklin	Goldman 1918:24
	Dorchester	Harris 1953:479–87		Jackson	Klimstra and Scott 1956:3
	Prince George's	Farner 1947:29		Johnson	McLaughlin and Robertson 1951:1
Virginia	Accomack	Goldman 1918:24		Union	Klimstra and Scott 1956:1
	Brunswick	Handley and Patton 1947:167		Washington	Casson 1984
	Nansemond	Goldman 1918:24		Williamson	Klimistra and Roseberry 1969:415
	Norfolk	Goldman 1918:24	Missouri	Bollinger	Goldman 1918:24
	North Hampton	Goldman 1918:24		Dunklin	Goldman 1918:28
	Westmoreland	Goldman 1918:24		New Madrid	Goldman 1918:28
	Richmond	Goldman 1918:24	Arkansas	Arkansas	Sealander 1979:149
North Carolina	Currituck	Goldman 1918:24		Ashley	Goldman 1918:28
	Wake	Goldman 1918:24		Benton	Davis and Lidicker 1955:298
South Carolina	Abbeville	Goldman 1918:24		Clay	Sealander 1979:149
	Aiken	Golley 1966:94		Craighead	Goldman 1918:28
	Barnwell	Golley 1966:94		Garland	Sealander 1979:149
	Calhoun	Golley 1966:94		Independence	Sealander 1979:149
	Darlington	Goldman 1918:24		Jefferson	Sealander and James 1958:221
	Greenville	Coleman 1948:294		Miller	Sealander 1979:149
	Ocohee	Golley 1966:94		Ouachita	Goldman 1918:28
	Orangeburg	Golley 1966:94		Pike	Goldman 1918:28
	Pickens	Goldman 1918:24		Polk	Cockrum 1952:281
Kentucky	Calloway	Barbour and Davis 1974:168		Pope	Sealander 1979:149
	Fulton	Barbour and Davis 1974:168		Prairie	Sealander 1979:149
	Hickman	Barbour and Davis 1974:168		Pulaski	Dellinger and Black 1940:190
	Knox	Goldman 1918:24		Washington	Sealander 1979:149
	Livingston	Barbour and Davis 1974:168	Oklahoma	Bryan	McCarley 1952:107
	Trigg	Barbour 1957:141		McCurtain	Whitaker 1937

assumed that none of the three occurrences are associated with human occupation(s).

Presented in Table 2 are provenience data and reference citations for archaeological rice rat remains in our zone of northern occurrence, as of ca. 1984 (see Endnote 4). Time span and culture period assignments in this table posed problems because many of the sites yielding rice rat remains are multicomponent. In such cases, the investigator's opinion, when given, was accepted as to the cultural affiliation of the faunal assemblages with rice rat remains; otherwise, they were assigned to the predominant cultural component. The time span assigned to each site or site component is presumed to encompass the age of the rice rat elements. In some instances, time span is based on multiple radiocarbon dates. In other cases, the time span represents our estimate of the age of the artifactual inventory associated with the faunal remains. Some "culture period" assignments in Table 2 were made in like manner.

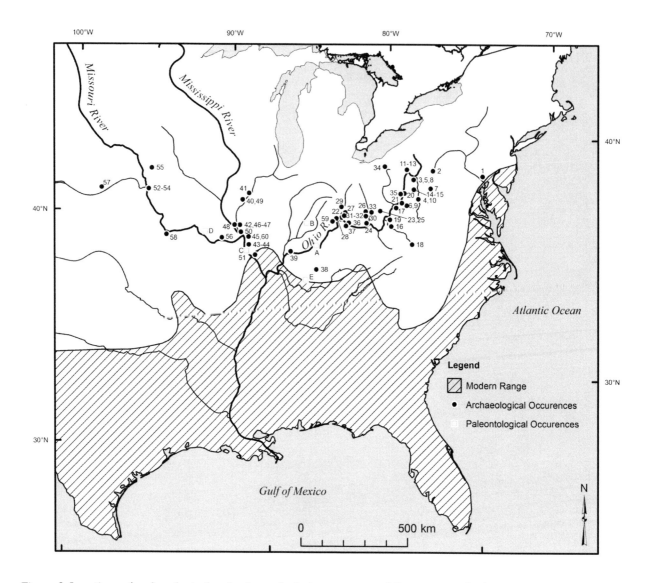

Figure 3. Locations of archaeological and paleontological occurrences of *Oryzomys* north of its modern range in the American Midwest. Archaeological occurrences identified in Table 2. Paleontological: A, Passenger Pigeon Cave and Raptor Roost, Harrison County, Indiana; B, Anderson Pit Cave, Monroe County, Indiana; C, Meyer Cave, Monroe County, Illinois; D, Brynjulfson Cave No. 2, Boone County, Missouri; E, Savage Cave, Logan County, Kentucky.

Consistent with Griffin's (1967) model, broad cultural labels such as "Middle Woodland" and "Mississippian" were used, rather than specific cultural affiliations such as "Hopewell" or "Oneota." It is acknowledged that the former often have temporal implications that vary from region to region, but the culture period labels used in this study refer only to the site-specific artifactual assemblages. This accounts for a lack of site-to-site correspondences between "culture period" and "time span" in Table 2.

Historical Perspective

Langdon's (1881:307) mention of "the recovery of two well-preserved crania [of the "rice-field mouse"] from the 'ashpits' in the Madisonville ancient cemetery," noting that they were "indubitable evidence of its *former* existence in the vicinity," represents the first reporting of archaeological rice rat remains in the American Midwest. This southwestern Ohio find was not, however, clearly represented by Langdon as an occurrence north of its modern range (see Endnote 5).

TABLE 2. ARCHAEOLOGICAL OCCURENCES OF RICE RATS NORTH OF THE MODERN RANGE LIMIT OF THE SPECIES.

State / Site	Fig. 3 Ref #	Site No.	County	No. of Bones[a]	MNI[a]	Referred Specimen Citation(s)[a]	Culture Period	Time Span	Archaeological References
Pennsylvania:									
Eschelman	1	36LA12	Lancaster	4	1	Guilday, et al. 1962	Historic	A.D. 1600–1625	Kinsey 1959
Johnston	2	36IN2	Indiana	15	4	Guilday 1955	Late Prehistoric	A.D. 1500–1600	Dragoo 1955b
McKees Rocks	3	36AL16	Allegheny	1	1	Guilday, pers. comm.	Late Prehistoric	ca. A.D. 1500	Buker 1968
Campbell	4	36FA26	Fayette	36	10	Guilday, pers. comm.	Late Prehistoric	A.D. 1350–1550	George 1974
Bunola	5	36AL4	Allegheny	1(+?)	1(+?)	Guilday, pers. comm.	Late Prehistoric	A.D. 1250–1450	George 1974
Varner	6	36GR1	Greene	6	1	Guilday 1961c, pers. comm.	Late Prehistoric	A.D. 1200–1400	Mayer-Oakes 1955
Fort Hill	7	36SO2	Somerset	2	1	Gilmore 1946; Guilday, pers. comm.	Late Prehistoric	A.D. 900–1600	Mayer-Oakes 1955
Guffey	8	36AL33	Allegheny	1	1	Guilday, pers. comm.	Late Prehistoric	A.D. 900–1600	None
Hartley	9	36GR23	Greene	4	2	Guilday, pers. comm.	Late Prehistoric	A.D. 900–1600	George 1974
Martin	10	36FA23	Fayette	1	1	Gilmore 1946	Late Prehistoric	A.D. 900–1600	Mayer-Oakes 1955
Mingo Rock Shelter	11	36BV81	Beaver	5	1	Guilday, pers. comm.	Late Prehistoric	A.D. 900–1600	None
Ohioview	12	36BV9	Beaver	2+	1	Guilday 1971, pers. comm.	Late Prehistoric	A.D. 900–1600	Alam 1961; Murphy 1971
Shippingport	13	36BV4	Beaver	2	1	Guilday, pers. comm.	Late Prehistoric	A.D. 900–1600	Mayer-Oakes 1955
Boyle	14	36WH19	Washington	1	1	Nale 1963	Late Prehistoric	A.D. 900–1000	Nale 1963
Meadowcroft Rock-shelter	15	36WH297	Washington	2	2	Adovasio, et al. 1980; Guilday, pers. comm.	Late Archaic/Early Woodland (?)	900–300 B.C. (?)	Adovasio et al. 1979, 1980; Carlisle and Adovasio 1982
West Virginia:									
Buffalo	16	46PU31	Putnam	66	17	Guilday 1971	Mississippian-Historic	ca. A.D 1680	Hanson 1975
Neale's Landing	17	46WD39	Wood	65	12	Tanner 1977	Mississippian	A.D. 1550–1650	Hemmings 1977
Mount Carbon	18	46FA7	Fayette	210	9	Guilday and Tanner 1965	Mississippian	A.D. 1200–1500	McMichael 1962
Miller	19	46JA55	Jackson	1	1	Murphy 1981	Mississippian	A.D. 1200–1400	Wilkins 1981
Speidel	20	46OH7	Ohio	8(+?)	3	Guilday and Mayer-Oakes 1952	Late Prehistoric	A.D. 900–1600	Mayer-Oakes 1954
Fairchance Mound	21	46MR13	Marshall	28	7	Guilday and Tanner 1968	Middle Woodland	A.D. 150–500	McMichael 1968; Hemmings 1984
Ohio:									
Madisonville	22	33HA36	Hamilton	2	2	Langdon 1881	Mississippian-Historic	A.D. 1300–1700	Griffin 1943
Gabriel	23	33AN6	Athens	2	1	Murphy 1975	Mississippian	A.D. 1200–1450	Murphy 1975
Feurt	24	33SC6	Scioto	21	2(+?)	Goslin 1950	Mississippian	A.D. 1200–1400	Griffin 1943
McCune	25	None	Athens	4	2	Murphy 1975, pers. comm.	Mississippian	A.D. 1200–1400	Murphy 1975
Cramer	26	33RO33	Ross	125	5	Goslin 1951, 1952	Mississippian	A.D. 1100–1700	Prufer and Shane 1970; Ullman 1985
Anderson	27	33WA4	Warren	3	1	Brainerd 1937	Mississippian	A.D. 1100–1300	Griffin 1943
State Line	28	33HA58	Hamilton	44	4	Ms. in possession of the authors	Mississippian	A.D. 1100–1300	Starr 1960; Essenpreis 1978
Incinerator	29	33MY57	Montgomery	80	12	Shane 1980	Mississippian	A.D. 1050–1350	Allman 1968; Heilman and Hoeffer 1981
Baum	30	33RO4	Ross	100+	24(+?)	Brainerd 1937; Hine 1910; Mills 1906	Mississippian	A.D. 1000–1300	Griffin 1943
Clough Creek	31	33HA16	Hamilton	10	3	Theler 1978	Mississippian	A.D. 1000–1300	Starr 1960

TABLE 2. (CONT.) ARCHAEOLOGICAL OCCURENCES OF RICE RATS NORTH OF THE MODERN RANGE LIMIT OF THE SPECIES.

State	Site	Fig. 3 Ref #	Site No.	County	No. of Bones[a]	MNI[a]	Referred Specimen Citation(s)[a]	Culture Period	Time Span	Archaeological References
	Sand Ridge (2)	32	33HA17	Hamilton	32	8	Theler 1978	Mississippian	A.D. 1000–1300	Griffin 1943; Starr 1960
	Blain	33	33RO49	Ross	62	11	Parmalee and Shane 1970	Mississippian	A.D. 950–1150	Prufer and Shane 1970
	Gillie Rockshelter	34	None	Summit	2	1	Shane 1973	Late Woodland	ca. A.D. 800	Bernhardt 1973
	Raven Rocks Rockshelter	35	None	Belmont	2	1	Shane and Parmalee 1981	Late Woodland	A.D. 750–950	Prufer 1981
	Sand Ridge (1)	32	33HA17	Hamilton	14	4	Theler 1978	Late Woodland	A.D. 450–800	Griffin 1943; Starr 1960
	Maple Creek	36	33CT32	Clermont	1	1	Vickery 1976	Late Archaic	1750–1000 B.C.	Vickery 1976
Kentucky:	Bintz	37	15CP1	Campbell	1(+?)	1(+?)	MacCord 1953	Mississippian	A.D. 1400–1600	Griffin 1953; MacCord 1953
	Salts Cave Vestibule	38	15ED4	Edmonson	1	1	Duffield 1974	Middle Woodland	1000–600 B.C.	Watson 1969, 1974
Indiana:	Angel	39	12VG1	Vanderburg	108+	23	Adams 1949, 1950; Richards 1980, pers. comm.	Mississippian	A.D. 1200–1500	Black 1967
	Jennison Guard	59	12D29	Dearborn	2	1	Breitburg, pers. comm.	Middle Woodland	A.D. 100–300	Black 1934
Illinois:	Emmons	40	11F286	Fulton	1	1	Guilday 1971	Mississippian	A.D. 1200–1400	Morse, et al. 1961
	Kingston	41	11P11	Peoria	4	1(+?)	Baker 1936; Parmalee 1962	Mississippian	A.D. 1100–1400	Simpson 1939
	Schild Cemetery	42	11GE15	Greene	1	1	Parmalee 1971	Mississippian	A.D. 1100–1400	Perino 1971
	Julien	43	11S63	St. Clair	4	1	Cross 1984	Mississippian	A.D. 1300–1400	Milner 1984
	Range (3)	44	11S47	St. Clair	2	1	L. Kelly 1980, 1981, pers. comm.	Mississippian	A.D. 1050–1150	Bareis 1977; J. Kelly 1979, 1980
	Cahokia, Mound 34 and/or village E. of Monks Mound	45	11MS2	Madison	141	12	Adams, pers. comm.; Guilday 1971; Parmalee 1957a	Mississippian	A.D. 950–1500	Brown 1975; Fowler 1975, 1977
	Kane	60	11MS194	Madison	9[b]	1(+?)[b]	Parmalee 1973	Late Woodland	A.D. 900–1000	Munson and Anderson 1973
	Cahokia, Merrell Tract	45	11MS2	Madison	6	4	L. Kelly 1979	Mississippian	A.D. 850–950	Kelly 1982; Salzer 1975
	Range (2)	44	11S47	St. Clair	5	2	L. Kelly 1980, 1981, pers. comm.	Late Woodland	A.D. 800–1000	Bareis 1977; J. Kelly 1979, 1980
	Cahokia, Powell Tract	45	11MS2-2	Madison	1	1	Parmalee 1963	Late Woodland-Mississippian	A.D. 600–1150	O'Brien 1972
	Range (1)	44	11S47	St. Clair	10	2	L. Kelly 1980, 1981, pers. comm.	Late Woodland	A.D. 600–800	Bareis 1977; J. Kelly 1979, 1980
	Apple Creek	46	11GE2	Greene	1	1	Parmalee, et al. 1972	Late Woodland (?)	A.D. 450–750(?)	Struever 1963, 1968b
	Newbridge	47	None	Greene	64[b]	1[b]	Styles 1981b	Late Woodland	A.D. 400–750	Styles 1981b
	Carlin	48	11C119	Calhoun	4[b]	1[b]	Styles 1981b	Late Woodland	A.D. 400–750	Stoner 1972; Styles 1981b
	Scovill	49	11F106	Fulton	25	1	Munson, et al. 1971	Middle Woodland	ca. A.D. 450	Munson, et al. 1971
	Macoupin	50	11JY70	Jersey	1	1	Hill 1970	Middle Woodland or Late Woodland	100 B.C.–A.D. 750	Rackerby 1973; Struever 1968a
	Modoc	51	11RA501	Randolph	4	2	Styles 1981a	Early and Middle Archaic	9000–5000 B.C.	Fowler 1959; Styles, et al. 1983

TABLE 2. (CONT.) ARCHAEOLOGICAL OCCURENCES OF RICE RATS NORTH OF THE MODERN RANGE LIMIT OF THE SPECIES.

State	Site	Fig. 3 Ref #	Site No.	County	No. of Bones[a]	MNI[a]	Referred Specimen Citation(s)[a]	Culture Period	Time Span	Archaeological References
Iowa:										
	Kuhl	52	13MI126	Mills	17(+?)[c]	17[c]	Bardwell 1981; Johnson 1972; Semken 1983	Woodland	A.D. 1000–1200	Hotopp 1978
	Johnson	53	13MI128 13MI129 13MI130	Mills	25(+?)[c]	25[c]	Bardwell 1981; Johnson 1972; Semken 1983	Woodland	A.D. 1000–1200	Hotopp 1978
	Institution Grounds	54	13MI131 13MI132 13MI135	Mills	13(+?)[c]	13[c]	Bardwell 1981; Johnson 1972; Semken 1983	Woodland	A.D. 1000–1200	Hotopp 1978
	McMinimee-Ahart-Denison	55	13CF102	Crawford	2	2	Semken 1983; Pyle, pers. comm.	Middle Woodland	ca. A.D. 150–250	None
Missouri:										
	Graham Cave	56	23MT2	Montgomery	2	1	Parmalee and Oesch 1972; Klippel, pers. comm.	Woodland	1000 B.C.–A.D. 900	Logan 1952; Klippel 1971
Nebraska:										
	Schmidt	57	25HW301	Howard	100+	37	Satorius-Fox 1982; Semken 1983	Plains Village	A.D. 1150–1500	None
Kansas:										
	Trowbridge	58	14WY1	Wyandotte	1[b]	1[b]	Johnson 1975	Middle Woodland	A.D. 150–450	Johnson 1979

[a] An MNI of "1(+1)" was assigned when only the number of bones was given in the literature. When only the number of individual rice rats was reported, the "number of bones" was recorded as the MNI with a "+" or '+(1)"

[b] Identifications are cf. (compares favorably).

[c] Bardwell (1981) reports a total of 351+ bones representing at least 128 individuals from various sites in the "Glenwood Locality," Mills County, Iowa, that includes the specimens from the Kuhl, Johnson, and Institution Grounds sites.

In reference to his excavations at the Baum village site, Mills (1906:71) commented that "The rice field mouse is found in great numbers in the refuse pits, attracted there evidently by the grain and nuts stored for food." In relating their presence specifically to the availability of food stored for human consumption, Mills was the first to offer an explanation for their occurrence in a prehistoric site context.

The earliest recognition that archaeological remains of the rice rat occurred well to the north of the species' historically known range is represented by Baker's (1936) identification of elements from the Kingston village in north-central Illinois. Adams (1949:Table 7) summarized archaeological occurrences of Midwestern rice rats as of 1949. He believed that the Kingston village specimens represented either a more northern range than had been suspected previously, or transportation from the south through trade or travel if the rice rats had been used as pets (Adams 1949:36, 1950:21). Adams noted an association of rice rat remains with Middle and Upper Mississippi sites exclusively, which he speculated may have been "due to the permanent agricultural life resulting in increased numbers of pests" (Adams 1949:36). This statement may have established an inferential precedent for later finds (see, for example, Goslin 1951:19–20; Guilday 1961b:3, 1961c:121; Guilday and Mayer-Oakes 1952:254–255; Guilday et al.1964:184). So entrenched was this belief by the mid-1960s that the presence of rice rat elements in the Mount Carbon faunal assemblage in West Virginia was cited as "strong internal evidence" for the existence of a "sedentary agricultural lifeway" (Guilday and Tanner 1965:6).

Goslin favored an accidental introduction of rice rats into southern Ohio by migrating or trading groups (Goslin 1950:21), speculating that the rice rat may have been transported in bundles of clothing, bags or baskets of corn or grain, etc. (Goslin 1951:21; see also Parmalee and Shane 1970:192). Goslin provided the first specific reference to corn as a possible food for rice rats in village site contexts. The finding of the remains of four individuals at the bottom of a refuse pit at the Cramer site in Ohio apparently prompted him to regard them as "plentiful around the areas where the corn was stored" (Goslin 1951:20).

Goslin (1950:17, 1951:21) further observed that the rice rat had neither continued to thrive in the vicinity of prehistoric villages, nor been reported recently from any area of Ohio. His reasoning that changing land use patterns (e.g., draining of low ground along streams and plowing of wet meadows) may have been responsible (Goslin 1951:21), represents the earliest cultural hypothesis concerning their disappearance

(see also Guilday 1955:144 and Parmalee and Shane 1970:192).

A non-cultural hypothesis for the range extension of the rice rat was offered by McLaughlin and Robertson (1951). Following a summary of archaeological finds, the authors state that "It seems possible that this former northward extension of the range of *Oryzomys palustris* may have been due to an increase in population pressure resulting in eruptive spread beyond the normal range limits" (McLaughlin and Robertson 1951:2).

Guilday and Mayer-Oakes (1952:255) viewed the non-occurrence of this species in the central and upper Ohio Valley today as "an extensive reduction in range from at least A.D. 1600 until the present time." Apparently favoring the idea of a single range reduction, Guilday expressed his belief that aboriginal villages provided a "specialized environmental niche" for the rice rat, the disappearance of which coincided with the "withdrawal" of the Indian (Guilday 1955:146, see also Bardwell 1981:38, 65, and Satorius-Fox 1982:39, 69). That this was a sufficient explanation for the species' range reduction was demonstrated by a presumed association of rice rats with the agricultural food stores of aboriginal populations: "It seemed as if the Rice Rat and the Indian were bound by some common bond, that as one became extinct so did the other. That common bond was, apparently, agriculture" (Guilday 1961b:3).

The literature has varied interpretations of the role of the rice rat in Guilday's "environmental niche." Guilday (1955:143–144, 146) believed their coexistence with aboriginal populations was "commensal" (see also Guilday 1961a:118, 1961c:121, 1971:18, 1972:906; Guilday et al. 1962:70), whereas Adams (1949:36) and Guilday and Parmalee (1965:47) regarded this species as a prehistoric "pest" and an "agricultural parasite."

The contrasting thoughts as to whether the rice rat was a "pest" or a "commensal" may have given rise to an idea concerning their disappearance that was initially expressed as an analogy between the native rice rat and Old World rat species. Guilday (1955:143) believed that the former filled the same niche in Native American villages as the Norway rat (*Rattus norvegicus*) does in our present society. This and similar statements (e.g., Guilday 1961b:25, 1971:18, 1972:906; Guilday and Tanner 1968:44) do not, however, imply contemporaneous coexistence of the two species at the same locations.

Guilday's (1961c:121–122) statement that "its present distribution may be limited because of interspecific competition with introduced Old World rats (*Rattus*)" is followed by specific reference to the association of

rice rats with Native American occupations. This suggests a cultural context for the competition, while another citation informs us that "The native rice rat is believed to have been replaced as a commensal with man by the Old World black rat (*Rattus rattus*) early in colonial history" (Guilday et al. 1962:70).

These statements suggest that, in aboriginal villages of the early contact period, rice rats competed unsuccessfully with European rat species and were eventually replaced by them. Guilday and Parmalee (1965:48) also expressed the possibility that the rice rat was incapable of competing with the native wood rat (*Neotoma*) in its own habitat. Both represent additional hypotheses for the disappearance of the rice rat from the zone of northern occurrence. Parmalee (1957a, 1957b) and Smith (1957) were the first to use the occurrence of rice rat elements from archaeological contexts for habitat reconstruction (see also Parmalee 1962:7; Parmalee and Oesch 1972:35, 49). Smith (1957:210) additionally inferred aspects of paleoclimate from these remains (see also Smith 1965:635).

Hypotheses

Emerging from these various discussions of the occurrence of the rice rat in archaeological contexts north of its modern range are several hypotheses for their presence or absence in this zone (graphically illustrated by Sarah A. R. Kingston):

1. The prehistoric range expansion may have been due to increasing rice rat population pressure resulting in an "eruptive spread" into the zone of northern occurrence.

2. Rice rats may have been accidental (or, if kept as pets, intentional) inclusions in items transported by groups moving northward.

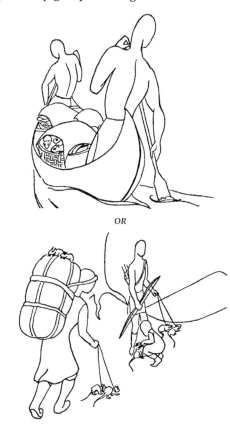

3. Agricultural products were probably among the items transported northward, and rice rats may have been with them. In aboriginal villages, it has been proposed that rice rats subsisted on stored foods, including corn; hence, their range extension may have been closely associated with, or dependent upon, the northward spread of agricultural peoples whose villages created a specialized niche for them. Because of the presumed dependence of rice rats on stored food, the "extinction" of these villages (initiated by European contact) was a factor contributing to rice rats' regional extirpation.

4. Changing land use patterns associated with European settlement may have been a contributing factor in the extirpation of rice rats. A corollary to this seems to be that, in addition to its presence in villages, the rice rat was part of resident local faunas.

5. In the postcontact period, rice rats may have competed unsuccessfully with European rats, and perhaps with native wood rats.

6. The disappearance of the rice rat may have been due to climatic differences in the prehistoric past. For example, Smith (1965:635) believed that a gradually cooling climate over the past one thousand years may have been a factor in the range reduction to the present day (see Parmalee 1968:111 for a similar statement). Such an hypothesis also assumes that rice rats were members of the resident local faunas.

The novelty of suggesting a direct connection between climatic variables and the past distribution of the rice rat north of its modern range is apparent upon reviewing previous statements that rejected climatic changes or variables as factors in the northern occurrences (see, for example, Guilday 1961a:118; Guilday et al. 1964:184; McLaughlin and Robertson 1951:2).

Assessment of Hypotheses

Hypothesis 1. McLaughlin and Robertson (1951) proposed that increasing population pressure resulted in the eruptive spread of rice rats into the zone of northern occurrence. This statement seems to suggest that some unspecified circumstance(s) caused rice rat populations to increase in number, exceed the carrying capacity of the habitats they occupied, and then invade new territory to the north. The phrase "eruptive spread" has been employed for certain insect infestations (Berryman 1986:72–75) and rarely, episodic bird invasions (e.g., snowy owls, *Nyctea scandiaca*). Our objection to this "explanation" for the rice rat's range extension is the investigators' failure to document population pressures on small mammal populations, or to discuss conditions that could have contributed to such pressure. Rice rats, like many other rodent species, have the capacity to rapidly reproduce. (See Semken 2016, this volume, Topic 1 for a discussion on eruptive spread and population dispersal.)

Hypothesis 2. The idea that rice rats were traded into the area for use as pets is abandoned in light of the fact that they do not occur in contexts suggesting captivity (cf. Bardwell 1981:37–38, 64), nor do we find ethnographic examples of their use as pets among North American Indian groups, as documented in comprehensive treatises (Driver 1969; Driver and Massey 1957; Hodge 1907, 1910; Swanton 1946; Trigger 1978).

The idea that rice rats were accidental inclusions in baggage transported by migrating groups or trading parties is feasible as a dispersal mechanism. However, the weakness of this explanation alone in accounting for their northern expansion is apparent when one considers that a modern analog—the northward transportation of grains and other commodities in barges, trucks, et cetera, has not produced such a result.

Hypothesis 3. An elaboration of the accidental inclusions hypothesis is represented by numerous references to the presence of corn and other stored foodstuffs

presumed to have met the subsistence needs of rice rats in aboriginal villages, creating specialized niches within which the species thrived. Most of the literatures suggests that this food supply was agricultural products; hence, the conceptual associations between (1) the northward spread of agricultural peoples and the northern range extension of rice rats, and (2) the extinction of the northern villages and extirpation of the rice rat upon European contact.

These related ideas would be at least partially substantiated if it could be documented that: (1) corn and other agricultural products formed an important part of the diet of rice rats; (2) there are no reported occurrences of rice rats in the northern zone prior to the adoption of agriculture; and (3) the rice rat was not part of resident local faunas, occurring, rather, only in association with aboriginal villages. Each of these is discussed below.

As its vernacular name implies, the rice rat may consume newly planted and growing non-native species of rice in the Southeastern United States, but other seeds as well as grasses, sedges, and fruits form part of its potential diet (Cahalane 1947:482; Hamilton and Whitaker 1979:180; Schwartz and Schwartz 1981:184–185; Walker 1975:759). Most authors who have discussed the feeding habits of this species, however, stress an apparent preference for virtually all types of animal matter when available (Barbour and Davis 1974:166, 168; Goldman 1918:4; Goodpaster and Hoffmeister 1952:368; Hamilton 1946:732; Hamilton and Whitaker 1979:180; Hoffmeister and Mohr 1957:167; Kale 1965:27, 29, Tables 8 and 9; Kincaid and Cameron 1982; Schantz 1943:104; Svihla 1931:239). Sharp documents the carnivorous nature of the rice rat:

> Because the *Oryzomys* examined in this study were feeding on animal material almost exclusively, it was concluded that they are preferentially carnivorous. The laboratory experiments strongly indicate that rice rats prefer animal material (Sharp 1967:561).

Given the feeding and other behaviors of rice rat populations observed by zoologists, and the unlikely possibility that they significantly depleted foods stored for human consumption, the idea that rice rats were parasitic upon aboriginal peoples seems unwarranted. The relationship seems rather to have been one of "commensalism," defined by Odum (1971:221) as a situation "in which one population is benefited, but the other is not affected" (see Emmel 1973:49 and Smith 1975:140 for similar definitions). Parasitism, by contrast, refers to a situation where one species "is benefited while the other species, the host, is harmed" (Emmel 1973:54). (See Semken 2016, this volume,

Topic 2 for a discussion on parasitism, commensalism, and procurement.)

As Table 2 shows, rice rat remains occur in Archaic contexts (Modoc Rock Shelter, Maple Creek site) and in Woodland sites and components lacking evidence of maize agriculture (e.g., Salts Cave Vestibule, Scovill, Apple Creek, Fairchance Mound, Carlin, Graham Cave). Other cultigens are reported for some of the latter, while corn was present at the Kane site (Cutler and Blake 1973), and in a late Late Woodland pit at the Range site (J. Kelly 1980:24). A partially carbonized maize ear was recovered from Macoupin (Struever and Vickery 1973:1200), and corn was present in "very low frequencies" at Newbridge, perhaps representing intrusions from an occupation later than early Late Woodland (Styles, 1981b:196). With the possible exception of Kane, where corn was abundant but dated to the Late Woodland–Mississippian transition, these site components cannot be considered representative of the "permanent" or "sedentary" lifeways to which Adams (1949:36) and Guilday and Tanner (1965:6), for example, referred. As we have documented, rice rats are omnivorous, eating meat and many plant foods other than maize. Thus, in the past, rice rats were as likely to have fed on pre-agricultural organic refuse as on the food debris of agricultural peoples. Importantly, the rice rat does not now occur in the American Corn Belt, north of its modern range (Jenkins 1941:318–319, Figure 5). Therefore, there is no necessary association of rice rats with maize, nor is there justification for the idea that rice rats were able to extend their range northward only when maize-growing peoples or agriculture spread north. It is equally unwarranted to infer the existence of an agriculturally based economy strictly from the presence of rice rats remains (as stated by Guilday and Tanner 1965:6).

Hypothesis 4. The idea that rice rats were extirpated from the zone of northern occurrence with the extinction of Native American villages is based on the assumption that the rice rat was not part of local or regional faunas but instead required the anthropogenic resources of Native villages. Rice rats, however, have not been extirpated from the Southeast, even though agriculturally based Native villages largely ceased to exist after Euro-American settlement, and extant rice rat populations are part of the native Southeastern fauna. Along the modern northern limit of distribution, McLaughlin and Robertson (1951), Klimstra and Scott (1956), and Cassen (1984) document rice rats living north of previous records in southern Illinois; comparable data exist for Arkansas since Goldman's (1918) study (see Table 1). These recent records appear to represent a northward expansion unassociated with human occupation.

Faunal evidence for the former existence of rice rat populations in the wild within the zone of northern occurrence is found at Anderson Pit Cave, Passenger Pigeon Cave, and Raptor Roost in southern Indiana; and Savage Cave in southern Kentucky. Meyer Cave, Illinois, and Brynjulfson Cave No. 2, Missouri, may represent additional examples.

While we conclude that commensal populations of rice rats inhabited prehistoric villages, the numerous and widespread occurrences documented in Figure 3 and Table 2 are suggestive of the contemporaneous existence of wild populations in the intervening areas (cf. Bardwell 1981:38, 65; Satorius-Fox 1982:39). The abandonment of Native American villages may have been a contributing factor in the extirpation of the rice rat from the zone of northern occurrence; however, by itself, that is insufficient to account for a total disappearance throughout the American Midwest.

An examination of the varied natural settings in which the rice rat occurs argues against the hypothesis that modern land use practices contributed to the species' extirpation. Excluding extremes of climate, its principal habitat requirement relates to the availability of suitable ground cover (Hamilton and Whitaker 1979:179; Schwartz and Schwartz 1981:184). The rice rat is well known within its range to be an inhabitant of damp meadows, marshes, and coastal flats (Goldman 1918:4; Goodpaster and Hoffmeister 1952:368; Handley 1971:298; Svihla, 1931:239). If there is suitable vegetation cover to afford protection, it can also be found in poorly drained uplands (Klimstra and Scott, 1956), woodland clearings (Goldman 1918:4; Hamilton and Whitaker 1979:179), and dry fields and upland slopes (Cahalane 1947:482; Hoffmeister and Mohr 1957:167; Schwartz and Schwartz 1981:184; Worth 1950:422). Furthermore, as noted above, rice rats have not been eliminated from local faunal assemblages in the Southeast, even though modern land use practices have altered the environment in much the same manner as in the zone of northern occurrence.

These observations indicate that the rice rat today thrives in a range of habitats, and its omnivorous diet accommodates a wide variety of foods. While modern agriculture and urban development may have diminished some habitats, many woodlots, brush-covered slopes, and marshes remain, in addition to numerous riparian settings. Stream corridors commonly utilized by this species provide suitable conduits for northward dispersal (Goldman 1918; Klimstra and Scott 1956).

Hypothesis 5. It is doubtful that competition between rice rats and European rat species in aboriginal villages during the early contact period can be invoked as a valid explanation for, or even a contributing factor in, the disappearance of rice rats from the zone of northern occurrence. Available ecological studies of these species suggest that they did not occupy the same niches, and valid instances of archaeological co-occurrence have not been found.

The first European rat species introduced into North America was the black rat, which became established in colonial settlements on the eastern seaboard in the seventeenth century (Silver 1927:59). The life history of the black rat indicates a dependence on the urban sources of food and shelter characteristic of Euro-American settlements (Doutt et al. 1966:167; Mumford 1969:79), but we have found no reference to black rats having invaded Native American villages during the seventeenth century. Although the black rat occurs as a wild animal in Asia, we have not located reports of feral populations in the United States. One such colony has been reported in coastal British Colombia (Banfield 1974:221). The second species of rat introduced from Europe, the Norway or brown rat, arrived on the east coast of North America about 1775 (Silver 1927:59) and spread rapidly throughout the settled portion of the continent north of Mexico.

Potential instances for examining possible displacement of rice rats following the introduction of European rats in eastern North America are available in faunal samples recovered from Native villages, such as Buffalo, Eschelman, and Neale's Landing, occupied during the late sixteenth or seventeenth centuries (see Table 2). The faunal assemblages of all three sites contained remains of rice rats, but none produced evidence of the European black rat. Because brown and black rats are very competitive, had either species of *Rattus* become firmly established in aboriginal villages, they would have been competitive with the rice rat.

We are aware of only one site yielding the remains of both rice rat and black rat (Meadowcroft Rockshelter), and two sites with occurrences of both rice rat and brown rat (Feurt and Raven Rocks). Adovasio et al. (1980:115) attribute the Meadowcroft black rat elements to mixing of the deposit, and Goslin (1950:16) notes that rice rat remains at Feurt occurred 2 to 4 feet deep in the cultural deposit. This argues for the latter's association with an undisturbed prehistoric occupation some 400 to 600 years earlier than the introduction of the brown rat into the continent. The brown rat must be intrusive in the Raven Rocks cultural deposit, there being no evidence of human habitation later than Late Woodland.

In attempting to evaluate Guilday and Parmalee's (1965:48) idea that rice rats may not have been able to compete with the wood rat "on his home grounds," it is necessary to examine the contexts within which

such competition might have taken place. The native habitat of the wood rat differs from that of the rice rat. According to Doutt et al. (1966:144), wood rats in Pennsylvania occur most commonly in high, rugged terrain with caves, dry ledges, and massive rock slides and outcrops. Nawrot and Klimstra (1976) list rock outcrops and overhangs along bluffs with numerous ledges, faults, and crevices as preferred habitats of the wood rat in southern Illinois.

Wood rat remains occur with those of rice rats at only four archaeological sites: Martin, Meadowcroft Rockshelter, Raven Rocks Cave, and Trowbridge. Even though some of the 60 sites included in this study are not represented by complete lists of identified fauna, and coarse-grained recovery techniques were employed at some sites, one might still expect more frequent co-occurrences if the two species had indeed competed prehistorically. Furthermore, Doutt et al. (1966:145) observe that the wood rat avoids civilized areas today. On these grounds, we reject the hypothesis that competition between wood rats and rice rats was a factor in the latter's disappearance from the zone of northern occurrence.

Hypothesis 6. The final hypothesis accounts for the rice rat's former distribution in terms of climates differing from those of the present day. We favor such a hypothesis and pursue the relationship between climatic variables and the rice rat's past and modern range in the section that follows.

Influence of Climate on the Rice Rat's Distribution

Range Limiting Factors

The rice rat's northern range boundary is not limited to particular vegetation zones (Handley 1971:298). Its present distribution cross-cuts several such zones, a fact that becomes apparent by referring to those portions of eastern North America (such as shown in Shelford 1963:19, Figure 2-1, and Braun 1950, Map of Forest Regions and Sections) that correspond with our revised modern range map in Figure 2. Furthermore, we have documented elsewhere that the rice rat today occupies a variety of habitats within major vegetation zones.

Examining the distribution of the rice rat in certain areas west of the Appalachians, we find no apparent barrier in the form of landscape features to impede its northward movement. In southern Illinois and southeastern Missouri, for example, large expanses of suitable habitat exist along stream corridors, where

both modern agricultural produce and abundant wild foods are available. These conditions seem entirely adequate for range expansion even further north than the advances documented by McLaughlin and Robertson (1951), Klimstra and Scott (1956), and Casson (1984).

What we observe, then, is a species on the margin of its range but with suitable food and habitat beyond it, a lack of obvious topographic barriers, and no known predators or competitors unique to the northern fringe. It is evident, we believe, that some condition, or set of conditions, exists that approaches or exceeds the physiological tolerance of the species.

Odum (1971:113) states: "Often a good way to determine which factors are limiting to organisms is to study their distribution and behavior at the edges of their ranges," and adds that "Temperature is often responsible for the zonation and stratification which occur in both water and land environments" (Odum, 1971:117). Similar viewpoints regarding the importance of temperature in the distribution of animals have been expressed by Andrewartha and Birch (1954:131, 176, 199); Ashworth (1980:210); Colinvaux (1973:286); Darlington (1961:326–327); Dice (1952:212, 440–441, 449); Udvardy (1969:102–103), and others. In assessing the rice rat's northern range margin, we suspect winter extremes to be limiting for this non-hibernating southern element of the North American mammalian fauna (Barbour and Davis 1974:168; Schwartz and Schwartz 1981:184). This is also the premise of Semken and his students, such as Johnson, Bardwell, and Satorius-Fox, who argue that reduction of temperature extremes during much of the last glacial episode was responsible for assemblages of non-analog faunas being created by warmer winter extremes and reduced summer extremes, resulting in sympatry of species now separated into separate biomes. (For further discussion, see also Semken 2016, this volume, Topic 3.)

In their study of rice rat populations on a Gulf Coast island, Negus et al. (1961) observed drastic and rapid declines in the number of individuals and their weight, and low reproductive activity, during the unusually harsh winter of 1957–1958. Hoffman and Jones (1970:367) predicted that species such as the rice rat might extend their ranges northward with a continued warming trend in North America, while Handley considered the distributional evidence itself in the following statement:

> However it [the rice rat] is known to have occurred further up the Potomac and Ohio Rivers in the recent past than it does now, and the boundary of its range seems to vacillate in the Great Plains, all perhaps in response to the vagaries of climate (Handley 1971:298).

Noting a parallel in the northern range extensions of both the rice rat and wood rat in southern Illinois, Nawrot and Klimstra (1976:9) attributed this phenomenon to "a past period of more favorable climatic conditions." Johnson (1972:27) believed that the presence of rice rat remains in various sites in Mills County, Iowa, could reflect northward expansion in response to climatic amelioration in the first few centuries A.D. while "the colder temperatures characterizing the subsequent Neo-Boreal may have been severe enough to cause constriction of its range" (Johnson 1972:28).

These observations and prehistoric distributional data lead one to expect a northward expansion of the rice rat's range during climatic episodes characterized by relatively mild winters, and range contraction during periods of severe winter weather. Ecological studies of other mammalian species having southern affinities may be cited in support of a parallel relationship between range fluctuation and winter conditions.

Other Species

The nine-banded armadillo (*Dasypus novemcinctus*), opossum (*Didelphis marsupialis*) and hispid cotton rat (*Sigmodon hispidus*) are all species of Neotropical origin that invaded the United States from the south (Schultz 1972:337–338; Sealander 1979:13; Jones et al. 1983:26). For all three species, Schultz (1972:338) argued that longer and colder winters during the past ten years resulted in their disappearance from the recent expansions along the northern margins of their ranges in the Central Great Plains. Attributing the northward movement of the armadillo to a warming trend from the late 1800s to the 1950s, Schultz noted that this species does not hibernate and is limited to a range where winters are fairly mild and not too long (Schultz 1972:337–338). Although attributing the armadillo's successful expansion in part to the decline of natural predators, Storrs (1982:827) agreed with the adverse impact of winter temperature on this species in her statement that "Frigid winters north and arid climes west contain the march."

In discussing the northern range changes of the opossum in the Great Lakes region, De Vos stated:

> It seems likely that range extensions of this species are correlated with successive years of mild winters. One or a series of severe winters may eradicate resident populations along the northern boundary of the range (De Vos 1964:22 2).

Similarly, Jones et al. (1983:22) are of the opinion that climatic amelioration on the Plains allowed for the range expansion of the opossum and the hispid cotton rat. For the latter species, they state that "the northern limits of the range seem to vary with the severity of winter, especially the prevalence of freezing rain and extended periods of sub-freezing temperatures" (Jones et al. 1983:203). This species "is so near its limits of tolerance on the Northern Plains that a single severe winter storm can alter its distributional limit by tens of miles" (Jones et al. 1983:22).

Hoffman and Jones (1970:382) agree that the northward spread of the cotton rat during the past century was possible under the influence of a warming trend, and that its distribution was probably limited by conditions accompanying "protracted sub-freezing temperatures" (Hoffman and Jones 1970:383). McClenaghan and Gaines (1978) documented marked declines in the abundance of cotton rat populations with severe winters in northeastern Kansas, while Davis and Barbour (1979) observed that a (newly established?) colony of cotton rats failed to survive the severe winter of 1977–1978 in Kentucky.

In reference to past northern populations of another southern species, the wood rat (*Neotoma floridana*), in southern Illinois, and the possible effects of the severe winters of 1912 and 1918, Nawrot and Klimstra speculated that

> Although all of the Shawnee Hills populations may not have been eliminated as a result of the severe weather conditions, they may have been reduced to such low levels that other mortality factors would have [had] a much greater influence in hindering or entirely eliminating recovery of the populations (Nawrot and Klimstra 1976:8).

These and other recent studies (see Endnote 6) indicate that several southern mammalian species are responsive to winter climatic stress on their northern range margins. Conditions exceeding the tolerances of such species, and hence limiting their distribution and abundance, probably include frozen ground, and precipitation-related variables such as depth and duration of snow cover, in addition to minimum temperature per se. It is the latter, however, that we wish to consider for possible correlations with the present and past distributions of the rice rat.

Climatic Variables.

The northern boundary of the rice rat was compared with a series of climatic variables presented in Climates of the States (National Oceanic and Atmospheric Administration, U. S. Department of Commerce 1974), including minima, maxima, and means. The climatic parameter that most closely fit the present distribution of the rice rat was mean minimum January temperature. Figures 2 and 4 show the mean minimum January temperature for the period 1931 to 1955

(or 1931 to 1961, the span varying from state to state) and the present (Figure 2) and past ranges (Figure 4) of the rice rat in the Midwest. It is apparent from Figure 2 that the modern northern range margin occurs primarily south of the -1.1° C to -2.2° C (28° F to 30° F) isotherms, marking the parameter of the rice rat's winter minima tolerance.

Given the necessity of daily foraging by this non-hibernating species, any northward expansion of the rice rat would be inhibited by protracted periods of subfreezing weather, represented either by in-situ climatic deterioration over time, or the progressively colder January mean temperatures encountered as one proceeds north. One would expect to find climatic amelioration of any appreciable magnitude and duration, at least during winters, to be accompanied by

northward expansion from a fluctuating range boundary. Conversely, the expected outcome of climatic deterioration of comparable magnitude and duration would be the southward regression of the species' margin to establish a new frontier, the specific configuration of which should correspond with parameters of winter extremes.

During favorable climatic episodes, we suspect the rice rat's northward expansion proceeded up stream corridors to the limits of its physiological winter tolerance. In its movement, the rice rat would have encountered aboriginal settlements providing an enhanced habitat niche where a commensal relationship could develop.

This model of past rice rat movements is at variance with the single range-reduction hypothesis of Guilday

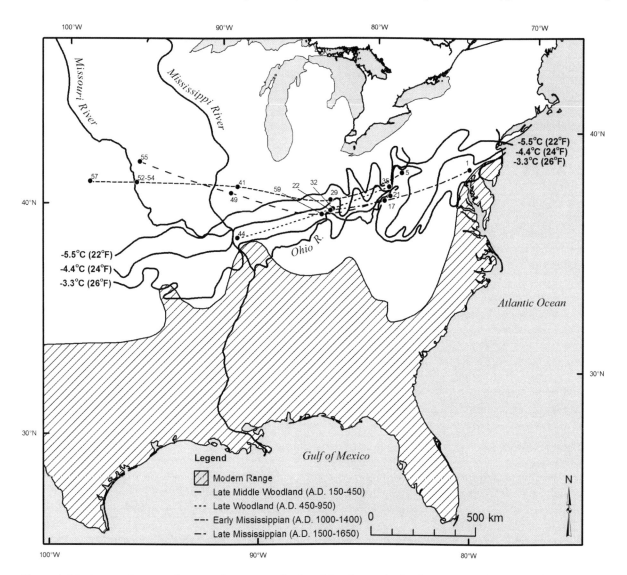

Figure 4. Modern and pre-modern northern range limits of the rice rat in the American Midwest in relation to modern mean minimum January isotherms. Numbers identify sites in Table 2.

and Mayer-Oakes (1952:255), Smith (1965:635), and Parmalee (1968:111). Occurrences of rice rat remains in archaeological contexts over the past several thousand years favor an alternative interpretation, that there have been several advances and retreats; this view is consistent with our current understanding of Holocene climate oscillations. The multiple advances are inferred by grouping sites with rice rat remains into culture periods and determining the northernmost occurrences for each period; these should approximate the northern range boundaries at different times in the past.

The problem of adequate site representation becomes increasingly acute with greater age because of reduced site densities, selective excavation, differential bone preservation, and so forth. There has also been a paucity of non-cultural Holocene excavations, making it difficult to draw inferences independent of human agency. The majority of sites with rice rat remains are of the Late Prehistoric/Mississippian cultural period. However, the Late Woodland period and even the latter part of the preceding Middle Woodland period are represented by a number of sites throughout the American Midwest. It is to these occurrences that we now turn for observations on the past distributions of the rice rat that constitute prehistoric range changes. When correlated with modern isotherms, these range changes provide the basis for a paleoclimatic reconstruction.

Paleoclimatic Reconstruction

The Midwestern archaeological occurrences of rice rats have been grouped into four major periods:

1. late Middle Woodland (A.D. 150–450);
2. Late Woodland (A.D. 450–950);
3. Early Mississippian (A.D. 1000–1400);
4. Late Mississippian–Historic (A.D. 1500–1650).

The northernmost occurrences for each period were determined and represented as northern range limits, and are shown on Figure 4 and listed in Table 2. A few occurrences at sites occupied between these periods, or for particularly long spans of time, are not included.

For the late Middle Woodland period, the northern boundary of the rice rat's range is defined on the west by the McMinimee-Ahart-Denison site in Iowa, and on the east by the Fairchance Mound in West Virginia. The Scovill site in Illinois and the Jennison Guard site in Indiana are located between the two. This range limit lies between 40° and 41° north latitude, and corresponds with the modern -5.6°C (22°F)

mean minimum January isotherm in Ohio, Indiana, and eastern Illinois. Further west, this range limit intersects modern mean minimum January isotherms ranging from -5.6°C (22°F) to -12.2°C (10°F) (see Figure 4).

Among the northernmost Late Woodland sites with rice rat remains, Gillie Rockshelter in northeastern Ohio may be anomalous because of its proximity to Lake Erie, with the possibility of ameliorated winter temperatures resulting from a lake effect in this area. Accordingly, we regard a line passing through Raven Rocks Cave to the south of Gillie Rockshelter as more representative of the rice rat's range limit during the Late Woodland period. Also serving to identify this northern boundary are the Sand Ridge site in southwestern Ohio, and the Apple Creek and Newbridge sites in Illinois. The rice rat, however, is dubiously affiliated with Late Woodland at Apple Creek, and its identification at Newbridge is uncertain. Therefore, the northernmost range extension during the period A.D. 450–950 may be slightly to the south in Illinois, perhaps represented by the occurrence of rice rats at Cahokia (Merrell Tract) in Madison County. These sites define a northern range extension that traverses the southern portions of Ohio, Indiana, and Illinois between 39° and 40° north latitude, corresponding with modern mean minimum January isotherms of -5.6° C to -4.4°C (22°–24°F).

During the Early Mississippian culture period, the distribution of the rice rat is defined by occurrences at many sites across the Midwest, the northernmost of which are the Schmidt site in Nebraska on the west; the Mills County, Iowa, sites; the Kingston site in Illinois; the Incinerator site in Ohio; and the Bunola site in Pennsylvania on the east. Located well to the north of the Late Woodland range limit, this line roughly corresponds with the earlier late Middle Woodland range limit.

Constituting the northernmost range extent during the Late Mississippian–Historic culture period are rice rat remains from the Madisonville site in southwestern Ohio on the west, the Neale's Landing site on Blennerhassett Island in the Ohio River, and the Johnston and Eschelman sites in Pennsylvania. Traversing only two Midwestern states, this range boundary is the southernmost of the four defined pre-modern range limits for the species. It lies between 38° and 40° north latitude, and falls between the modern -4.4°C (24°F) and -3.3°C (26°F) mean minimum January isotherms.

This latest culture period corresponds with the initial phase of the Neo-Boreal climatic episode, dated by Bryson and Wendland (1967) between A.D. 1550 and 1850. Temperatures colder than those of the modern era are well documented for the Neo-Boreal, an

observation that seemingly conflicts with a Late Mississippian and Historic range limit to the north of the rice rat's present distribution. We speculate, however, that the northern occurrences are early in the Neo-Boreal and that an insufficient amount of time had elapsed since the onset of cooling for the full effects to be realized in terms of the southward contraction of the rice rat's range. Furthermore, the cooling trend was apparently progressive, with the most severe winter conditions occurring sometime after the onset of the Neo-Boreal, eventually resulting in the disappearance of the rice rat from the zone of northern occurrence.

We doubt that the age of any rice rat remains from the archaeological sites considered in this paper postdates A.D. 1650. Among the latest sites, only Madisonville in Ohio and Buffalo in West Virginia have spans of occupation that may extend to a later date. Perusal of the illustrated cultural material from these sites (Griffin 1943; Hanson 1975; Hooton and Willoughby 1920) reveals the presence of diagnostic artifacts earlier than the European contact period. Judging from the proportional representation of trade goods, the historic components of both sites appear to have been minor, and it is likely that the rice rat specimens were associated with one or more pre-eighteenth century occupations.

Fritts et al. (1979) provided quantitative estimates of temperature differences throughout the Neo-Boreal that suggest cooler conditions in the post–A.D. 1700 period, relative to those of the period 1602–1700. In their Great Lakes and Midwest region, Fritts et al. (1979:Figure 10) estimated that winter temperatures for the period 1602–1900 averaged 2.1°C lower than the mean winter temperature from 1901 to 1962. Winter temperature in the same area for the period 1602–1700 is estimated to have averaged only 1°C lower than that of the period 1901–1970, with a smaller area including most of Ohio, Indiana, Illinois, and a part of Iowa having had average winter temperatures 1.5°C lower from 1602 to 1650 (Fritts et al. 1979:Figure 6). These data suggest that for nearly a century of the first half of the Neo-Boreal (i.e., until ca. A.D. 1700), winters were cool but not as cold, on average, as they were later in the Neo-Boreal.

Increasingly cool winters associated with the onset of the Neo-Boreal would have adversely affected at least non-commensal populations in and along valley corridors. Forest clearance related to human habitation, however, would have provided ideal rice rat habitat (Smith 1975:141), and colonies established at loci of human occupation may have survived mild fluctuations in climate. Therefore, we cannot discount the possibility that rice rat specimens in Late Mississippian–Historic contexts north of the modern range constituted relict populations that temporarily survived the initial climatic deterioration associated with the Neo-Boreal.

Warmer temperatures toward the end of the Neo-Boreal may be indicated by Wahl's (1968) study based on observational records. During the 1830s and 1840s, annual temperatures in Indiana, Ohio, and Kentucky are estimated to have averaged about 1.1°C (2°F) lower than the mean annual temperature of the period 1931–1960 (Wahl 1968:79, Figure 11). By this part of the twentieth century, we suspect that the rice rat's range had already been depressed well to the south.

We conclude that rice rat populations disappeared from the zone of northern occurrence between A.D. 1500 and 1700 in response to progressively colder climatic conditions. Populations might have survived locally for short periods as commensals at aboriginal habitation sites. Fluctuating northern range margins to the south of the line reconstructed for the Late Mississippian–Historic period would be expected for the post–A.D. 1700 period. Occurrences cited by Goldman (1918) after the end of the Neo-Boreal might represent one or more range limits north of the line imposed by earlier winter conditions. A still more recent range boundary than Goldman's is currently being established as milder winters persist, with advances northward in southern Illinois and Arkansas.

If, as we believe, the distribution of rice rats is controlled by minimum winter temperature, then the range changes documented in this paper allow paleoclimatic reconstructions based on the assumption that the -1.1°C to -2.2°C (28°–30°F) mean minimum January isotherms defining the modern range margin also determined the northern limits of distribution in the past.

Although evidence is lacking, we speculate that during the last glacial maximum episode (22,000–16,500 yrs. B.P.), rice rats would have been distributed far to the south of their present-day range. Perhaps their habitat included the refugia of the eastern deciduous forest along the lower Mississippi Valley, and along the Gulf Coast of the Southeastern United States (Davis 1976; Delcourt and Delcourt 1979).

During late glacial times and continuing into the early Holocene, the rice rat's range presumably expanded to the north as winter conditions ameliorated and suitable habitats became available within the northward-migrating elements of deciduous forest (Davis 1976). However, the Late-Glacial Holocene transition was represented by a series of rapidly changing climatic events. Northward expansion, expected for postglacial warming trends, is perhaps represented by one rice rat element in an Early Archaic cultural zone (Stratum 15) at Modoc Rockshelter

in southern Illinois (Styles 1981a). Rice rat remains were also recovered from Strata 4 and 5 at this site, attributed by Styles (l981a:120) to the Middle Archaic period. A rice rat element from the Late Archaic Maple Creek site in southwestern Ohio may be associated with a later episode of warm-dry conditions that existed in this portion of the Midwest ca. 2000 or 1500 B.C. (Ogden 1966:396; Wright 1971:451). The rice rat remains in Archaic deposits at Modoc Rockshelter and Maple Creek offer supporting evidence of individualistic response as proposed by Graham and Lundelius (FAUNMAP Working Group 1996) as opposed to a climatic shift of biomes. (For further discussion see Semken 2016, this volume, Topic 4.) The paucity of comparably early occurrences may be due to poor preservation, or selection of later Woodland and Mississippian sites for excavation; few Archaic sites with large and adequately analyzed faunal collections have been excavated in the zone of northern occurrence.

Uncertainties exist in this climatic reconstruction. It should be cautioned that paleoclimatic fluctuations may well have been a rapid series of events, and may not have resulted in an identical distribution of shifted isotherms. Temperature gradients may have been steeper in the past, for example, with the north-south distances between isotherms having been less than those separating them today. Furthermore, the undulations of particular isotherms in their east–west traverse across the Midwest may not have coincided with those of today, which would have produced many localized variations in climatic conditions (Satorius-Fox 1982:33, 69).

The various northern range limits postulated are of unequal extent: those that traverse fewer states in an east–west direction and are based on fewer occurrences are less certain than the better documented and more extensive northern boundaries. Correlation of northern range extensions with modern mean minimum January isotherms seems more credible in the central portion of the Midwest than toward the fringes. On the west, archaeological sites with rice rat remains tend to correspond with particularly low isotherms in comparison to the Midwestern "heartland." The eastern termini of the various reconstructed range limits, except that defined by the Eschelman site, tend to converge at the Appalachian Plateau.

Discussion

In this section, we discuss the appropriateness of our approach to reconstructing a climatic parameter by citing similar studies, and considering certain

problems and assumptions associated with this zoogeographic method.

Bryson (1985:275) identified two basic methods in which past climates are reconstructed: (1) developing physical models based on direct climatic field evidence; and (2) postulating analogs of past climatic conditions through the use of "proxies." A climate proxy is a "nonclimatic variable that covaries with climate" (Bryson 1985:285). The development of the climate proxy method was prompted by the rarity of direct field evidence, and the relative unreliability of most physical models derived from there (Bryson 1985:275–276). When no modern analog can be found for a past climatic regime, "transfer functions" may be used to postulate "partial analogs." A transfer function is "an empirically determined quantitative relationship between a proxy 'data vector' and a climatic 'data vector'" (Bryson 1985:275).

We assume correspondence of our approach with Bryson's concept of a transfer function in that our proxy data vector is the occurrence of rice rat remains north of the modern range; our climatic data vector is winter temperature; and the quantitative relationship between the two is expressed in terms of specific isotherms of mean minimum January temperature that we believe existed at various latitudes during different times in at least portions of the Midwest. One might also consider that a qualitative relationship between proxy and climatic data vectors may be expressed in relative terms, such as "warmer," "colder," "wetter," or "drier." Examples of the latter, including references to rice rats, are abundantly represented in the literature. We cite only a few that we believe are representative and that parallel our approach. A few archaeologists have attempted qualitative paleoclimatic inferences based specifically on the prehistoric presence of rice rat remains in the zone of northern occurrence.

In a discussion of several animal species, including rice rats, in archaeological contexts north of the modern range, Smith (1957:210) inferred higher temperatures for the time span that he (erroneously) believed accommodated the prehistoric specimens. Hill (1970: Preface) states that "Rice rat remains … indicate that the temperature was slightly warmer during the occupation of the [Macoupin] site than it is now." Johnson (1975:29) believed that average temperatures during the period of the Trowbridge site occupation (Middle Woodland) would have been somewhat warmer than those of today. Warmer and/or wetter conditions during the Merrell Tract occupation were inferred by L. Kelly (1979:18) from rice rat remains at the Cahokia site in Illinois.

In the American Southwest, Holbrook's (1977) observations on changes in the composition of ten

small rodent species in archaeological sites provided an example of a qualitative study that, like the present paper, illustrated the potential of small rodent recovery and analysis for understanding changing climatic conditions in the prehistoric past. Among species presently on the northern margins of their ranges in her study area, Holbrook documented a replacement of mesic-adapted rodents by more xeric-adapted species, suggesting less winter precipitation and increasing summer warmth through time. Her findings supplemented pollen evidence for increasing aridity.

Williams and Wigley (1983) combined glacier, ice-core, tree-line, tree-ring, and pollen data for North America, Greenland, and Europe to define three climatic episodes over the past 2000 years. They concluded "that there is good agreement of various proxy climate records within regions at specific times and that climatic change has differed in detail between regions" (Williams and Wigley 1983:299).

Degerbl and Krog (1951) use occurrences of the European pond tortoise (*Emys orbicularis*) north of its modern distribution to document both range extension and contraction in postglacial times. Because this species hibernates during the winter, the authors reasoned that summer temperature was the limiting factor in its distribution. They correlated two episodes of northward migration with climatic conditions characterized by warm, dry summers, and subsequent range contractions with periods of climatic deterioration (cooler and damper summers). Although declining to assign a definite summer temperature at the former northernmost range margin of *Emys* in Sweden, the authors noted that the present-day northern limit is south of the 20°C (68°F) July isotherm in France, Spain, and parts of the Balkan Peninsula. Degerbl and Krog used multiple species as biological proxies of past climates by correlating *Emys'* latest range contraction with the disappearance of one plant, one fish, and two beetle species.

As an example of a quantitative approach to reconstructing past climatic parameters using biological proxies, Galloway (1983) collected tree remains above the timberline in the Southwest, then compared mean July temperature differences between the altitudes of the highest specimens and the present timberline in his study area. On this basis, Galloway inferred full-glacial temperatures about 10°C below present levels.

In the Midwest, Wayne (1967) used Wisconsin-age molluscan species to infer a mean annual temperature of ca. -3°C within about 10 km (6 miles) of the ice margin, based on the dominance of species whose northern limits now lie north of the -7°C mean annual isotherm. Elsewhere, the distribution of fossil snails

was used to place the 5°C mean annual isotherm ca. 200 km (125 miles) to the south.

Ashworth (1980) found the modern distribution of populations of two species of arctic-alpine beetles that were present as Quaternary fossil assemblages in northwestern Minnesota to be geographically separated in regions where summer thermal regimes were similar. For the area containing the fossil beetles, Ashworth postulated a climatic analog with the more northern modern population, with mean July temperatures ranging from 11° to 14°C if the Quaternary environment were regional. If localized, a mean July temperature of 17°C would be implied, consistent with the present thermal regime of the area now inhabited by the more southern population.

Ashworth's concern that any particular fossil assemblage used as a biological proxy of climate reflects localized, but not necessarily regional, climatic conditions was one of two "limitations" he discussed in relation to the method of characterizing past climates by mean temperatures derived from comparison of distribution patterns and isotherms. As the author points out, however, thermal conditions in microenvironments generally reflect those of the regional climate, and the probability of finding a fossil assemblage in a microenvironment unlike the regional setting is extremely small (Ashworth 1980:210–211). Ashworth also cautioned that meteorological averages cannot be assumed to be factors controlling distribution, by which statement we assume acknowledgment on Ashworth's part that it was the lethal temperature extremes that controlled distribution. Even though thermal environments deduced from studies employing biological proxy data are reported in terms of mean temperatures (Ashworth 1980:210), it is commonly the case that the warmest or coldest months of the year (July or January) are selected where heat or cold, respectively, are suspected to be relevant limiting factors. Paleoclimatic reconstruction has yet to reach a level of sophistication whereby temperature ranges can be specified in temporal increments shorter than months or, in some cases, seasons.

Bryson (1985:277) also expressed concern about the use of biological proxies for inferring past environments, based as it is on several assumptions. One of these assumptions is that proxy occurrences reflect the regional macroclimate and are not "outlier" populations reflecting only microclimatic conditions. Such a concern parallels that of Ashworth, and we acknowledge the possibility of disjunct rice rat populations surviving for periods of time in aboriginal villages where food in the form of habitation refuse was available. Although not to our knowledge observed for rice rats in the field, it is also possible that individuals

or populations at the northern margin of their range could occupy the burrows of other animals below the frost line, as Jones et al. (1983:203) documented for the hispid cotton rat on the Plains. However, given the daily foraging habits and short life span of the rice rat, we find it difficult to conceive how populations could have avoided for extended periods of time the cold winter conditions that would have exceeded their physiological tolerances, even if food and shelter were available.

The problem of isolated populations living in a suitable habitat beyond the "true" (i.e., more representative) range limit seems to us more acute for organisms such as trees that have a much greater longevity. Thus, Bryson (1985:285) argues there is a longer delay in biological response to climatic change that is related to the length of the reproductive cycle of the species involved, as well as the time required for reproductive stock to be present. This delay is minimal for mobile and short-lived rodent species in comparison with longer lived trees. In this regard, it is significant that Bryson addressed most of his cautionary notes to the use of pollen data rather than animals (see Endnote 7).

With respect to the representativeness of biological proxy data, we are of the opinion that a geographically extensive and numerically large database increases the interpretation that a regional climatic regime is reflected by rice rat elements in archaeological and paleontological contexts.

Bryson (1985:277) questions the assumption that range maps may be used to identify limiting values of specific climatic variables for various species, partly because of the potential outlier population and reproductive lag problems, and partly because multiple factors may be involved rather than a single climatic variable. One of Bryson's examples—the interplay between temperature and precipitation in the distribution of maize—reflects his bias toward plants rather than animals. Although we acknowledge the probable influence of precipitation-related variables (e.g., depth and duration of snow cover), we find a better fit for the rice rat's modern range margin with isotherms than with isohyets. Furthermore, we believe that animals like the rice rat respond more rapidly to temperature than to other variables such as precipitation; i.e., temperature was perhaps the most "controlling" of various potentially limiting factors. Finally, it should be recognized that our objective, unlike Bryson's, was to reconstruct one parameter of past climate—mean minimum January temperature—and not an entire paleoclimatic regime. In this regard, we also avoided biasing our results towards summer conditions, which Bryson (1985:281) and Williams and Wigley (1983:287) noted is common when biological proxy evidence is used for paleoclimatic reconstruction.

Summary

In this paper, we have revised the modern range limit of the rice rat by reference to recent sightings and captures, and have documented archaeological and paleontological occurrences north of this boundary in the American Midwest. We have summarized hypotheses concerning the appearance of the rice rat in our defined zone of northern occurrence as well as its subsequent disappearance. Each of these hypotheses was evaluated, and most were rejected as unsuitable or inadequate explanations for past range extensions and contractions when aspects of the species' behavior, habitat, contexts of occurrence, and distribution were examined. The possible influence of climate on the rice rat's distribution was, however, one hypothesis that can account for its former presence and current absence in the zone of northern occurrence, it was therefore singled out for further consideration.

We evaluated ecological factors other than climate that might affect the rice rat's range, noting that there is only slight northward movement in the modern era despite the fact that there are neither topographic barriers nor known predators/competitors unique to the northern fringe that might impede its northern spread; nor is the species limited to habitats occurring only south of the modern range limit. We concluded that climate is the controlling factor in the establishment of the rice rat's northern range margin, and we used analogy to show that climate also influences the ranges of four other species of southern origin: the armadillo, opossum, cotton rat, and wood rat. Acknowledging that the rice rat does not hibernate and forages for food throughout the year, we identified one aspect of winter temperature, and attendant variables such as amount and duration of snow cover, as the factors most likely to have imposed limits on the distribution of this species in the prehistoric past, as they apparently do today. At least partial confirmation of this conclusion was derived from a correlation of the present northern boundary of the rice rat with mean minimum January temperature (-1.1° to -2.2°C [28° to 30°F] isotherms).

We modeled fluctuating range margins for the rice rat by plotting the northernmost occurrences with present-day mean minimum January isotherms. From this we proposed the following climatic reconstruction: the late Middle Woodland period (A.D. 150–450) was characterized by mild winters averaging ca. 4.2°C (7°F) warmer; Late Woodland (A.D. 450–950) winters were ca. 0.6°C (1°F) cooler; a return to milder winters approximating those of late Middle Woodland occurred in Early Mississippian (A.D. 1000–1400) times; and colder winters during the Late

Mississippian–Historic period (A.D. 1500–1650) are evidenced by a ca. 2.4°C (4°F) decrease corresponding with the initial phase of the Neo-Boreal climatic episode. We concluded that cold temperatures during this episode resulted in a regression of the rice rat's range to a margin south of its present northern limit.

Conclusion

Noteworthy in this study is the general agreement between our results and those of other approaches to reconstructing climate in the American Midwest. For example, we find agreement with various climatic episodes derived in part from observational data of the historic period. Such models are exemplified by the studies of Baerreis and Bryson (1965), Bryson and Wendland (1967), Bryson, Baerreis, and Wendland (1970), Wendland and Bryson (1974), and Wendland (1978). Bernabo's (1981) climatic reconstruction based on pollen data is one of several palynological schemes in the Midwest and Great Lakes region in which concordance with the results of our study is particularly striking.

Because the zoogeographical approach adopted in this paper uniquely reconstructs one parameter of climate—mean minimum January temperature—it may be used to complement and/or supplement other approaches. Illustrating such a possibility is Harris's (1970) study of range changes of the yellow-bellied marmot (*Marmota flaviventris*) in the American Southwest. Remains of this mammal in archaeological and paleontological contexts were used to infer high effective moisture due primarily to summer precipitation greater than that of the present, while dominant winter precipitation was inferred from pollen and alluvial studies for the same period. Thus, the latter two approaches gave an incomplete picture of the precipitation regime; the hidden importance of summer precipitation was detected only by the zoogeographical data.

Many approaches to climatic reconstruction fail to discriminate seasonal differences such as those revealed by Harris's data, yet instances of climatic episodes characterized by seasons that were not synchronized with respect to relative warmth or coldness are documented in the literature. For example, the paleoclimatic study of Fritts et al. (1979) based on tree ring data documents a coincidence of relatively cool winters and warm summers in portions of the United States.

We regard the zoogeographical approach adopted in this paper as a tool for reconstructing an elusive parameter of past climate that gains significance when articulated with approaches treating botanical and geological data. We emphasize that much of its potential usefulness, however, lies in the realm of applying such reconstructions to the investigation of climate's impact on human behavior in one area of eastern North America—the Midwest—that witnessed the development and decline of such influential cultures as Adena, Hopewell, and Fort Ancient in the prehistoric past.

Acknowledgments

The authors are indebted to the following individuals, who made available unpublished data on rice rat identifications: W. R. Adams, Emanuel Breitburg, John E. Guilday, Lucretia S. Kelly, James L. Murphy, Katherine Pyle, Ronald L. Richards, and Marsha Satorius-Fox. John E. Guilday and Walter E. Klippel responded to requests for information about the contexts of rice rat elements from the Meadowcroft Rockshelter and Graham Cave sites, respectively. Others who assisted in providing useful information include David Benn, Carl Falk, Richard L. George, Jeffrey R. Graybill, James M. Heilman, Walter E. Klippel, James W. Porter, Holmes A. Semken, Jr., and Donald P. Tanner.

We give special thanks to Sarah A. R. Kingston for doing the descriptive rice rat drawings, and Matthew G. Hill for redrawing the maps, Figures 2–4.

The authors are especially grateful to David A. Baerreis, John E. Guilday, Holmes A. Semken, Jr., and Matthew G. Hill for their critical reading of the manuscript and their helpful comments and suggestions. Holmes A. Semken, Jr., is also thanked for his insightful commentary that brought this paper into the current era! We also wish to thank several anonymous reviewers for their most helpful comments, suggestions, and corrections. Katherine Stevenson, Susan Nowland, Suzanne Harris, and Constance Arzigian provided editorial comment and draft typing. Errors and omissions remain the responsibility of the authors.

This paper is dedicated to the memory of John E. Guilday, a pioneer in analyzing Midwestern faunal remains who paved the way for modern studies seeking to understand relationships among past human populations, environments, and resources.

Endnotes

(1) Hall and Kelson (1959:555) state "The northern limit of range of this species [*Oryzomys palustris*] seems to fluctuate, probably owing to fluctuations of population densities, and

is less precisely known than most common North American mammals." Some modifications were made of Hall's (1981) Map 358. For example, the sole record for modern rice rats in Kansas is here disregarded based on Cockrum's (1952:281) argument and the lack of recently documented occurrences (Bee et al. 1981:231). Studies of mammalian distributions in Ohio (Bole and Moulthrop 1942; Gottschang 1981) and Indiana (Mumford and Whitaker 1982) discount other reports of rice rats in those states (Dragoo 1955a:8; Langdon 1881:307; Mumford 1969:67).

(2) Research using mitochondrial and nuclear DNA in molecular studies by Hanson et al. (2010) argues that within the *Oryzomys palustris* complex in the United States there are two distinct species, with *O. p. texensis* now elevated to species status as *O. texensis*, largely found west of the Mississippi River. See also the work of Indorf and Gaines (2013). No attempt was made to document occurrences of the extinct Pleistocene form *O. p. fossilis*, the remains of which have been found in Kansas, Texas, and elsewhere (Kurten and Anderson 1980:239; Richards 1980:426).

(3) Presumed paleontological occurrences include 30 rice rat elements at Meyer Cave in Monroe County, Illinois (Parmalee 1967:141, Table 2) and two bones at Brynjulfson Cave No. 2 in Boone County, Missouri (Parmalee and Oesch 1972:35, Table 4). In both cases, mixing of the deposits was evidenced by bioturbation and the presence of bones from domesticated animals of European origin. Furthermore, prehistoric cultural material occurred within the deposits and the radiocarbon dates (one from Meyer Cave and two from Brynjulfson Cave No. 2) are relatively recent. A single rice rat element at Savage Cave in Logan County, Kentucky, is believed by Guilday and Parmalee (1979) to be associated with a post-Pleistocene human occupation that is represented by undated cultural remains in deposits extensively disturbed by vandals.

The initial identification of a human parietal fragment (Richards 1972, Tables 1 and 2) from Anderson Pit Cave was erroneous (Richards, personal communication, 1981).

(4) Researchers seeking data on rice rat remains in archaeological contexts since the early 1980s are directed to FAUNMAP (Graham et al. 1994) and the numerous Midwestern faunal reports published in the last 30 years.

(5) Langdon (1881:307) states:

Hesperomys Palustris, Baird. [*Oryzomys palustris*] — *Rice-field Mouse* — On December 18, 1876, I took from the stomach of a Red-shouldered Hawk killed at Madisonville, [Hamilton County, Ohio] the posterior half of a body with the tail attached, which I referred to this species. Indubitable evidence of its *former* existence in this vicinity is afforded by the discovery of two well-preserved crania from the "ash-pits" in the Madisonville ancient cemetery. For verifications of the identity of the latter I am indebted to Dr. Elliot Coues, U.S.A. [emphasis in original]

(6) Recent studies by Myers et al. (2009) document the opossum's range boundary movement 200 km (125 miles) northward in Michigan between 1968 and 1990, this movement linked to the amelioration of winter extremes as a result of climatic warming. In addition, this study found white-footed mice (*Peromyscus leucopus*) and southern flying squirrels (*Glaucomys volans*) extending their ranges northward by 225 km in the 30-year period since 1980, with these species replacing northern counterparts (Myers et al. 2009:1444–1445,1448). Beatty et al. (2014) assess the opossum's range in Indiana in relation to anthropogenic resources at its northern boundary. Taulman and Robbins (2014:1629) found that the nine banded armadillo is limited at its northern range boundary in Kansas and Illinois by mean minimum January temperature and factors related to winter extremes.

As a future research question, given Myers et al.'s (2009) demonstration of small mammal replacements, did the rice rat replace any rodent species in its northward movements?

(7) Some terrestrial snail species have disjunct or relict populations beyond their defined range boundary in suitable microhabitats. Many snail species appear to have a very small home range and the ability to withstand some adverse conditions, particularly dry conditions, by estivating for long periods. Theler has recorded the minute native snail *Vertigo gouldi* (A. Binney) estivating under dry conditions at moderate temperatures for more than six years before emerging from its long dormancy under increased moisture.

References Cited

Adams, William R.
  1949   Faunal Remains from the Angel Site. Unpublished Master's thesis, Department of Anthropology, Indiana University, Bloomington.
  1950   Food Animals Used by the Indians at the Angel Site. *Proceedings of the Indian Academy of Science* 59:19–24. Indianapolis.

Adovasio, J. M., J. D. Gunn, J. Donahuey R. Stuckenrath, J. Guilday, and K. Lord
  1979   Meadowcroft Rockshelter — Retrospect 1977: Part 1. *North American Archaeologist* 1:3–44.

Adovasio, J. M., J. D. Gunn, J. Donahue, R. Stuckenrath, J. Guilday, K. Lord, and K. Volman
  1980   Meadowcroft Rockshelter — Retrospect 1977: Part 2. *North American Archaeologist* 1:99–137.

Alam, Emil A.
  1961   A Preliminary Report on a Stratified Site at Ohioview, Pa. *Pennsylvania Archaeologist* 31(2):61–77.

Allman, John C.
  1968   The Incinerator Village Site. *Ohio Archaeologist* 18(2):50–55.

Andrewartha, H. G., and L. C. Birch
  1954   *The Distribution and Abundance of Animals*. University of Chicago Press, Chicago.

Ashworth, Allan C.
  1980   Environmental Implications of a Beetle Assem-
         blage from the Gervais Formation (Early Wiscon-
         sinan?), Minnesota. *Quaternary Research* 13:200–212.

Baerreis, David A., and Reid A. Bryson
  1965   Climatic Episodes and the Dating of the
         Mississippian Cultures. *The Wisconsin Archeologist*
         46(4):203–220.

Baker, Frank Collins
  1936   Remains of Animal Life From the Kingston Kitch-
         en Midden Site Near Peoria, Illinois. *Transactions of
         the Illinois State Academy of Science* 29:243–246.

Banfield, A. W. F.
  1974   *The Mammals of Canada*. University of Toronto
         Press, Toronto and Buffalo.

Barbour, Roger W.
  1957   Some Additional Mammal Records from Ken-
         tucky. *Journal of Mammalogy* 38(1):140–141.

Barbour, Roger W., and Wayne H. Davis
  1974   *Mammals of Kentucky*. University Press of Ken-
         tucky, Lexington.

Bardwell, Jennifer
  1981   The Paleoecological and Social Significance of the
         Zooarchaeological Remains from Central Plains Tra-
         dition Earthlodges of the Glenwood Locality, Mills
         County, Iowa. Unpublished Master's Thesis, Depart-
         ment of Social Studies, University of Iowa, Iowa City.

Bareis, Charles J.
  1977   *Report of Investigations and Proposed Mitigation for
         the Range Site (11-S-27), St. Clair County, Illinois*. FAI-
         270 Archaeological Mitigation Project. Department of
         Anthropology, University of Illinois, Urbana.

Beatty, William S., James C. Beasley, and Olin E. Rhodes, Jr.
  2014   Habitat Selection by a Generalist Mesopredator
         near its Historic Range Boundary. *Canadian Journal of
         Zoology* 92:41–48.

Bee, James W., Gregory E. Glass, Robert S. Hoffman, and
Robert R. Patterson.
  1981   *Mammals in Kansas*. Public Education Series No.
         7. University of Kansas Museum of Natural History,
         Lawrence.

Bernabo, J. Christopher
  1981   Quantitative Estimates of Temperature Changes
         over the Last 2700 Years in Michigan Based on Pollen
         Data. *Quaternary Research* 15:143–159.

Bernhardt, Jack E.
  1973   Gillie Rockshelter: A Late Woodland Phase in
         Summit County, Ohio. Unpublished Master's thesis,
         Department of Anthropology, Kent State University,
         Kent, Ohio.

Berryman, Alan A.
  1986   *Forest Insects: Principles and Practice of Population
         Management*. Plenum Press, New York.

Black, Glenn A.
  1934   Archaeological Survey of Dearborn and Ohio
         Counties. *Indiana History Bulletin* 11(7).
  1967   *Angel Site*. Indiana Historical Society, Indianapolis.

Bole, B. Patterson, Jr., and Philip N. Moulthrop
  1942   The Ohio Recent Mammal Collection in the
         Cleveland Museum of Natural History. *Scientific
         Publications of the Cleveland Museum of Natural History*
         5(6):83–181. Cleveland.

Brainerd, George Walton
  1937   *Animal Remains of the Anderson Village Site*. Unpub-
         lished Ph.D. dissertation, Department of Zoology,
         Ohio State University, Columbus.

Braun, E. Lucy
  1950   *Deciduous Forests of Eastern North America*. Macmil-
         lan, New York.

Brown, James A. (editor)
  1975   *Perspectives in Cahokia Archaeology*. Bulletin No. 10.
         Illinois Archaeological Survey, University of Illinois,
         Urbana.

Bryson, Reid A.
  1985   On Climatic Analogs in Paleoclimatic Reconstruc-
         tion. *Quaternary Research* 23:275–286.

Bryson, Reid A., David A. Baerreis, and Wayne M. Wendland
  1970   The Character of Late-Glacial and Post-Glacial
         Climatic Changes. In *Pleistocene and Recent Environ-
         ments of the Central Great Plains*, edited by Wakefield
         Dort, Jr., and J. Knox Jones, Jr., pp. 53–74. University
         Press of Kansas, Lawrence.

Bryson, Reid A., and Wayne M. Wendland
  1967   Tentative Climatic Patterns for Some Late Glacial
         and Post-Glacial Episodes in Central North America.
         In *Life, Land and Water*, edited by William J. Mayer-
         Oakes, pp. 271–298. University of Manitoba Press,
         Winnipeg.

Buker, William E.
  1968   The Archaeology of McKees Rocks Late Prehis-
         toric Village Site. *Pennsylvania Archaeologist* 38:3–49.

Cahalane, Victor H.
  1947   *Mammals of North America*. Macmillan, New York.

Carlisle, R. C., and J. M. Adovasio (editors)
  1982   *Meadowcroft Collected Papers on the Archaeology of
         Meadowcroft Rockshelter and the Cross Creek Drainage*.
         Cultural Resource Management Program, Depart-
         ment of Anthropology, University of Pittsburgh.

Casson, John E.
  1984   A New Distribution Suggested for the Rice Rat
         (*Oryzomys palustris*) in Southern Illinois. *Transactions
         of the Illinois State Academy of Science* 77:285.

Cockrum, E. Lendell
  1952   *Mammals of Kansas*. University of Kansas
         Publications, Vol. 7(1). Museum of Natural History,
         Lawrence.

Coleman, Robert H.
1948   Some Mammal Notes from South Carolina. *Journal of Mammalogy* 29(3):293–294.

Colinvaux, Paul A.
1973   *Introduction to Ecology.* John Wiley and Sons, New York.

Conaway, Clinton H.
1954   The Reproductive Cycle of Rice Rats (*Oryzomys palustris palustris*) in Captivity. *Journal of Mammalogy* 35(2):263–266.

Cross, Paula G.
1984   Vertebrate Faunal Remains from the Julien Site. In *The Julien Site (11-S-63)*, by George R. Milner, pp. 223–243. American Bottom Archaeology, FAI-270 Site Reports, Vol. 7. University of Illinois Press, Urbana.

Cutler, Hugh C., and Leonard W. Blake
1973   Plant Materials from the Kane Village Site (11 Msl94), Madison County, Illinois. Appendix B: A Preliminary Report on Kane Village: A Late Woodland Site in Madison County, Illinois, by Patrick J. Munson and James P. Anderson. In *Late Woodland Site Archaeology in Illinois I: Investigations in South-Central Illinois*, edited by James A. Brown, pp. 34–57. Bulletin No. 9. Illinois Archaeological Survey, Urbana.

Darlington, Philip J., Jr.
1961   *Zoogeography.* John Wiley and Sons, New York.

Davis, Margaret Bryan
1976   Pleistocene Biogeography of Temperate Deciduous Forests. *Geoscience and Man* 13:13–26.

Davis, Wayne H., and Roger W. Barbour
1979   Distributional Records of Some Kentucky Mammals. *Transactions of the Kentucky Academy of Science* 40(3–4):111.

Davis, Wayne H., and William Z. Lidicker, Jr.
1955   The Rice Rat, *Oryzomys palustris texensis*, in Northwestern Arkansas. *Journal of Mammalogy* 36(2):298.

Degerbl, Magnus, and Harald Krog
1951   *Den Europaeiske Sumpskildpadde (Emys orbicularis L.) i Danmark.* Danmarks Geologiske Undersgelse, Series II, 18.

Delcourt, Paul A., and Hazel R. Delcourt
1979   Late Pleistocene and Holocene Distributional History of the Deciduous Forest in the Southeastern United States. *Veroffentlichungen des Geobotanischen Institutes der ETH.* 68:79–107. Zurich.

Dellinger, S. C., and J. D. Black
1940   Notes on Arkansas Mammals. *Journal of Mammalogy* 21(2):187–191.

De Vos, Antoon
1964   Range Changes of Mammals in the Great Lakes Region. *American Midland Naturalist* 71:210–231.

Dice, Lee R.
1952   *Natural Communities.* University of Michigan Press, Ann Arbor.

Doutt, J. Kenneth, Caroline A. Heppenstall, and John E. Guilday
1966   *Mammals of Pennsylvania.* Pennsylvania Game Commission, Harrisburg.

Dragoo, Don W.
1955a *An Archaeological Survey of Gibson County, Indiana.* Indiana Historical Bureau, Indianapolis.
1955b Excavations at the Johnston Site, Indiana County, Pennsylvania. *Pennsylvania Archaeologist* 25(2):85–141.

Driver, Harold E.
1969   *Indians of North America.* 2d rev. ed. University of Chicago Press, Chicago.

Driver, Harold E., and William C. Massey
1957   Comparative Studies of North American Indians. *Transactions of the American Philosophical Society*, New Series, Vol. 47, Pt. 2, Philadelphia.

Duffield, Lathel F.
1974   Nonhuman Vertebrate Remains from Salts Cave Vestibule. In *Archeology of the Mammoth Cave Area*, edited by Patty Jo Watson, pp. 123–133. Academic Press, New York .

Emmel, Thomas C.
1973   *An Introduction to Ecology and Population Biology.* W. Norton, New York.

Essenpreis, Patricia S.
1978   Fort Ancient Settlement: Differential Response at a Mississippian–Late Woodland Interface. In *Mississippian Settlement Patterns*, edited by Bruce D. Smith, pp. 141–167. Academic Press, New York.

Farner, Donald S.
1947   New Records for *Oryzomys palustris palustris* (Harlan) and *Acariscus masoni Ewing. Proceedings of the Biological Society of Washington* 60:29–30.

FAUNMAP Working Group
1996   Spatial Response of Mammals to Late Quaternary Environmental Fluctuations. *Science* 272:1601–1606.

Fowler, Melvin L.
1959   *Summary Report of Modoc Rock Shelter.* Report of Investigations No. 8. Illinois State Museum, Springfield.

Fowler, Melvin L. (editor)
1975   *Cahokia Archaeology: Field Reports.* Papers in Anthropology No. 3. Illinois State Museum Research Series, Springfield.
1977   *Explorations into Cahokia Archaeology.* 2d rev. ed. Bulletin No. 7. Illinois Archaeological Survey, University of Illinois, Urbana.

Fritts, Harold C., G. Robert Lofgren, and Geoffrey A. Gordon
1979   Variations in Climate Since 1602 as Reconstructed from Tree Rings. *Quaternary Research* 12:18–46.

Galloway, R. W.

1983   Full-Glacial Southwestern United States: Mild and Wet or Cold and Dry? *Quaternary Research* 19:236–248.

George, Richard L.

1974   Monogahela Settlement Patterns and the Ryan Site. *Pennsylvania Archaeologist* 44(1–2):1–22.

Gilmore, Raymond M.

1946   Mammals in Archeological Collections from Southwestern Pennsylvania. *Journal of Mammalogy* 27:227–234.

Goldman, Edward A.

1918   *The Rice Rats of North America* (*Genus* Oryzomys). North American Fauna, No. 43. Bureau of Biological Survey, U. S. Department of Agriculture, Government Printing Office, Washington, D.C.

Golley, Frank B.

1966   *South Carolina Mammals*. Contributions from the Charleston Museum 15.

Goodpaster, Woodrow W., and Donald F. Hoffmeister

1952   Notes on the Mammals of Western Tennessee. *Journal of Mammalogy* 33(3):362–371.

Goslin, Robert M.

1950   Animal Remains from a Prehistoric Ohio Indian Site. *Ohio Indian Relic Collectors Society Bulletin* 25:16–22.

1951   Evidence of the Occurrence of the Rice Rat in Prehistoric Village Sites in Ohio. *Ohio Indian Relic Collectors Society Bulletin* 26:19–22.

1952   Mammal and Bird Remains from the Cramer Village Site, Ross County, Ohio. *Ohio Archaeologist* 2(4):20–21.

Gottschang, Jack L.

1981   *A Guide to the Mammals of Ohio*. Ohio State University Press, Columbus.

Griffin, James B.

1943   *The Fort Ancient Aspect: Its Cultural and Chronological Position in Mississippi Valley Archaeology*. University of Michigan Press, Ann Arbor.

1953   Comments on the Cultural Position of the Bintz Site, Campbell County, Kentucky. *American Antiquity* 18(3):262.

1967   Eastern North American Archaeology: A Summary. *Science* 156:175–191.

Guilday, John E.

1955   Animal Remains from an Indian Village Site, Indiana County, Pennsylvania. *Pennsylvania Archaeologist* 25(2):142–147.

1961a   Prehistoric Record of *Scalopus* from Western Pennsylvania. *Journal of Mammalogy* 42:117–118.

1961b   The Rice Rat Riddle. *SPAAC [Society for Pennsylvania Archaeology, Allegheny Chapter] Speaks* 1:23–25.

1961c   Vertebrate Remains from the Varner Site (36-Gr-1). *Pennsylvania Archaeologist* 31(3–4):119–124.

1971   *Biological and Archeological Analysis of Bones from a 17th Century Indian Village (46 Pu 31), Putnam County, West Virginia*. Report of Archeological Investigations, No. 4. West Virginia Geological and Economic Survey, Morgantown.

1972   Archaeological Evidence of *Scalopus aquaticus* in the Upper Ohio Valley. *Journal of Mammalogy* 53(4):905–907.

Guilday, John E., Paul S. Martin, and Allen D. McCrady

1964   New Paris No. 4: A Late Pleistocene Cave Deposit in Bedford County, Pennsylvania. *Bulletin of the National Speleological Society* 26(4):121–194.

Guilday, John E., and William J. Mayer-Oakes

1952   An Occurrence of the Rice Rat (*Oryzomys*) in West Virginia. *Journal of Mammalogy* 33(2):253–255.

Guilday, John E., and Paul W. Parmalee

1965   Animal Remains from the Sheep Rock Shelter (36 Hu 1), Huntingdon County, Pennsylvania. *Pennsylvania Archaeologist* 35:34–49.

1979   Pleistocene and Recent Vertebrate Remains from Savage Cave (15Lo110), Kentucky. In *Western Kentucky Speleological Survey, Annual Report 1979*, edited by John E. Mylroie, pp. 5–10. Murray State University Printing Services, Murray, Kentucky.

Guilday, John E., Paul W. Parmalee, and Donald P. Tanner

1962   Aboriginal Butchering Techniques at the Eschelman Site (36 La 12), Lancaster ,County, Pennsylvania. *Pennsylvania Archaeologist* 32:59–83.

Guilday, John E., and Donald P. Tanner

1965   Vertebrate Remains from the Mount Carbon Site (46-Fa-7), Fayette County, West Virginia. *The West Virginia Archeologist* 18:1–14.

1968   Vertebrate Remains from the Fairchance Mound (46 Mr 13), Marshall County, West Virginia. *West Virginia Archeologist* 21:41–54.

Graham, Russell W., Ernest L. Lundelius, and the FAUNMAP Working Group

1994   *Faunmap: A Database Documenting Late Quaternary Distributions of Mammal Species in the United States*. Scientific Papers No. 25(2). Illinois State Museum, Springfield.

Hall, E. Raymond

1981   *The Mammals of North America*. 2d rev. ed. John Wiley and Sons, New York.

Hall, E. Raymond, and Keith R. Kelson

1959   *The Mammals of North America*. Ronald Press, New York.

Hamilton, W. J., Jr.

1946   Habits of the Swamp Rice Rat, *Oryzomys palustris palustris* (Harlan). *American Midland Naturalist* 36:730–736.

Hamilton, William J., Jr., and John O. Whitaker, Jr.

1979   *Mammals of the Eastern United States*. 2d rev ed. Cornell University Press. Ithaca.

Handley, Charles O., Jr.
1971   Appalachian Mammalian Geography — Recent Epoch. In *The Distributional History of the Biota of the Southern Appalachians, Part III: Vertebrates*, edited by Perry C. Holt, pp. 263–303. Research Division Monograph 4. Virginia Polytechnic Institute and State University, Blacksburg.

Handley, Charles O., Jr., and Clyde P. Patton
1947   *Wild Mammals of Virginia*. Commonwealth of Virginia Commission of Game and Inland Fisheries, Richmond.

Hanson, J. Delton, Jane L. Indorf, Vicki J. Swier, and Robert D. Bradley
2010   Molecular Divergence within the *Oryzomys palustris palustris* Complex: Evidence for Multiple Species. *Journal of Mammalogy* 91(2):336–347.

Hanson, Lee H., Jr.
1975   *The Buffalo Site: A Late 17th Century Indian Village Site (46Pu31) in Putnam County, West Virginia*. Report of Archeological Investigations No. 5. West Virginia Geological and Economic Survey, Morgantown.

Harlan, R.
1837   Description of a New Species of Quadruped, of the Order Rodentia, Inhabiting the United States. *American Journal of Science and Arts* 31:385–386.

Harris, Arthur H.
1970   Past Climate of the Navajo Reservoir District. *American Antiquity* 35:374–377.

Harris, Van T.
1953   Ecological Relationships of Meadow Voles and Rice Rats in Tidal Marshes. *Journal of Mammalogy* 34(4):479–487.

Heilman, James M., and Roger R. Hoeffer
1981   Possible Astronomical Alignments in a Fort Ancient Settlement at the Incinerator Site in Dayton, Ohio. In *Archaeoastronomy in the Americas*, edited by Ray A. Williamson, pp. 157–171. Ballena Press Anthropological Papers No. 22. Los Altos, California.

Hemmings, E. Thomas
1977   *Neale's Landing: An Archeological Study of a Fort Ancient Settlement on Blennerhassett Island, West Virginia*. Open-File Report OF807. West Virginia Geological and Economic Survey, Morgantown.
1984   Fairchance Mound and Village: An Early Middle Woodland Settlement in the Upper Ohio Valley. *West Virginia Archeologist* 36(1):3–51.

Hill, Frederick C.
1970   Animal Remains from the Macoupin Site, Illinois. Unpublished Master's thesis, Department of Biological Sciences, Illinois State University, Normal.

Hine, James S.
1910   Ohio Species of Mice. *The Ohio Naturalist* 10(4):65–72.

Hodge, Frederick Webb (editor)
1907, 1910   *Handbook of American Indians North of Mexico* 2 pts. Bulletin 30. Bureau of American Ethnology, Washington, D.C.

Hoffmann, Robert S., and J. Knox Jones, Jr.
1970   Influence of Late-Glacial and Post-Glacial Events on the Distribution of Recent Mammals on the Northern Great Plains. In *Pleistocene and Recent Environments of the Central Great Plains*, edited by Wakefield Dort, Jr., and J. Knox Jones, Jr., pp. 355–394. University Press of Kansas, Lawrence.

Hoffmeister, Donald F., and Carl O. Mohr
1957   *Fieldbook of Illinois Mammals*. Manual 4. Illinois Natural History Survey, Urbana.

Holbrook, Sally J.
1977   Rodent Faunal Turnover and Prehistoric Community Stability in Northwestern New Mexico. *The American Naturalist* 111:1195–1208.

Holman, J. Alan, and Ronald L. Richards
1981   Late Pleistocene Occurrence in Southern Indiana of the Smooth Green Snake, *Opheodrys vernalis*. *Journal of Herpetology* 15:123–125.

Hooton, Earnest A., and Charles C. Willoughby
1920   *Indian Village Site and Cemetery near Madisonville, Ohio*. Papers of the Peabody Museum of American Archaeology and Ethnology 8(1). Cambridge, Massachusetts.

Hotopp, John
1978   Glenwood: A Contemporary View. In *The Central Plains Tradition: Internal Development and External Relationships*, edited by Donald J. Blakeslee, pp. 109–133. Report 11. Office of the State Archaeologist, University of Iowa, Iowa City.

Howell, Arthur H.
1927   The Rice Rat in Maryland. *Journal of Mammalogy* 8(4):312.

Howell, J. C., and C. H. Conaway
1952   Observations on the Mammals of the Cumberland Mountains of Tennessee. *Journal of the Tennessee Academy of Science* 27(2):153–158.

Indorf, Jane L., and Michael S. Gaines
2013 Genetic Divergence of Insular Marsh Rice Rats in Subtropical Florida. *Journal of Mammalogy* 94(3):897–910.

Jenkins, Merle T.
1941   Influence of Climate and Weather on Growth of Corn. In *Climate and Man*, U.S. Department of Agriculture, pp. 308–320. Yearbook of Agriculture. U.S. Government Printing Office, Washington, D.C.

Johnson, Alfred E.
1979   Kansas City Hopewell. In *Hopewell Archaeology: The Chillicothe Conference*, edited by David S. Brose and N'omi Greber, pp. 86–93. Kent State University Press, Kent, Ohio.

Johnson, Eileen McAllister
1975   *Faunal and Floral Material from a Kansas City Hopewell Site: Analysis and Interpretation*. Occasional Papers No. 36. The Museum, Texas Tech University, Lubbock.

Johnson, Paul Curtis
1972   Mammalian Remains Associated with Nebraska Phase Earth Lodges in Mills County, Iowa. Unpublished Master's thesis, Department of Geology, University of Iowa, Iowa City.

Jones, J. Knox, Jr., David M. Armstrong, Robert S. Hoffmann, and Clyde Jones
1983   *Mammals of the Northern Great Plains*. University of Nebraska Press, Lincoln.

Kale, Herbert W., II
1965   *Ecology and Bioenergetics of the Long-billed Marsh Wren*, Telmatodytes palustris griseus (*Brewster*), in *Georgia Salt Marshes*. Publications of the Nuttall Ornithological Club 5. Cambridge, Massachusetts.

Kelly, John E.
1979   Annual Report of 1978 Investigations at the Range Site (11-S-47). In *Annual Report of 1978 Investigations by the University of Illinois-Urbana FAI-270 Archaeological Mitigation Project*, edited by Charles J. Bareis, pp. 16–34. Archaeological Field Laboratory, University of Illinois-Urbana, Columbia, Illinois.
1980   Annual Report of 1979 Investigations at the Range Site (11-S-47). In *Annual Report of 1979 investigations by the University of Illinois-Urbana FAI-270 Archaeological Mitigation Project*, edited by Charles J. Bareis, pp. 18–28. Department of Anthropology, University of Illinois, Urbana–Champaign.
1982   *Formative Development at Cahokia and the Adjacent American Bottom: A Merrell Tract Perspective*. 2 vols. Archaeological Research Laboratory, Western Illinois University, Macomb.

Kelly, Lucretia S.
1979   *Animal Resource Exploitation by Early Cahokia Populations on the Merrell Tract*. Circular No. 4. Illinois Archaeological Survey, Urbana.
1980   September Monthly Progress Report—FAI-270 Project. Manuscript on file, Department of Anthropology, University of Illinois, Urbana.
1981   Annual Report of the Faunal Analysis Laboratory. In *Annual Report of 1980 Investigations by the University of Illinois at Urbana–Champaign FAI-270 Archaeological Mitigation Project*, edited by Charles J. Bareis, pp. 96–104. Department of Anthropology, University of Illinois at Urbana–Champaign.

Kincaid, W. Bradley, and Guy N. Cameron
1982   Dietary Variation in Three Sympatric Rodents on the Texas Coastal Prairie. *Journal of Mammalogy* 63:668–672.

Kinsey, W. Fred, III

1959   Historic Susquehannock Pottery. In *Susquehannock Miscellany*, edited by John Witthoft and W. Fred Kinsey III, pp. 61–98. Pennsylvania Historical and Museum Commission, Harrisburg.

Klimstra, W. D., and J. L. Roseberry
1969   Additional Observations on Some Southern Illinois Mammals. *Transactions of the Illinois State Academy of Science* 62:413–417.

Klimstra, Willard D., and Thomas G. Scott
1956   *Distribution of the Rice Rat in Southern Illinois*. Natural History Miscellanea, No. 154. Chicago Academy of Sciences, Chicago.

Klippel, Walter E.
1971   *Graham Cave Revisited, A Reevaluation of Its Cultural Position during the Archaic Period*. Memoir No. 9. Missouri Archaeological Society, Columbia.

Kurten, Bjorn, and Elaine Anderson
1980   *Pleistocene Mammals of North America*. Columbia University Press, New York.

Langdon, Frank W.
1881   The Mammalia of the Vicinity of Cincinnati, a List of Species with Notes. *Journal of the Cincinnati Society of Natural History* 3:297–313.

Logan, Wilfred D.
1952   *Graham Cave, an Archaic Site in Montgomery County, Missouri*. Memoir No. 2. Missouri Archaeological Society, Columbia.

MacCord, Howard A.
1953   The Bintz Site. *American Antiquity* 18(3):239–244.

Mayer-Oakes, William J.
1954   *The Speidel Site (46-Oh 7) Ohio County, West Virginia*. Special Publication No. 2. West Virginia Archeological Society, Moundsville, West Virginia.
1955   *Prehistory of the Upper Ohio Valley*. Annals of Carnegie Museum, Vol. 34. Pittsburgh.

McCarley, W. H.
1952   The Ecological Relationships of the Mammals of Bryan County, Oklahoma. *The Texas Journal of Science* 4(1):102–112.

McClenaghan, Leroy R., Jr., and Michael S. Gaines
1978   *Reproduction in Marginal Populations of the Hispid Cotton Rat* (Siqmodon hispidus) *in Northeastern Kansas*. Occasional Papers No. 74. University of Kansas Museum of Natural History, Lawrence.

McLaughlin, Charles A., and William B. Robertson
1951   A *New Record of the Rice Rat*, Oryzomys palustris palustris, *from Southern Illinois*. Natural History Miscellanea, No. 80. Chicago Academy of Sciences, Chicago.

McMichael, Edward V.
1962   Preliminary Report on Mount Carbon Village Excavations, 46-Fa-7. *West Virginia Archeologist* 14:36–51.

1968   *Introduction to West Virginia Archeology*. 2d rev. ed. West Virginia Geological and Economic Survey, Morgantown.

Mills, William C.
1906   Baum Prehistoric Village. *Ohio Archaeological and Historical Society Publications* 15:44–136.

Milner, George R.
1984   *The Julien Site (11-S-63)*. American Bottom Archaeology, FAI-270 Site Reports, Vol. 7. University of Illinois Press, Urbana.

Morse, Dan, Phyllis Morse, and Merrill Emmons
1961   The Southern Cult, the Emmons Site, Fulton County, Illinois. *Central States Archaeological Journal* 8:124–140.

Mumford, Russell E.
1969   *Distribution of the Mammals of Indiana*. Monograph No. 1. Indiana Academy of Science, Indianapolis.

Mumford, Russell E., and John O. Whitaker, Jr.
1982   *Mammals of Indiana*. Indiana University Press, Bloomington.

Munson, Patrick J., and James P. Anderson
1973   A Preliminary Report on Kane Village: A Late Woodland Site in Madison County, Illinois. In *Late Woodland Site Archaeology in Illinois I: Investigations in South-Central Illinois*, edited by James A. Brown, pp. 34–57. Bulletin No. 9. Illinois Archaeological Survey, Urbana.

Munson, Patrick J., Paul W. Parmalee, and Richard A. Yarnell
1971   Subsistence Ecology of Scovill, a Terminal Middle Woodland Village. *American Antiquity* 36:410–431.

Murphy, James L.
1971   36 Bv 9 and the Monongahela Complex. *Society for Pennsylvania Archaeology Newsletter* 3:2–5. Amockwi Chapter No. 17.

1975   *An Archeological History of the Hocking Valley*. Ohio University Press, Athens.

1981   Faunal Remains from the Miller Site (46-Ja-55), Jackson County, West Virginia. *West Virginia Archeologist* 31:20–30.

Myers, Philip, Barbara L. Lundrigan, Susan M. G. Hoffman, Allison Poor Haramin, and Stephanie H. Seto
2009 Climate-Induced Changes in the Small Mammal Communities of the Northern Great Lakes Region. *Global Change Biology* 15:1434–1454.

Nale, Robert F.
1963   The Salvage Excavation of the Boyle Site (36 Wh 19). *Pennsylvania Archaeologist* 33(4):164–194.

National Oceanic and Atmospheric Administration, U.S. Department of Commerce
1974   *Climates of the States*. 2 vols. Water Information Center, Port Washington, New York.

Nawrot, J. R., and W. D. Klimstra
1976   *Present and Past Distribution of the Endangered Southern Illinois Woodrat* (Neotoma floridana illinoensis). Natural History Miscellanea, No. 196. Chicago Academy of Sciences, Chicago.

Negus, Norman C., Edwin Gould, and Robert K. Chipman
1961   Ecology of the Rice Rat, *Oryzomys palustris* (Harlan), on Breton Island, Gulf of Mexico, with a Critique of the Social Stress Theory. *Tulane Studies in Zoology* 8(4).

O'Brien, Patricia Joan
1972   *A Formal Analysis of Cahokia Ceramics from the Powell Tract*. Monograph No. 3. Illinois Archaeological Survey, Urbana.

Odum, Eugene P.
1971   *Fundamentals of Ecology*. 3rd ed. W. B. Saunders, Philadelphia.

Ogden, J. Gordon, III
1966   Forest History of Ohio. I. Radiocarbon Dates and Pollen Stratigraphy of Silver Lake, Logan County, Ohio. *Ohio Journal of Science* 66(4):387–400.

Parmalee, Paul W.
1957a   Vertebrate Remains from the Cahokia Site, Illinois. *Transactions of the Illinois State Academy of Science* 50:235–242.

1957b   Zoology. In *The Identification of Non-Artifactual Archaeological Materials*, edited by Walter W. Taylor, pp. 45–46. Publication 565. National Academy of Sciences–National Research Council, Washington, D.C.

1962   Additional Faunal Records from the Kingston Lake Site, Illinois. *Transactions of the Illinois State Academy of Science* 55(1):6–12.

1963   Identification of Faunal Remains. In *Second Annual Report: American Bottoms Archaeology, July 1, 1962–June 30, 1963*, Melvin L. Fowler, editor, pp. 14–16. Illinois Archaeological Survey, Urbana.

1967   A Recent Cave Bone Deposit in Southwestern Illinois. *Bulletin of the National Speleological Society* 29(4):119–147.

1968   Cave and Archaeological Faunal Deposits as Indicators of Post-Pleistocene Animal Populations and Distribution in Illinois. In *The Quaternary of Illinois*, edited by Robert E. Bergstrom, pp. 104–113. University of Illinois, Urbana.

1971   Faunal Materials from the Schild Cemetery Site, Greene County, Illinois. Appendix A, for The Mississippian Component at the Schild Site (No. 4), Greene County, Illinois, by Gregory H. Perino, pp. 1–148. In *Mississippian Site Archaeology in Illinois I*, edited by James A. Brown, pp. 142–143. Bulletin No. 8. Illinois Archaeological Survey, Urbana.

1973   Faunal Remains from the Kane Village Site (Ms 194), Madison County, Illinois. Appendix A, in A Preliminary Report on Kane Village: A Late Woodland Site in Madison County, Illinois, by Patrick J. Munson and James P. Anderson, pp. 34–57. In *Late*

Woodland Site Archaeology in Illinois I: Investigations in South-Central Illinois, edited by James A. Brown, pp. 49–52. Bulletin No. 9. Illinois Archaeological Survey, Urbana.

Parmalee, Paul W., and Ronald D. Oesch
1972   *Pleistocene and Recent Faunas from the Brynjulfson Caves*, Missouri. Reports of Investigations No. 25. Illinois State Museum, Springfield.

Parmalee, Paul W., Andreas A. Paloumpis, and Nancy Wilson
1972   *Animals Utilized by Woodland Peoples Occupying the Apple Creek Site, Illinois*. Reports of Investigations No. 23, Illinois State Museum, Springfield. Research Papers, Vol. 5, Illinois Valley Archaeological Program, Springfield.

Parmalee, Paul W., and Orrin C. Shane III
1970   The Blain Site Vertebrate Fauna. In *Blain Village and the Fort Ancient Tradition in Ohio*, by Olaf H. Prufer and Orrin C. Shane III, pp. 185–206. Kent State University Press, Kent, Ohio.

Perino, Gregory H.
1971   The Mississippian Component at the Schild Site (No. 4), Greene County, Illinois. In *Mississippian Site Archaeology in Illinois I*, edited by James A. Brown, pp. 1–148. Bulletin No. 8. Illinois Archaeological Survey, Urbana.

Prufer, Olaf H.
1981   *Raven Rocks: A Specialized Late Woodland Rock Rockshelter Occupation in Belmont County, Ohio*. Kent State Research Papers in Archaeology No. 1. Department of Sociology and Anthropology, Kent State University, Kent, Ohio.

Prufer, Olaf H., and Orrin C. Shane, III
1970   *Blain Village and the Fort Ancient Tradition in Ohio*. Kent State University Press, Kent, Ohio.

Rackerby, Frank
1973   A Statistical Determination of the Black Sand Occupation at the Macoupin Site, Jersey Co., Illinois. *American Antiquity* 38:96–101.

Richards, Ronald L.
1972   The Woodrat in Indiana: Recent Fossils. *Proceedings of the Indiana Academy of Science* 81:370–375.

1980   Rice Rat (*Oryzomys cf. palustris*) Remains from Southern Indiana Caves. *Proceedings of the Indiana Academy of Science* 89:425–431.

Salzer, Robert J.
1975   Excavations at the Merrell Tract of the Cahokia Site: Summary Field Report, 1973. In *Cahokia Archaeology: Field Reports*, edited by Melvin L. Fowler, pp. 1–8. Papers in Anthropology No. 3. Illinois State Museum Research Series, Springfield.

Satorius-Fox, Marsha R.
1982   Paleoecological Analysis of Micromammals from the Schmidt Site, a Central Plains Tradition Village in Howard County, Nebraska. Unpublished Master's Thesis, Department of Geology, University of Iowa, Iowa City.

Schantz, Viola S.
1943   The Rice Rat, *Oryzomys palustris palustris*, in Delaware. *Journal of Mammalogy* 24(1):103–104.

Schultz, C. Bertrand
1972   Holocene Interglacial Migrations of Mammals and Other Vertebrates. *Quaternary Research* 2:337–340.

Schwartz, Charles W., and Elizabeth R. Schwartz
1981   *The Wild Mammals of Missouri*. Rev. ed. University of Missouri Press and Missouri Department of Conservation, Columbia.

Sealander, John A.
1979   *A Guide to Arkansas Mammals*. River Road Press, Conway, Arkansas.

Sealander, John A., and Douglas James
1958   Relative Efficiency of Different Small Mammal Traps. *Journal of Mammology* 39(2):215–223.

Semken, Holmes A., Jr.
1983   Holocene Mammalian Biogeography and Climatic Change in the Eastern and Central United States. In *Late-Quaternary Environments of the United States, Vol. 2 – The Holocene*, edited by H. E. Wright, Jr., pp. 182–207. University of Minnesota Press, Minneapolis.

2016   The Zooarchaeological Significance of the Rice Rat in the Midwest: A Response to "Archaeological Remains of the Rice Rat as a Climatic Proxy in the American Midwest," by Kent D. Vickery, James L. Theler, and Orrin C. Shane, III. *The Wisconsin Archeologist* 97(2):81–84.

Shane, Orrin C., III
1973   Vertebrate Remains. In *Gillie Rockshelter: A Late Woodland Phase in Summit County, Ohio*, by Jack E. Bernhardt, pp. 33–38. Unpublished Master's thesis, Department of Sociology and Anthropology, Kent State University, Kent, Ohio.

1980   Fort Ancient Hunting Practices. Paper presented at the 45th Annual Meeting of the Society for American Archaeology, Philadelphia.

Shane, Orrin C., and Paul W. Parmalee
1981   Vertebrate Remains. In *Raven Rocks: A Specialized Late Woodland Rockshelter Occupation in Belmont County, Ohio*, by Olaf H. Prufer, pp. 57–72. Kent State Research Papers in Archaeology No. 1. Department of Sociology and Anthropology, Kent State University, Kent, Ohio.

Sharp, Homer F., Jr.
1967   Food Ecology of the Rice Rat, *Oryzomys palustris* (Harlan), in a Georgia Salt Marsh. *Journal of Mammalogy* 48(4):557–563.

Shelford, Victor E.
1963   *The Ecology of North America.* University of Illinois Press, Urbana.

Silver, James
1927   The Introduction and Spread of House Rats in the United States. *Journal of Mammalogy* 8(1):58–60.

Simpson, A. M.
1939   *The Kingston Village Site.* The Peoria Academy of Science, Peoria, Illinois.

Smith, Bruce D.
1975   *Middle Mississippi Exploitation of Animal Populations.* Anthropological Papers No. 57. Museum of Anthropology, University of Michigan, Ann Arbor.

Smith, Philip W.
1957   An Analysis of Post-Wisconsin Biogeography of the Prairie Peninsula Region Based on Distributional Phenomena among Terrestrial Vertebrate Populations. *Ecology* 38(2):205–218.
1965   Recent Adjustments in Animal Ranges. In *The Quaternary of the United States,* edited by H. E. Wright, Jr., and David G. Frey, pp. 633–642. Princeton University Press, Princeton, New Jersey.

Starr, S. F.
1960   The Archaeology of Hamilton County, Ohio. *Journal of the Cincinnati Museum of Natural History* 23(1). Cincinnati.

Stoner, Louis J.
1972   The Carlin Site: Salvage Archaeology on a Late Woodland Village. *Quarterly Newsletter* 4:21–22. Illinois Association for the Advancement of Archaeology.

Storrs, Eleanor E.
1982   The Astonishing Armadillo. *National Geographic* 161(6):820–830.

Struever, Stuart
1963   *Excavations in a Hopewell Community.* Archaeological Research, Chicago.
1968a   *A Re-examination of Hopewell in Eastern North America.* Ph.D. dissertation, Department of Anthropology, University of Chicago, Chicago.
1968b   Flotation Techniques for the Recovery of Small-Scale Archaeological Remains. *American Antiquity* 33:353–362.

Struever, Stuart, and Kent D. Vickery
1973   The Beginnings of Cultivation in the Midwest-Riverine Area of the United States. *American Anthropologist* 75(5):1197–1220.

Styles, Bonnie W.
1981a   Analysis of Faunal Remains from the 1980 Excavations. In *Modoc Rock Shelter Archaeological Project, Randolph County, Illinois 1980–81,* by Bonnie W. Styles, Melvin L. Fowler, Steven R. Ahler, Frances B. King, and Thomas R. Styles, pp. 115–131. Completion Report to the Department of the Interior, Heritage Conservation and Recreation Service, and the Illinois Department of Conservation. Illinois State Museum, Springfield.
1981b   *Faunal Exploitation and Resource Selection: Early Late Woodland Subsistence in the Lower Illinois Valley.* Scientific Papers No. 3. Northwestern University Archeological Program, Evanston.

Styles, Bonnie W., Steven R. Ahler, and Melvin L. Fowler
1983   Modoc Rock Shelter Revisited. In *Archaic Hunters and Gatherers in the American Midwest,* edited by James L. Phillips and James A. Brown, pp. 261–297. Academic Press, New York.

Svihla, Arthur
1931   Life History of the Texas Rice Rat (*Oryzomys palustris texensis*). *Journal of Mammalogy* 12:238–242.

Swanton, John R.
1946   *The Indians of the Southeastern United States.* Bulletin 137. Bureau of American Ethnology, Washington, D.C,

Tanner, Donald P.
1977   Analysis of Vertebrate Remains from Neale's Landing. Appendix A. In *Neale's Landing: An Archeological Study of a Fort Ancient Settlement on Blennerhassett Island, West Virginia,* by E. Thomas Hemmings, pp. A-1–A-28. Open-File Report OF807. West Virginia Geological and Economic Survey, Morgantown.

Taulman, James F., and Lynn W. Robbins
2014   Range Expansion and Distributional Limits of the Nine-Banded Armadillo in the United States. *Journal of Biography* 41:1626–1630.

Theler, James L.
1978   The Vertebrate Faunal Remains from Sand Ridge (33Ha17): A Stratified Habitation Site in Southwestern Ohio. Unpublished Master's thesis, Department of Anthropology, University of Wisconsin–Madison.

Theler, James L., and Suzanne M. Harris
1988   Faunal Remains from the Turpin Site (33Ha19), Hamilton County, Ohio. *West Virginia Archeologist* 40(2):1–23.

Trigger, Bruce G. (editor)
1978   *Northeast.* Handbook of North American Indians, Vol. 15. Smithsonian Institution, Washington, D.C.

Udvardy, Miklos D. F.
1969   *Dynamic Zoogeography.* Van Nostrand Reinhold, New York.

Ullman, Kyle L.
1985   *The Ceramics from the Kramer Village Site (33Ro33), Ross County, Ohio.* Kent State Research Papers in Archaeology No. 5. Department of Sociology and Anthropology, Kent State University, Kent, Ohio.

Ulmer, Frederick A., Jr.
1944   Further Notes on the Rice Rat in Delaware. *Journal of Mammalogy* 25(4):411.

1951   Notes on the Rice Rat in New Jersey and Pennsylvania. *Journal of Mammalogy* 32 (1):121–122.

Vickery, Kent D.
1976   *An Approach to Inferring Archaeological Site Variability.* Ph.D. dissertation, Department of Anthropology,
Indiana University, Bloomington.

Wahl, E. W.
1968   A Comparison of the Climate of the Eastern
United States During the 1830s with the Current
Normals. *Monthly Weather Review* 96:73–82.

Walker, Ernest P.
1975   *Mammals of the World.* 3rd ed. Vol. II. Johns Hopkins University Press, Baltimore and London.

Watson, Patty Jo
1969   *The Prehistory of Salts Cave, Kentucky.* Reports of
Investigations No. 16. Illinois State Museum, Springfield.

Watson, Patty Jo (editor)
1974   *Archeology of the Mammoth Cave Area.* Academic
Press, New York.

Wayne, William J.
1967   Periglacial Features and Climatic Gradient in
Illinois, Indiana, and Western Ohio, East-Central
United States. In *Quaternary Paleoecology,* edited by
E. J. Cushing and H. E. Wright, Jr., pp. 393–414. Yale
University Press, New Haven.

Wendland, Wayne M.
1978   Holocene Man in North America: The Ecological
Setting and Climatic Background. *Plains Anthropologist* 23:273–287.

Wendland, Wayne M., and Reid A. Bryson
1974   Dating Climatic Episodes of the Holocene. *Quaternary Research* 4:9–24.

Whitaker, H. L.
1937   Occurrence of the Texas Rice Rat in Oklahoma.
Journal of Mammalogy 18:102.

Wilkins, Gary R.
1981   The Miller Site (46-Ja-55): A Fort Ancient Component. *West Virginia Archaeologist* 31:2–19.

Williams, L. D., and T. M. L. Wigley
1983   A Comparison of Evidence for Late Holocene
Summer Temperature Variations in the Northern
Hemisphere. *Quaternary Research* 20:286–307.

Worth, C. Brooke
1950   Observations on the Behavior and Breeding of
Captive Rice Rats and Woodrats. *Journal of Mammalogy* 31(4):421–426.

Wright, H. E., Jr.
1971   Late Quaternary Vegetational History of North
America. In *The Late Cenozoic Glacial Ages,* edited by
Karl K. Turekian, pp. 425–464. Yale University Press,
New Haven.

Wolfe, James L.
1982   *Oryzomys palustris.* Mammalian Species No. 176.
The American Society of Mammalogists.

The Zooarchaeological Significance of the Rice Rat in the Midwest:

A Response to "Archaeological Remains of the Rice Rat (*Oryzomys*) as a Climatic Proxy in the American Midwest," by Kent D. Vickery, James L. Theler, and Orrin C. Shane III

Holmes A. Semken, Jr.

This interesting paper is still apt even though it was prepared over three decades ago. It evaluates the explanations, many still in vogue as possibilities, that have been proposed to explain the "anomalous" presence of *Oryzomys*, the rice rat, north of its present geographic distribution in Midwestern archaeological sites. It also has implications for the Gleasonian model (individualistic species response to climatic change) of biogeography, a concept not fully recognized by paleozoologists at the time of preparation. Following are musings on a few topics, among many, that emerged while reviewing a draft of the manuscript.

Topic 1: Eruptive Spread vs. Population Dispersal. I concur with the authors that "eruptive spread" is a confusing term. Events where super-abundances of a single species suddenly appear are commonly known as eruptions, outbreaks, or population explosions (Ehrlich and Ehrlich 1990). These terms reference rapid increases in species density and accompanying range expansion, usually followed by crashes to normal densities within a year. These can be of three different types:

- Erratic, as exemplified by the cotton rat explosion in 1957 in Texas, probably a result of a very unusual rainfall event (Davis and Schmidly 1997)
- Cyclic, as with the collared lemming (Wilson and Ruff 1999:658), where population densities periodically change from one individual per hectare to more than 50 in a year

- Permanent, frequently exemplified by invasive species, e. g., the Norway rat (Armitage 1993), expanding across broad geographic areas of North America

Population explosions do result in greater dispersal distances, but usually only push a species temporarily into less favorable local habitats. Invasive species aside, "explosions" rarely result in significant changes in normal range, certainly not of the magnitude exhibited by the rice rat during the late Holocene across the eastern half of the United States.

However, as noted in the manuscript, species distributions are not static, and marginal ranges can progressively expand or contract within decades (Hoffman and Jones 1970). The cotton rat, *Sigmodon hispidus* (Cameron and Spencer 1981), the armadillo, *Dasypus novemcinctus* (Jasinsk and Wallace 1914), and the opossum, *Didelphis virginiana* (Hoffmeister 1989) have substantially expanded their ranges over the past century. Effective population dispersal does not occur at eruptive speed, but as distribution adjustments on the margins of dynamic populations responding to changing climatic conditions within and between episodes, as proposed in this paper. Thus, eruptions can be excluded from the rice rat's Late Holocene changes in distribution.

Topic 2: Parasitism, Commensalism, and Procurement. Parasitism, commensalism, and procurement have been documented as sources for micromammals in numerous archaeological contexts and used to

Holmes A. Semken, Jr., Department of Earth and Environmental Sciences, University of Iowa, Iowa City

establish them as contemporaneous with occupation. Semken and Falk (2014) concluded that either or both the deer and white-footed mouse, attracted by food and shelter, were parasites in many Northern Plains earth lodge villages, much to the disgust of the inhabitants. Commensalism, here including marginal mutualism, was predicted by Rhodes and Semken (1986), who attributed ground squirrel/gopher remains to both ridding the garden of pests and supplying the villagers with a food source. Szuter (1994) used a lagomorph index (cottontail/jackrabbit) to predict land management practices and feeding strategies among the Hohokam; and Parmalee (1965) documented procurement through butcher marks on squirrels and woodrat remains in Tick Creek Cave, Missouri. Thus, micromammal/human relationships are documented in the archaeological record, and rice rats cannot be labeled automatically as an exception. Exploitation, in whichever (or both) direction(s), was possible because all involved were residents.

However, the introduction of rice rats and their subsequent establishment in scores of villages north of their present range via Native American commerce is unlikely because of scale. Comparing backpacks and canoes to the keel and steam boats that were infested with invasive European species is not realistic for rice rat–sized animals. However, saying that the rice rat's preferred food was not corn, as noted in the article, is a questionable objection, because corn was still a major part of the village diet and was stored for year-round use in almost all of the sites with rice rat remains. Most rodents are very opportunistic, and rice rats could still have done well in the absence of favorite foods. That being said, their presence in these sites is still enigmatic because a survey of the literature indicates that the rice rat does not have a propensity for rural dwellings, farm products, or villages. I only found one entry for *Oryzomys* on the topic. Whitaker and Hamilton 1998:281) opined that:

> The rice rat is such a widespread species and often so abundant within its distributional limits that we would expect it to be much better known. That it is not, perhaps, at least partly because it is usually of little consequence to humans.

It is unlikely that its preferences have changed from the time in question. A more likely scenario is that, when it immigrated into the region as a result of suitable climatic conditions, a new delicacy appeared in the neighborhood. The numbers of *Oryzomys*, like *Neotoma*, could have been enhanced in sites because of procurement. Whitaker and Hamilton (1998:332) state that the meat of the woodrat is excellent. The evidence

for the use of micromammals as a food source has been well documented in Falk and Semken (1998).

Topic 3: Climatic Change and Zooarchaeology. One of the more intriguing aspects of this paper is that it confirms that micromammals in archaeological associations can be a valuable asset to the study of Neogene biogeography, where there are two basic biogeographic models of faunal and botanical responses to changing climates, Clementsian and Gleasonian. The Pleistocene and Holocene, because of a more concise time scale and having the archaeological chronology, offer fertile ground to test these concepts.

The Clementsian model holds that the modern biomes remained intact, and drifted north and south in response to fluctuating glacial–interglacial conditions. Boreal and tundra megamammals that were discovered well south of their present distribution were explained by this model. However, stratigraphic juxtaposition of these species later suggested that megamammals of mixed ecological heritage were co-inhabitants on a continental scale during Wisconsinan glacial advance and retreat. Over the past half-century, increasing interest in glacial-age micromammals has revealed that rodent-sized species representative of distinct modern biomes also were co-inhabitants and were part of a widespread non-analog glacial community (FAUNMAP Working Group 1996; Semken 1988). Radiocarbon dating of representative non-analog micromammals has documented this relationship (Semken et al. 2010) and reinforced the Gleasonian model of community structure, where each species within a community responded independently to changing climates, rather than as part of a superorganism (FAUNMAP Working Group 1996). Because archaeological sites are finely divided chronologically, at least in a geological framework, animal remains, if properly collected, can provide an excellent database for biogeographic trends and paleoenvironmental information at the time of site occupation.

Topic 4: Individual Response. This study of the rice rat seems to present a classic example of individualistic response during the Late Holocene. The animal's appearance and disappearance in an otherwise stable micromammal community during succeeding cultural contexts, and its apparent response to changing climate, is a convincing argument for Gleasonian biogeography in the Midwest. The cotton rat, opossum, and armadillo, along with the rice rat, are presently expanding to the north and to the west in varying degrees at different rates. A FAUNMAP II survey of archaeological sites in the region did not reveal the

presence of cotton rats, armadillos, or opossums in rice rat-bearing localities. The rub is that the faunal lists for most of the *Oryzomys*-bearing sites are scanty. While the absence of evidence is not always evidence of absence, specialists who identified the rice rat in better documented sites certainly would recognize the cotton rat, which also has a distinct dental pattern. Opossums and armadillos would not escape any person interested in faunal remains in sites where larger mammals were identified. Thus, it is unlikely that these taxa were co-inhabitants with the rice rat.

Proving that archaeologically associated rice rats were present because of their regional occurrence at the time would be enhanced if Holocene non-cultural sites were excavated. Except for a few cave sites in the upper Midwest, this has not happened. Admittedly, microvertebrate and plant macrofossil recovery requires a considerable effort in the field and laboratory, and willing specialists for identification are rare. However, the 58 archaeological localities with rice rats recorded in this paper provide convincing evidence that the rice rat was established periodically in the region during the late Holocene.

Guilday Tribute. Although the zooarchaeology of micromammls dates prior to the last century (Cope 1875), there was a dearth of activity in this area until John E. Guilday, along with Ernest L. Lundelius, reintroduced the analysis of Quaternary micromammal paleoecology in North America in the early 1960s with an emphasis on cultural as well as non-cultural sites. Although I may be biased because John and Ernie were (are) both friends as well as mentors, the authors are correct in lauding John's tireless contributions, despite a dehabilitating illness, to the paleoecological value of micromammals. John's work with the rice rat is a prime example of the value of micromammal zooarchaeology. Unfortunately, many archaeologists still regard all of these remains as intrusions, and some are. However, this article and others over the last half century demonstrate their potential.

An Aside. I frequently have been asked about the origin of the term micromammal. I presented a paper in a 1986 ICAZ (International Council for Archaeozoology) symposium in Bordeaux dedicated to "small mammals." During the following discussion of my paper on shrews and rodents, I mentioned that I felt out of place because all of the other papers focused on deer, goats, gazelles, etc. To that audience, now laughing, large mammals were elephants, hippos, and giraffes; small mammals were cattle, deer, and sheep. Christine Denys (National Museum Natural History, France), said "let's call them micromammals." It stuck!

References Cited

Armitage, Philip L.
  1993   Commensal Rats in the New World, 1492–1992. *Biologist* 40:174–178.

Cameron, Guy N., and Stephan R. Spencer
  1981   *Sigmodon hispidus. Mammalian Species* 158:1–9.

Cope, Edward D.
  1875   On an Indian Kitchen Midden. *Proceedings of the Philadelphia Academy of Science* 27:25.

Davis, William B., and David J. Schmidly
  1997   *The Mammals of Texas*. Online edition, Texas Tech University, http://www.nsrl.ttu.edu/tmot1/copyrigh.htm, accessed July 24, 1015.

Ehrlich, P., and A. Ehrlick
  1990   *The Population Explosion*. Simon and Schuster, New York.

FAUNMAP Working Group
  1996   Spatial Response of Mammals to Late Quaternary Environmental Fluctuations. *Science* 272:1601–1606.

Falk, Carl R., and Holmes A. Semken, Jr.
  1998   Taphonomy of Rodent and Insectivore Remains in Archaeological Sites: Selected Examples and Interpretations. In *Quaternary Paleozoology in the Northern Hemisphere*, edited by J. J. Saunders, B. W. Styles, and G. F. Baryshnikov, pp. 285–321. Scientific Papers 27. Illinois State Museum, Springfield.

Hoffman, R. S., and J. A. Jones, Jr
  1970   Influence of Late-Glacial and Post-Glacial Events on the Distribution of Recent Mammals on the Northern Great Plains. In *Pleistocene and Recent Enviroments of the Central Great Plains*, edited by W. Dort, Jr., and J. K. Jones, pp. 355–394. University of Kansas Press, Lawrence.

Hoffmeister, Donald F.
  1989   *Mammals of Illinois*. University of Illinois Press, Urbana.

Jasinsk, Steven E., and Steven C. Wallace
  1914   Investigation into the Paleobiology of *Dasypus bellus* Using Geometric Morphometrics and Variation of the Calcaneus. *Journal of Mammalian Evolution* 21:285–298.

Parmalee, Paul W.
  1965   The Food Economy of Archaic and Woodland Peoples at the Tick Creek Cave Site, Missouri. *Missouri Archaeologist* 27:1–34.

Rhodes, Richard S. II, and Holmes A. Semken, Jr.
  1986   Quaternary Biostratigraphy and Paleoecology of Fossil Mammals from the Loess Hill Region of Western Iowa. *Proceedings of the Iowa Academy of Sciences* 93:94–129.

Szuter, C. R.
  1994   Nutrition, Small Mammals, and Agriculture.
          In *Paleonutrition: The Diet and Health of Prehistoric
          Americans*, edited by K. D. Sobolik, pp. 55–65.
          Occasional Paper 22. Center for Archaeological
          Investigations, Southern Illinois University,
          Carbondale.

Semken, Holmes A., Jr.
  1988   Environmental Interpretations of the
          "Disharmonious" Late Wisconsin Biome of
          Southeastern North America. In *Late Pleistocene and
          Early Holocene Paleoecology and Archaeology of the
          Eastern Great Lakes Region*, edited by R. S. Laub, N. G
          Miller, and D. W. Steadman, pp. 185–194. Bulletin of
          the Buffalo Society of Natural Sciences 33.

Semken, Holmes A., Jr., and Carl R. Falk
  2014   Ecology and Environmental Degradation of Two
          Little Ice-Age Earthlodge Villages in Central North
          Dakota: The Environmental Evidence. In *Archaeology,
          Biogeography, and Zooarchaeology: A Tribute to
          the Legacy and Career of James L. Theler*, edited by
          Matthew G. Hill. *The Wisconsin Archeologist* 95(2):249–
          268.

Semken, Holmes A., Jr., Russell W. Graham, and Thomas
  W. Stafford, Jr.
  2010   AMS ^{14}C analysis of Late Pleistocene Non-Analog
          Faunal Components from 21 Cave Deposits in
          Southeastern North America. *Quaternary International*
          217:240–255.

Vickery, Kent D., James L. Theler, and Orrin C. Shane, III
  2016   Archaeological Remains of the Rice Rat
          (*Oryzomys*) as a Climatic Proxy in the American
          Midwest. *The Wiscosnsin Archeologist* 97(2):49–80.

Whitaker, J. O., Jr., and W. J. Hamilton, Jr.
  1998   *Mammals of the Eastern United States*. Cornell
          University Press, Ithaca.

Wilson, Don E., and Sue Ruff
  1999   *The Smithsonian Book of North American Mammals*.
          Smithsonian Institution Press, Washington, D.C.

A Retrospective of Harris A. Palmer's Excavations at Preston Rockshelter (47GT157)

Michael J. Roy and Danielle M. Benden

Abstract

Preston Rockshelter (47GT157) is a shallow, natural rockshelter formed in St. Peter Sandstone, located on a hillside above a small stream in northeastern Grant County, Wisconsin. Harris A. Palmer, a geologist at the University of Wisconsin–Platteville, directed archaeological field schools and site excavations there between 1966 and 1969. The senior author served as one of Palmer's undergraduate field school participants during the 1969 field season. Nearly 40 years have passed, and little data from Preston – save for a handful of radiocarbon dates, short summaries, and a recent article on the fauna – has been published. This paper reviews the discovery and excavation of Preston Rockshelter and highlights significant analyses undertaken by James B. Stoltman, James L. Theler, and myriad University of Wisconsin–Madison students after the collections were transferred there for curation in 1975. Using original notes, maps, photographs, and compiled analytical data, we present an overview of the excavations at Preston. Finally, we provide a retrospective of Palmer, an important avocational archaeologist whose work in Wisconsin archaeology was influential, and at times stimulated lively discussion.

Introduction

People have inhabited Grant County, Wisconsin, and the Upper Mississippi River valley for at least the last 12,000 years (Theler and Boszhardt 2003). As of 2016, 864 archaeological sites have been recorded in the county, of which the overwhelming majority contain a prehistoric occupation (Wisconsin Archaeological Site Inventory 2016). Discoveries such as Paleoindian points from Withington (47GT158) (Loebel 2009), Archaic quarrying activity at Bass (47GT25) (Stoltman et al. 1984), and occupations at Brogley (47GT156) (Benden

2010) and Osceola (47GT24) (Ritzenthaler 1957), Woodland communities at Brogley (Alhambra 2010; Maus 2010) and Millville (47GT53) (Freeman 1969), and the Late Woodland/Mississippian settlement at Fred Edwards (47GT377) (Finney 2013) attest to the lengthy and rich prehistoric human history in Grant County. Many additional Driftless Area sites within 100 km of Preston have helped to further develop the regional cultural chronology.

In the 1960s, a flurry of avocational archaeological activity was undertaken in Grant County, with individuals actually competing to find evidence of prehistoric occupation (University of Wisconsin–Platteville Archives, Harris Palmer Collection [UW-P Archives, HPC]). During this time, new sites were reported frequently, with Preston serving as a notable example.

Harris A. Palmer was an Associate Professor of Geology at Wisconsin State College Platteville (later renamed the Wisconsin State University–Platteville, and finally the University of Wisconsin–Platteville). He first learned of and visited Preston Rockshelter in 1964. Palmer, a geologist with an educational background in anthropology and a keen interest in archaeology, had previously identified many sites, worked at Bass and Withington, and collected and described artifacts his entire life, beginning in his youth in Sawyer County (UW-P Archives, HPC). In 1964, using a posthole digger equipped with sectional pipe as an auger, he and colleagues discovered enough artifacts and information about the cultural deposits at Preston to encourage additional work. Palmer visited the site again in 1965, and in early 1966 he submitted a research proposal to the Wisconsin State University–Platteville, with the intention of exploring the strata at Preston Rockshelter for four consecutive years. Lack of funding in 1967 allowed investigations to take place only during the 1966, 1968, and 1969 field seasons. Palmer's primary

objective, one that appeared frequently in his writings and was expressed regularly to students, was to confirm and further demonstrate Paleoindian occupation of the Driftless Area, particularly at Preston Rockshelter. He also intended to introduce students to the field of archaeology through his summer excavation course, Geology 306: Field Archaeology Workshop.

Artifact collections and field documentation from the Preston excavations were donated by Palmer to the University of Wisconsin–Madison [UW–Madison] Department of Anthropology in 1975, asking only that they be used for research and as teaching aids. The collections remain there for permanent curation. These materials have been studied and described by several students under the direction of James B. Stoltman, UW–Madison. In 2015, the site records were digitized, and diagnostic artifacts were rehoused in archival bags and boxes to preserve them long-term. Re-curation of the remaining site collection housed at UW–Madison is ongoing. Extensive supporting documentation is also located in the Harris Palmer Collections at the University of Wisconsin–Platteville Archives.

Site Setting

Preston Rockshelter is located near the small village of Preston, on a north-trending spur of Military Ridge in Grant County, Wisconsin (Figure 1). It lies in the unglaciated Driftless Area, which is characterized by ridges, steep wooded hillsides, and valleys containing numerous spring-fed streams (Martin 1965). The regional bedrock geology consists of stratified deposits of sandstone and karst-affected dolomite and limestone. Preston Rockshelter, at an elevation of 305 meters above sea level, formed within the St. Peter Sandstone formation immediately above Oneota/Prairie du Chien dolomite (Smith and Simo 1997). Here, the Ancell formation of the St. Peter Sandstone is capped by layers of limestone, shale, and dolomite, and limestone also underlies the sandstone. The arched roof of the Preston shelter conforms to a collapsed sandstone cave (Boszhardt 2003a; Cronon 1970). An unnamed stream, only 0.5 meters wide, lies 30 meters east of the shelter; it flows intermittently, running northward as a tributary of Fennimore Branch Creek, which then flows north into the Blue River, eventually draining into the Wisconsin River. The rockshelter has an earthen embankment in front of the drip line that formed from slope wash. The stream does not flow into the shelter; however, runoff from the loess-capped hill above drains into the cave and has contributed sediment to the otherwise sandy floor deposits, which slope down toward a crevice in

the rear. Between 1966 and 1969, when excavations were ongoing, the rockshelter was surrounded by agricultural fields for a dairy farm (Figure 2a). Today, the property is privately owned and contains farmed hilltops and largely undisturbed grasslands and forests (Figure 2b).

Preston Rockshelter (Figures 2 and 3) is more or less symmetrical at the entrance and measures 22.5 meters (68.5 feet) across and 5 to 6 meters (15–18 feet) in height near the center, and extends 14.5 meters (44.5 feet) back from the drip line. The entrance faces to the east and is within and well below a large sandstone and limestone ridge, thus providing excellent protection from the prevailing weather—rain, wind, and snow—from the west. At the time of discovery, the floor of the shelter had an approximately 20 percent (11°) slope from northeast to southwest toward the rear of the shelter. Soil within the cave is sandy loam, having originated from slow decay of the sandstone as well as loess and decomposed vegetative material that was dropped, washed, or blown into the cave; the situation is similar to that seen at Raddatz Rockshelter (Black 1959).

Due to the weak and friable nature of the St. Peter Sandstone at Preston, there have been numerous collapses from the ceiling and rear wall. Many of the buried sandstone fragments had decomposed to white, tan, or light yellow sand pockets, while other stone pieces were largely intact. Hence, solid pieces of sandstone roof fall were frequently encountered, mapped, and then removed during excavations. Rock fall was particularly noticeable on the west wall of the shelter where a "rear overhang" had developed due to the erosion of sandstone at lower levels, and there was significant rock fall immediately south of the excavation. Deep excavation units in 1969 encountered relatively large sandstone boulders. Palmer considered these to be the result of more intensive cave-ins, and they seemed to represent the base of cultural deposits in some units. The larger roof fall deposits might also represent more active erosion during the Mid-Holocene Altithermal or the terminal Pleistocene climatic regimes.

The climate of the Driftless Area prior to 11,000 years ago was dominated by the Laurentide Ice Sheet to the north, west, and east. As the ice sheet receded between 14,000 and 10,000 years ago, the vegetation was largely sub-arctic, dominated in the late Pleistocene by spruce forest (Chumbley et al. 1990; Wright et al. 1963). During this period, the Wisconsin River experienced catastrophic floods (Clayton and Attig 1989; Knox and Attig 1988) that carried massive amounts of meltwater, carved walls of tributaries, and deposited sandy outwash terraces (MacClintock

Figure 1. Location of the Preston Rockshelter in Grant County, Wisconsin. (Base map Wisconsin Geological and Natural History Survey.)

1922) in the lower portion of its valley, although these did not reach the elevation of Preston. As demonstrated by palynological studies, temperatures rose rapidly around 10,000 B.P., resulting in a more temperate climate (Chumbley et al. 1990; Wright et al. 1963). Baker et al. (1996), describing the upper Roberts Creek Basin, a Driftless Area drainage in eastern Iowa 70 km (44 miles) west of Preston, suggested that the climate had been relatively stable over the past 10,000 years but with distinct reductions in long-term precipitation in the Mid to Late Holocene. From studies of pollen, microfossils, and insect remains in stratified sediments of Roberts Creek Basin, Baker et al. (1996) described the postglacial transition from spruce forest to oak and elm. Next, between 6,500 and 5,500 B.P., mesic forest, sugar maple, basswood, and hornbeam replaced spruce forest in lower areas, with prairie appearing in nearby warmer areas. Between 5,500 and 3,000 B.P., which included a period of warmer and moister conditions (4,000–3,000 B.P.),

Figure 2. Preston Rockshelter: (a) 1960s photograph of Preston Rockshelter, looking west; (b) view of the shelter in 2016. Note the changes in vegetation.

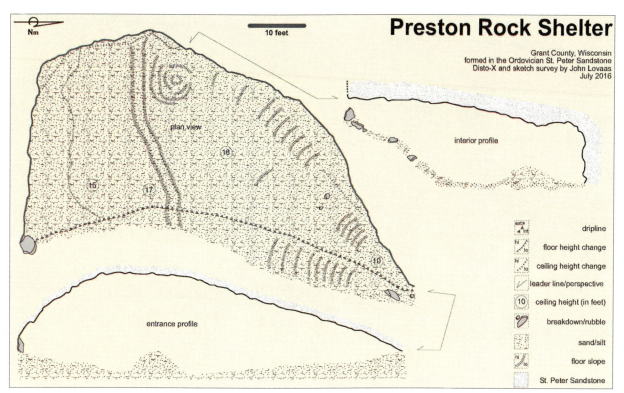

Figure 3. Map of Preston Rockshelter, 2016. (Map drawn by John Lovaas.)

this portion of the Driftless Area was dominated by prairie. Then, at 3,000 B.P., oak returned with accompanying non-tree pollens suggesting oak savanna; this flora remained until the time of Euro-American settlement. Bryson (2007) included the Preston area in the "Prairie Peninsula," a wedge of grasslands characterized by dry western air dissecting the eastern woodlands. Climatic models developed for Brogley Rockshelter (Benden 2010), a cave located approximately 30 km (19 miles) south of Preston, suggest a

relatively consistent climate, temperature, and precipitation over the past 3,000 years.

The vegetation near Preston Rockshelter was recorded between 1830 and 1850, during early Euro-American settlement. The Government Land Office survey data (GLO Wisconsin Land Survey Records 2016) used to create the "original" vegetation maps (Finley 1993) that were interpreted by Curtis (1965), indicated that the area around Preston was largely oak openings or savanna dominated by burr, white, and

black (yellow) oaks on hilltops and gentle slopes, with various other hardwoods in a gallery forest on valley walls and alongside rivers. Hilltops and wide valleys were covered by grasslands and subject to periodic fires. This is consistent with undisturbed or recovered areas in the Driftless Area today, and with models developed by both Baker (1996) and Bryson (2007). This region is still characterized by moist woodland with oak savanna, and, in the narrow, often steep valleys, gallery mixed hardwood forests that provide abundant deciduous woodland edges, and plentiful running streams. The locality has a temperate climate, with a mean annual temperature of 10° C (Moran and Hopkins 2002). Temperatures can be seasonally extreme, with summer days going well above 32°C (90°F), and winter nights dropping below -30°C (-22°F). The freeze-free season is about 5 months, from May through October. Total precipitation is about .8 meters (31 inches), which includes .8 to 1.5 meters (30-60 inches) of snow. Westerly winds dominate, blowing southwesterly in summer and northwesterly in winter.

History of Excavations

Palmer's work with student teams at Preston Rockshelter represented his third archaeological dig in Wisconsin. A lease was drawn with the landowner, Mr. Mel Holub, for June 1966 through 1969. Excavations were conducted for 6 weeks in June and July of 1966 (9 students), 1968 (11 students), and 1969 (6 students).

The log of activities in the summer of 1966 suggests backbreaking work on the part of the excavation team as they initially hauled tools and plywood for bracing, cleared brush, and fenced the rockshelter from ranging cattle. Using an end loader, they carefully removed approximately 30 inches (.8 meters) of an organic, sandy loam slope wash that had gathered in the shelter in historic times. Inspection and screening of the upper deposit yielded modern artifacts—remnants of agricultural materials or bones of domestic animals—and one broken projectile point. The exposed soil surface ranged from .5 m (1.6 feet) deep in the northeast corner to 1.2 m (4 feet) in the southwest corner, measured below a datum (post) aligned with a scribe cut into the sandstone wall.

A baseline was established as a north–south line running approximately parallel to the upper cave opening. A rectangular grid of 4 x 4 foot (1.2 x 1.2 m) units was established (Figure 4) just north of the rockshelter's center, and encompassed an area of 32 by 24 feet (9.75 by 7.32 m). The datum post was located at section 4N36W and can be seen in Figure 5. Immediately

below the historic fill, a sterile layer of approximately 1 foot (30 cm) of dark, organic soil was identified; this soil was troweled to a depth of 3 to 4 feet (.9 to 1.2 m) below the datum. During the first year, a deep stratigraphic test pit (referred to as the "foxhole") was excavated near the north center of the grid outlined in Figure 4. The rear wall of the rockshelter was not fully perpendicular but had a sandstone "overhang" along that western wall that sloped down and to the rear. The area beneath the overhang was excavated as the soil surface became exposed. Plywood sheathing, cut in 4-foot squares or 4 x 1 foot rectangles, was used to provide a solid floor in each excavation unit, with the narrower pieces braced to reinforce section walls. In deeper excavations, additional wall bracing was used to retain exposed profile walls of adjacent units. Excavation levels within the units were arbitrary 6-inch (15 cm) intervals. All levels were troweled, with shovels used only to remove blocks of sandstone roof falls. Soil was screened (Figure 5) through ¼ inch mesh. Cultural materials were recorded in a log, and then reviewed by Palmer (Figure 6).

At the end of the first season, July 22, 1966, excavated unit depths ranged from 2 feet (.6 m) to 12 feet (3.6 m), with the "fox-hole" reaching 19.5 feet (5.9 m) below datum (Figure 4). Excavations reaching below 9 feet (2.7 m) below datum (e.g., 16N40W or 16N36W) produced only pieces of charcoal and animal bone. Consequently, the second and third seasons focused on removing the deposits between 3 and 10 feet (.9 to 3 m) in units adjacent to those excavated in 1966. Excavation proceeded deeper with each season, with the greatest depths occurring at the center and near the rear, notably in Units 16N24W to 16N16W (see Figure 4).

During the 1966 season, exposed walls occasionally exceeded 5 feet (1.5 m). Despite shoring of unit walls, the significant differences between excavated depths in the various units contributed to at least two cave-ins during the first season. Further erosion occurred on some walls during the inactive period from July 1966 to June 1968, during which water entered the shelter. Additional precautions implemented in the 1968 and 1969 seasons succeeded in reducing, though not completely eliminating, wall slumping. Caved-in deposits were carefully removed and recorded, but likely resulted in some mixing of artifacts from cultural strata. In addition, animal burrowing and digging by previous human occupants undoubtedly contributed to artifact movement over time.

The sloping nature of the living floors was demonstrated early during the 1966 season. Stratigraphic mapping revealed that "the entire dig was a succession of inclined living floors where hearth material had been spread out" (UW–P Archives, HPC, M870020).

Solid Sandstone Rear Wall

	12N 48W 5' *12'* <u>12'</u>	16N 48W 5' *7'* <u>11'</u>			
8N 44N - <u>12'</u>	12N 44W 5' *7'* <u>10'</u>	16N 44W 5' *7'* <u>12'</u>	20N 44W 5' *7'* <u>12'/7.2'</u>	24 N 44W 5' - <u>10.5'</u>	
8N 40W - - <u>8.5"</u>	12N 40W 5' *7'* <u>11.5"</u>	16N 40W* 19.5' *19.5'* <u>19.5</u>	20N 40W 5' *7'* <u>11'</u>	24N 40W 5' *6'* <u>7.5'</u>	28N 40W - - <u>8.0'</u>
8N 36W - - <u>10'</u>	12N 36W - *10'* <u>10'</u>	16N 36W 12.0' *12'/16'* <u>14.5'</u>	20N 36W 5' *9'/7'* <u>12.5</u>	24N 36W 5' *5'* <u>11'</u>	28N 36W - - <u>8.5'</u>
8N 32W - - <u>10'</u>	12N 32W 9.5' *11'* <u>11'</u>	16N 32W 9.5' *12'/16'* <u>14'</u>	20N 32W 5' *9'/7'* <u>11'</u>	24N 32W 5' *5'* <u>11'</u>	28N 32W - - <u>8.5'</u>
8N 28W - - <u>10'</u>	12N 28W 9.5' *11'* <u>11.5'</u>	16N 28W 9.5' *12'* <u>12'</u>	20N 28W 5' *9'/7'* <u>11'</u>	24N 28W 5' *5'* <u>7'</u>	28N 28W - - <u>6.8'</u>
8N 24W - - <u>9'</u>	12N 24W 2' *8'* <u>11.5'</u>	16N 24W 2' *5'* <u>11.5'</u>	20N 24W 2' *6'/5'* <u>9'</u>	24N 24W 2' *5'* <u>7.8'</u>	28N 24W - - <u>5.8'</u>
8N 20W	12N 20W - - <u>9'/4'</u>	16N 20W - *4'* <u>9'</u>	20N 20W - *4'* <u>5'/4'</u>	24N 20W - *4'* <u>6.5'/4'</u>	24N 18W

N ➤   N-S Baseline.   Rockshelter Opening to East

Depths listed as maximum by end of season; from top to bottom, 1966, 1968 in italics, 1969, underlined.
Dash (-) no data recorded or no excavation performed
*"Foxhole" dug in 1966; ---, dashed line is location rear overhang; solid line on south side is "caved-in area"

Figure 4. The sectional grid established at the Preston Rockshelter with maximum depths reached in each year of excavation: 1966, 1968 (italics) and 1969 (underline).

The floor sloped toward the rear (west) and, with excavations made in 6-inch horizontal increments, the inclination made for "difficult interpretation of a dig conducted on a level basis" (UW–P Archives, HPC, M870020). Further, the steeper strata at the rear of the cave contained ceramic sherds that had apparently washed out of higher units to the east during flash flooding of the cave (Fay 1975) from the creek or from above. Careful mapping and removal of sandstone roof-collapse pieces was unexpected and laborious. Narrow steel rods judiciously probed the sandy soil to identify significant and deeply buried sandstone, and the vertical walls allowed mapping of the natural stratification and facilitated interpretation. The excavation units were backfilled with screened soil at the end of the 1969 final season.

Figure 5. Photograph of Harris Palmer standing at entrance of Preston Rockshelter, with students excavating and sifting in July 1969. Note the datum stake on top of the profile wall, in front and to the left of Palmer.

Figure 6. Harris Palmer logging cultural artifacts at Preston Rockshelter, 1969.

Excavation Results

Preston Rockshelter was especially rich in features and faunal remains, produced a variety of important lithic artifacts, and yielded important information regarding Woodland and Late Archaic cultures. Even though Preston Rockshelter has been known to professional archaeologists since 1966, a full site report has never been published; the following analyses have been conducted largely by Stoltman and his students at UW–Madison.

Radiocarbon Samples

Charcoal samples were collected from hearths, carefully handled, and then dried for three days prior to wrapping in aluminum foil. Five radiocarbon dates (Bender et al. 1979) were obtained from wood charcoal samples (Table 1).

Features

Once excavation commenced, the first evidence of occupation was a hearth feature encountered in a central unit at a depth of 4.3 feet (1.3 m) below datum (or about one-half foot (.15 m) below the level of sterile topsoil). Hearths, many of which contained stones, artifacts, and ecofacts, were common in the upper levels where the stratigraphy was complex but also where sterile layers made it possible to separate ceramic-bearing strata. Only the better-defined hearths were mapped as features in the first year. More features, and less distinct ones, were mapped in the second and third field seasons. Though the features were mapped, they have not been analyzed other than to identify locations of cultural artifacts.

Lithic Artifacts

In an analysis of Preston lithic artifacts, Santure (1978) first proposed the presence of four cultural components based upon unique lithic and ceramic assemblages (Figures 7 and 8); they were further described by Theler and Chalkley-Hubbell (2016). From top to bottom, Santure identified Cultural Level 1 as Middle and Late Woodland, based in part on Madison Triangular points, and with no evidence of Early Woodland diagnostics. Cultural Level 2 was initially recognized as a zone that produced both Woodland ceramics and Late Archaic Durst Stemmed points, but is now understood to comprise mixed or combined components. Cultural Level 3 represented a Late Archaic zone with Durst Stemmed points but no ceramics. The lowest recognized, Cultural Level 4, also lacked pottery but did contain a high frequency of scrapers and knives, and the unique Preston Corner Notched points (Boszhardt 2003b; Stoltman 1997). This lowest zone did not contain Raddatz points, supporting Stoltman's placement of the Preston phase between Middle Archaic (Raddatz) and terminal Archaic (Durst).

TABLE 1. RADIOCARBON DATES FROM PRESTON ROCKSHELTER.*

Association	WIS-Number	Square	Depth (m)	Radiocarbon Age (B.P.)	Calibrated Age (2σ)**	Cultural Period
Pre-ceramic level associated with Preston Corner-Notched projectile points	941	16N 36W	2.96–3.02	2780 ± 65	1108–810 B.C.	Archaic Pre-Durst
Hearth, Feature 23; Pre-ceramic levels with Durst projectile points	946	20N 32W	2.6	2710 ± 65	1007–793 B.C.	Archaic Durst
Transition levels	943	16N 40W	2.2	1670 ± 65	A.D. 230–544	Late Middle Wd./ Early Late Wd.
Associated with Madison Ware ceramics and small triangular projectile points	944	16N 32W	1.4-1.5	1220 ± 60	A.D. 669–961	Late Woodland
Late Woodland level	932	12N 36W	1.5	1150 ± 60	A.D. 717–1015	Late Woodland

All samples were wood charcoal.
*Originally published in Bender et. al. 1979:124-125.
**Based on OxCal Version 4.2.

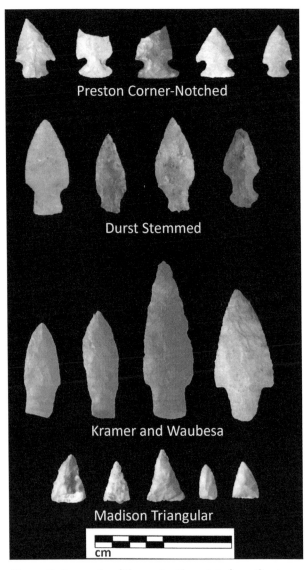

Figure 7. A sample of the projectile points from Preston.

Ceramics

Ceramic analysis was performed by Robert Fay (1975). A total of 2,574 sherds, including 146 rims (representing 60 individual vessels) and 183 decorated and 2,249 undecorated body fragments, were examined, classified, and sorted by horizontal and vertical provenience (Figure 8). Table 2 summarizes the count and percent of each ceramic type. Rim profiles were drawn for every vessel (Figure 9). Decorative techniques included dentate stamped, incised, punctated, and cord impressed, done as simple bands or in complex designs. Many of the diagnostic sherds were identified as at least three variations of Havana ware; others were attributed to Linn and Madison ware. Most of the ceramics were recovered from western units in the rear of the shelter, from the easternmost entrance area, and from the northernmost units. The majority were found in levels corresponding to Middle and Late Woodland periods; however, a few sherds in the rear units were mixed into Late Archaic levels. Fay concluded that Woodland people inhabited the Preston site during Middle and Late Woodland periods, perhaps seasonally. Stoltman incorporated ceramics from Preston in two syntheses for southwestern Wisconsin: his 1979 review of the Middle Woodland stage, and Stoltman and Christiansen's (2000) Late Woodland analysis.

Faunal Remains

The Preston excavation provided an extensive array of faunal remains. In his study of the mussel remains, Theler (1987a, 1987b) documented that the dominant mussel species found at Preston favored low-energy environments, which suggested that streams in the immediate vicinity may have been impounded, perhaps by beavers (Theler 1983; Theler

TABLE 2. SUMMARY OF CERAMICS RECOVERED FROM PRESTON (AFTER FAYE 1975).

Category	Rimsherds	Decorated Body Sherds	Undecorated Body Sherds	Total	Percent
Havana ware	4	3	–	7	.3
Linn ware	36	76	89	201	7.8
Madison ware	68	71	16	155	6.0
Unclassified rim and body sherds	38	2	7	47	1.8
Decorated body sherds	–	31	–	31	1.2
Undecorated body sherds	–	–	1890	1890	73.3
Unclassified sherds	–	–	247	247	9.6
Total	146	183	2249	2578	100.0

Figure 8. A sample of ceramics from Preston.

and Chalkley-Hubbell 2016:37). In a recently published synthesis based on earlier analyses, Theler and Chalkley-Hubbell (2016) reported over 3,000 individual faunal specimens representing 67 taxa, including a wide variety of mammalian species, with white-tailed deer dominating. Based upon analysis of the dentition, many deer were harvested from late fall through spring (Theler and Chalkley-Hubbell 2016:17–18). Baker (2009) further examined fragmented bones of white-tailed deer and argued for bone grease production, a process that likely reflected cold season occupation. The bird remains (Chalkley-Hubbell 1976; Theler and Chalkley-Hubbell 2016) included a variety of large species, most if not all harvested for food rather than for ceremonial purposes. The abundance of turkey, grouse, and pigeon suggested a deciduous forest and forest-edge habitat during periods of habitation.

The vertical distribution of faunal remains corroborates the argument that Preston represents four cultural components (Santure 1978; Theler and Chalkley-Hubbell 2016). An increased variety of faunal species that indicate year-round activity during the Late Woodland component also supports an interpretation of human landscape packing during the Effigy Mound period (Theler and Boszhardt 2006; Theler and Chalkley-Hubbell 2016:36).

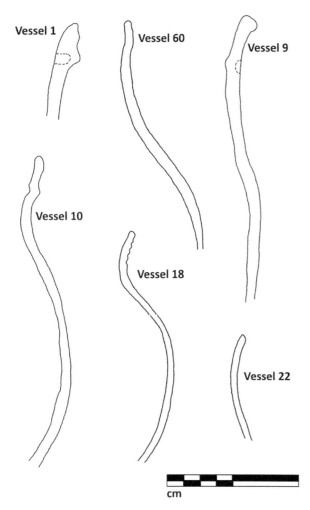

Figure 9. Rim profiles of sherds illustrated in Figure 8.

Summary

Preston had a significant number of hearths, hearth-stones, charcoal, artifacts, and ecofacts, with material coming predominantly from 3 to 10 feet (.9 to 3 m) below datum. Analysis of lithic artifacts by Santure (1978) and Stoltman (1997), and of faunal remains by Theler (1983:Table 2, 1987a, 1987b, 2000) and Theler and Chalkley-Hubbell (2016), suggested that Preston Rockshelter had been occupied during four distinct cultural periods. Ceramic and lithic artifact analyses placed the Late and Middle Woodland cultures within the two upper components. The third component was affiliated with the Late Archaic Durst phase at ca. 3000 B.P. Of particular significance was the stratigraphic position of these Durst points above the fourth and lowest component, where the presence of a distinctive corner-notched point type led Stoltman (1997:134) to define Preston Notched points and the Preston phase.

Preston is considered the earliest known Late Archaic phase in southwest Wisconsin and is dated to ca. 3,500 B.P. (Stoltman 1997:134). Radiocarbon dating of five charcoal samples taken at various depths (Table 1) generally supported the cultural sequence, although Stoltman (1997:134) acknowledged some mixing in the sandy soil and also recognized the potential for deeper cultural deposits.

Harris A. Palmer and Prehistoric Archaeology: Grant County, Wisconsin, from the 1960s to the 1980s

The 1960s to 1980s were an interesting time for avocational archaeologists such as Palmer to actively pursue their interest in southwestern Wisconsin. Documents suggest there was, particularly during the 1960s, a dominant theme of finding evidence for Paleoindian cultures in southwestern Wisconsin. This goal is expressed in Palmer's 1966 research proposal entitled, "An Archeological Investigation of Paleo-Indian Occupation in the Driftless Area of Wisconsin" (UW–P Archives, HPC, M870020), which aimed "to determine in terms of absolute time, when the fluted point people lived in the Driftless Area," a goal he also conveyed to his students at the Preston field schools.

Many people, including some landowners, collected artifacts and had family collections that consisted mostly of lithic artifacts. Others, especially in the 1960s, were "explorers," entrepreneurial types driven to find new sites and identify, usually by word-of-mouth, new opportunities for excavation. Many of the "explorers" had been surface collectors and some became avocational archeologists, that is, individuals willing to perform excavations under accepted protocols and involving a team of participants.

Correspondence in the UW–Platteville archives suggests both competition and cooperation between people with these varied interests. Often, individuals shared news of discoveries and, sometimes, advice and labor. In the 1960s, initial archaeological excavations of several sites in Grant County were somewhat hastily planned, even spontaneous. Records suggest that the Brogley and Preston Rockshelter excavations fit this mold, at least in their initial stages. At Brogley, Harris Palmer, local high school teacher Robert Nelson, and student Robert Willey conducted a site survey during the summer of 1966 (coincidentally the first year of Palmer's excavations at Preston). Subsequent excavations by Nelson at Brogley were more carefully planned (Benden 2010; Nelson 2010). While their approach to excavation was not always "textbook," the efforts of these avocational archaeologists

nonetheless provided meaningful results that otherwise might not be available today.

In the 1970s and 1980s, university-based professional archaeologists and their students explored sites with increasing frequency in southwest Wisconsin and re-examined the discoveries and excavations of the 1960s. At Brogley and then at Preston, high-school and university students again participated in the excavations, furthering the scope of interest in archaeology and resulting in publicity (e.g., *Janesville Gazette* 1969; *Milwaukee Journal* 1969; *Platteville Journal*, 17 July 1969 for Preston; 26 July1970 for Brogley). A few of these students went on to become avocational archaeologists, while others continued an appreciation and interest in prehistory and archaeology.

Palmer's interest in early cultures is probably best explained by his 1964 letter to the President of Wisconsin State University–Eau Claire: "You will no doubt recall my late father's keen interest in Indian relics at Lake Lipsie [Lipette Lake, Burnett County, WI], and one that he fostered in me at an early age. I consider it a tribute to him that I continue this interest today, and have the opportunity to pursue it on a professional level" (UW–P Archives, HPC). Between 1935 and 1940, Palmer was trained at UW–Madison as a geologist with studies in anthropology. He then served as a consulting geologist with the Wisconsin Geological Survey, U.S. Army Corps of Engineers, and private engineering firms. In 1947, Palmer began a career in higher education, first as Associate Professor in Iowa and, from 1956 until his retirement in 1975, as a Professor of Geology at the University of Wisconsin–Platteville. In addition to teaching geology he taught Prehistoric Man and Field Archeology, which included his field schools at Preston.

His geology background provided Palmer several advantages because, as a consulting geologist and then as a professor leading field trips, he had professionally explored "hidden" rural locations throughout southwest Wisconsin. As he did so, Palmer kept a trained eye out for evidence of past human activity. For example, he identified geological formations, former quarries, and other natural resources that might have been of use to prehistoric peoples. He also established contact with local informants who might provide archaeological leads. His knowledge of southwestern Wisconsin was both broad and detailed, and he kept copious notes, sometimes synthesizing findings into plans (UW–P Archives, HPC, M870020). In 1975, Harris Palmer reported 51 sites, 16 of which were in Grant County (UW–P Archives, HPC).

Throughout his lifetime, Harris Palmer pursued professional correspondence, both at meetings and by mail, and published several interesting or unique findings, including late Pleistocene fauna in Iowa (Palmer 1953), a prehistoric bison in northwest Wisconsin (Palmer 1954), fossil goat remains from North America (Palmer 1956), truncated barbed points from northern Illinois (Palmer and Palmer 1962a), Indian mounds in Sawyer County, Wisconsin (Palmer and Palmer 1962b), peccary bones in possible Early Archaic context (Palmer 1974), a possible location for the Battle of the Brule (Palmer 1978), and a fluted point perhaps associated with the Boaz mastodon in Richland County, Wisconsin (Palmer and Stoltman 1976). He excavated at Dwyer Rockshelter at Silver Mound in 1964 (Carr and Boszhardt 2010:12). He was an active member in scientific, geological, and mining associations, including the Wisconsin Archeological Society. In 1981, he was awarded the Increase A. Lapham Research Medal by the Society.

Palmer often led archaeological explorations in Wisconsin. While at Platteville, Palmer showed a deep interest in Paleoindian occupation in southwest Wisconsin. As he put it, he "specialized in Archaic and Paleo-Indian problems" and "the relationship of extinct Pleistocene faunas" of this period (UW–P Archives, HPC). In 1962, Palmer identified the Withington site (Loebel 2009; Stoltman 1991), located near the Platte River, and the nearby Bass site (Stoltman et al. 1984). In 1964, Withington became his first formal archaeological excavation, which yielded a significant number of Early Paleoindian tools from surface and plowzone contexts (Loebel 2009; Stoltman 1991). That experience further stimulated his interest in Paleoindian culture. The brief excavation at Withington seemed to lack the organized approach he displayed in later years such as at Preston, which had a significant, disciplined, and multiyear effort. An interesting side-note was his discovery of a stone, possibly the drop-stone of an ancient deadfall trap, at a solution cavern about 0.7 miles from Withington (UW–P Archives, HPC M870020). Although Palmer carefully investigated this find and described possible schemes for the trap's operation, including radiocarbon dating of underlying bone, that work was never published.

His discovery of Early Archaic Hardin Barbed points at the Galena chert quarry/workshop Bass site inspired 1976 excavations there by Stoltman (Stoltman et al. 1984). Also during this period, Palmer corresponded with others about Paleoindian points found at Silver Mound in Jackson County, Wisconsin (UW–P Archives, HPC, M870020). Thus, when he came upon the Preston Rockshelter in 1964, a site within 30 kilometers (19 miles) of Bass and Withington, he logically considered Preston as a probable stratified site with the potential for a sealed Paleoindian component. Although his efforts at Preston did not

produce evidence of Paleoindian occupation, this site provided a wealth of information on Late Archaic and Woodland cultures, and it is possible that Paleoindian deposits are still present at the site.

Health considerations in the mid-1970s forced Harris Palmer to reduce his archeological efforts somewhat. Beginning in 1970 and continuing until his death in 1986 at the age of 73, he spent considerable time in Burnett County exploring the landscape for evidence of historic fur trading posts. Notably, he is credited with finding and helping to excavate the XY Trading Company post on the Yellow River in Northwest Wisconsin (Oerichbauer 1981, 1982; UW–P Archives, HPC). His discoveries led, in part, to the development of Forts Folle Avoine Historical Park, in Burnett County, Wisconsin, which today houses the Harris Palmer Historical Library and Research Center.

Conclusions

Preston Rockshelter was excavated during an era of significant activity by avocational and professional archaeologists in southwestern Wisconsin and has provided considerable insight into Late Archaic and Woodland cultural traditions. The objective of excavating rapidly, yet carefully, to a substantial depth was confounded in practice by the occasional cave-in of an excavation wall, obstructions by sandstone from ancient ceiling cave-ins, and inclination of strata toward the rear of the cave, all of which probably caused some mixing of sediment and artifacts, especially near the rear of the rockshelter. While Palmer considered the stratigraphic mapping challenging, the record is largely consistent, as all levels were troweled, recorded, and the artifacts and records curated. At the conclusion of the excavations, approximately one-third of the rockshelter surface had been opened, and it is possible that older cultural deposits remain at lower depths. There is clearly an opportunity to further explore this site, perhaps by future excavations.

Palmer's excavations at Preston Rockshelter and the subsequent analyses of recovered materials at UW–Madison under the direction of James Stoltman, and later by James Theler, have added significant information to our understanding of prehistoric activity in southwestern Wisconsin, especially the Late Archaic. Information considered in this paper, background on discovery and excavation of Preston Rockshelter 50 years ago, and a review of the analyses of cultural artifacts over the past 40 years, is provided thanks in large part to the efforts and skills of Harris A. Palmer in the 1960s and his donation of records and cultural artifacts to the Department of Anthropology Collections at UW–Madison. Indeed, studies of cultural artifacts from Preston are ongoing and there is still much to be examined and learned from the collection in the future.

Acknowledgments

The authors wish to thank Robert "Ernie" Boszhardt for reading earlier drafts of this manuscript and providing thoughtful commentary. Many thanks to Donn and Sheila Barber, the current landowners, who allowed us to visit the site in July of 2016. We are also grateful to John Lovaas, who created the map of Preston (Figure 3). We extend our thanks to James Hibberd, Archivist, at UW–Platteville, for his assistance identifying Palmer's records, and to Cody Schmitt, who created the digitized rim profiles that appear in this report.

References Cited

Alhambra, Dominique V.
    2010   An Analysis of Five Ceramic Vessels from the Brogley Rockshelter (47GT156). *The Wisconsin Archeologist* 91(2):27–40.

Baker, R, G., E. A. Bettie III, D. P. Schwert, D. G. Horton, C. A. Chumbley, L. A. Gonzalez, and M. K. Reagen.
    1996   Holocene Paleoenvironments of Northeast Iowa. *Ecological Monographs* 66(2):203–234.

Baker, Jonathon D.
    2009   Prehistoric Bone Grease Production in Wisconsin's Driftless Area: A Review of the Evidence and Its Implications. Master's thesis, University of Tennessee, Knoxville.

Benden, Danielle M.
    2010   The Brogley Rockshelter (47GT156) Revisited: A History of Excavation and the Impacts of the Curation Crisis. *The Wisconsin Archeologist* 91(2):7–26.

Bender, Margaret M., David A. Baerreis, and Reid A. Bryson
    1979   University of Wisconsin Radiocarbon Dates XVI. *Radiocarbon* 21(1):120–130.

Black, Robert F.
    1959   Geology of Raddatz Rockshelter Sk5, Wisconsin. *The Wisconsin Archeologist* 40(2):69–82.

Boszhardt, Robert F.
    2003a *Deep Cave Rock Art in the Upper Mississippi Valley.* Prairie Smoke Press, St. Paul, Minnesota.
    2003b Preston Corner Notched. In *A Projectile Point Guide for the Upper Mississippi River Valley*, p. 55. University of Iowa Press, Iowa City.

Bryson, Reid A.
2007   The Prairie Peninsula. In *A Paleoclimatology Workbook: High Resolution, Site-Specific, Macrophysical Climate Modeling*, edited by Reid A. Bryson and Katherine McE. DeWall, pp. 75–80. The Mammoth Site of Hot Springs, Inc., Hot Springs, South Dakota.

Carr, Dillon, and Robert F. Boszhardt
2010   Silver Mound Wisconsin: Source of Hixton Silicified Sandstone. *Midcontinental Journal of Archaeology* 35(1):5–36.

Chalkley-Hubbell, Sarah
1976   The Avifauna of Preston Rockshelter: A Study in Bird Exploitation in the Driftless Area. Master's thesis, Department of Anthropology, University of Wisconsin–Madison.

Chumbley, C. A., R. G. Baker, and E. A. Bettis
1990   Midwestern Holocene Paleoenvironments Revealed by Floodplain Deposits. *Science* 249:272–274.

Clayton, Lee., and John W. Attig
1989   *Glacial Lake Wisconsin*. Geological Society of America Memoir 173. Geological Society of America Books, Boulder, Colorado.

Cronon, Bill
1970   The Sandstone Caves of Wisconsin. *The Wisconsin Speleologist* 9(3):53–99.

Curtis, John T.
1965   *The Vegetation of Wisconsin, An Ordination of Plant Communities*. University of Wisconsin Press, Madison, Wisconsin.

Fay, Robert P.
1975   A Report on Ceramic Material Recovered from the Preston Rockshelter (Gt157): A Middle Archaic to Late-Woodland Rockshelter in Grant County, Wisconsin. Undergraduate senior thesis, University of Wisconsin–Madison. Anthropology Permanent Collections Storage, Preston Rockshelter Archives, Madison, Wisconsin.

Finley, Robert W.
1993   *Original Vegetation Cover of Wisconsin*. Map. Wisconsin Department of Natural Resources, Madison.

Finney, Fred A.
2013   Intrasite and Regional Perspectives on the Fred Edwards Site and the Stirling Horizon in the Upper Mississippi Valley. *The Wisconsin Archeologist* 94(1&2):3–248.

Freeman, Joan
1969   The Millville Site: A Middle Woodland Village in Grant County, Wisconsin. *The Wisconsin Archeologist* 50(2):37–87.

Government Land Office (GLO) Wisconsin Land Survey Records
2016   Electronic documents, http://digicoll.library.wisc.edu/SurveyNotes, accessed April 10, 2016.

Janesville Gazette
1969   Janesville Man Assists Excavate Indian Shelter. 24 July: pg. 6A. Janesville, Wisconsin.

Knox, James C., and Attig, John W.
1988   Geology of the Pre-Illinoian Sediment in the Bridgeport Terrace, lower Wisconsin River Valley, Wisconsin. *Journal of Geology* 96:505–513.

Loebel, Thomas J.
2009   Withington (47-Gt-158): A Clovis/Gainey Campsite in Grant County, Wisconsin. *Midcontinental Journal of Archeology* 34(2):223–248.

MacClintock, Paul
1922   The Pleistocene History of the Lower Wisconsin River. *The Journal of Geology* 30(8):673–689.

Martin. Lawrence
1965   *The Physical Geography of Wisconsin*. University of Wisconsin Press.

Maus, Matthew
2010   The Projectile Points of Brogley Rockshelter (47GT156). *The Wisconsin Archeologist* 91(2):41–62.

Milwaukee Journal
1969   Youths Dig Project, Uncover Artifacts. 27 July. Milwaukee, Wisconsin.

Moran, Joseph M., and Edward J. Hopkins.
2002   *Wisconsin's Weather and Climate*. University of Wisconsin Press, Madison, Wisconsin.

Nelson, Robert
2010   The Brogley Rockshelter (47GT156): A Personal Reminiscence. *The Wisconsin Archeologist* 91(2):77–80.

Oerichbauer, Edgar S.
1981   An Interim Report: The 1970, 1978, and 1979 Archeological Excavations at the Site of the Northwest and XY Company Wintering Post. Wisconsin State Historical Society, Madison.
1982   Archaeological Excavations at the Site of a North West and XY Company Winter Post (47–Bt–26): A Progress Report. *The Wisconsin Archeologist* 63(3):153–236.

Palmer, Harris A.
1953   A Late Pleistocene Fauna from the Des Moines Area. *Proceedings of the Iowa Academy of Science* 60:399–402.
1954   A Review of the Interstate Park, Wisconsin Bison Find. *Proceedings of the Iowa Academy of Science* 61:313–319.
1956   *Ibex iowensis* First Evidence of a Fossil Goat in North America. *Proceedings of the Iowa Academy of Science* 63:450–452.

1974   Implications of an Extinct Peccary–Early Archaic Artifact Association from a Wisconsin Cave. *The Wisconsin Archeologist* 55(3):218–230

1978   Search for the Battle of the Brule. *The Wisconsin Archeologist* 59(2):246–252

Palmer, Charles, and Harris A. Palmer

1962a   Truncated Barb Points from Northeastern Illinois. *The Wisconsin Archeologist* 43(1):9–12.

1962b   Occurrence of Indian Mounds in Northern Sawyer County, Wisconsin. *The Wisconsin Archeologist* 43(1):25.

Palmer, Harris A., and James B. Stoltman

1976   The Boaz Mastodon: A Possible Association of Man and Mastodon in Wisconsin. *Midcontinental Journal of Archeology* 1(2):163–177.

Platteville Journal

1969   Students Excavating 3,000-year-old Rockshelter. 17 July, pp 6–7. Platteville, Wisconsin.

1970   Ancient Cave Reveals History of Area. 26 July. Platteville, Wisconsin.

Ritzenthaler, Robert

1957   The Old Copper Culture of Wisconsin. *The Wisconsin Archeologist* 38(4):186–329.

Santure, Sharron K.

1978   An Analysis of the Lithic Artifacts from Preston Rockshelter (47Gt157). Unpublished student paper. University of Wisconsin–Madison, Anthropology Permanent Collections Storage, Preston Rockshelter Archives, Madison, Wisconsin.

Smith, George L., and J. Antonio Simo

1997   Carbonate Diagenesis and Dolomitization of the Lower Ordovician Prairie du Chien Group. *Geoscience Wisconsin* 16:1–16.

Stoltman, James B., Jeffery A. Behm, and Harris A. Palmer.

1984   The Bass Site: A Hardin Quarry/Workshop in Southern Wisconsin. In *Prehistoric Chert Exploitation: Studies from the Midcontinent*, edited by B. M. Butler and E. E. May, pp 197–224. Occasional Paper 2. Center for Archaeological Investigations, Southern Illinois University, Carbondale.

Stoltman, James B.

1979   Middle Woodland Communities of Southwestern Wisconsin. In *Hopewell Archaeology: The Chillicothe Conference*, edited by David S. Brose and N'omi Greber, pp. 122–139. Kent State University Press, Kent, Ohio.

1991   A Reconsideration of Fluted Point Diversity in Wisconsin. *The Wisconsin Archeologist* 72(3&4):245–264.

1997   The Archaic Tradition. *The Wisconsin Archeologist* 78(1&2):112–139.

Stoltman, James B., and George W. Christiansen

2000   The Late Woodland Stage in the Driftless Area of the Upper Mississippi Valley. In *Late Woodland Societies: Tradition and Transformation across the Midcontinent*, edited by Thomas Emerson, Dale McElrath, and Andrew Fortier, pp. 497–524. University of Nebraska Press, Lincoln.

Theler, James L.

1983   *Woodland Tradition Economic Strategies: Animal Resource Utilization in Southwestern Wisconsin and Northeastern Iowa*. PhD dissertation, Department of Anthropology, University of Wisconsin–Madison. ProQuest, Ann Arbor, Michigan.

1987a   The Prehistoric Freshwater Mussels (Naiades) from Brogley Rockshelter in Southwestern Wisconsin. *American Malacological Bulletin* 5(2):165–171.

1987b   *Woodland Tradition Economic Strategies: Animal Resource Utilization in Southwestern Wisconsin and Northeastern Iowa*. Report 17. Office of the State Archaeologist, University of Iowa, Iowa City.

2000   Animal Remains from Native American Archeological Sites in Western Wisconsin. *Transactions of the Wisconsin Academy of Sciences, Arts and Letters* 88:121–142.

Theler, James L., and Robert F. Boszhardt

2003   *Twelve Millennia, Archaeology of the Upper Mississippi River Valley*. University of Iowa Press, Iowa City.

2006   Collapse of Crucial Resources and Culture Change: A Model for the Woodland to Oneota Transformation in the Upper Midwest. *American Antiquity* 71(3):433–472.

Theler, James L., and Sarah Chalkley-Hubbell

2016   Faunal Remains from Preston Rockshelter (47GT157), Grant County, Wisconsin. *The Wisconsin Archeologist* 97(1):5–46.

Wright, H. E. Jr., T. C. Winter, and H. L. Patten

1963   Two Pollen Diagrams from Southeastern Minnesota: Problems in the Late- and Post-glacial Vegetational History. *Geological Society of America Bulletin* 74:1371–1396.

Aberrant Earthworks? A Contemporary Overview of Oneota Mound Ceremonialism

Colin M. Betts and Dale R. Henning

Abstract

Mound ceremonialism has historically served as one of the primary taxonomic traits used to differentiate the Woodland and Upper Mississippian traditions. Despite over a century of archaeological research that has repeatedly produced evidence for Oneota mound construction and use, it has often been dismissed as either anomalous occurrences or short-term cultural survivals. A comprehensive examination of mound construction and use by Oneota and related groups reveals it to have been a minor yet durable phenomenon that occurred across the entire temporal and spatial scope of the Upper Mississippian period. Within this general span, two periods of intensification occurred at A.D. 1100–1400 and A.D. 1600–1725. When considered within the larger framework of the ritual and secular purposes of mound ceremonialism, these occurrences are shown to be associated with the primary cultural processes that define each period, notably the establishment of broad interaction networks as well as cultural attempts to mitigate the impacts of European contact.

Introduction

The relationship between the Oneota tradition and mound ceremonialism has constituted a long-standing paradox. From its inception, the Oneota cultural manifestation has been distinguished from the preceding Woodland period in part by the absence of earthen mound construction. Despite this seemingly clear taxonomic distinction, Oneota materials have had the temerity to repeatedly appear in mound contexts. Even as this evidence has been acknowledged, it has generally been dismissed as a minor or secondary aspect of Oneota culture, often considered to be an anomalous and short-term holdover from the preceding Woodland period. However, this perspective is largely an illusion based on a limited perspective—most considerations of Oneota mounds have occurred at the regional level—and as a consequence Oneota mounds have the appearance of being a temporally and spatially isolated phenomenon. This paper offers an assessment of the temporal, spatial, and cultural dimensions of the occurrence of mound construction and use by Oneota and related groups. An examination of these varying contexts shows that it was a widespread phenomenon that varied significantly in intensity and form across time and space. Oneota mounds, and those found among Oneota-related groups, occur across the Upper Midwest, with two general increases in intensity from A.D. 1100–1400 and again from A.D. 1600–1725. This examination provides important insights into mound ceremonialism as a dynamic tradition with a continuous legacy among Oneota groups that extends well beyond the Woodland tradition. The reasons behind these occurrences are embedded in the ritual function of mound ceremonialism through the establishment and maintenance of intergroup relations, the role of mortuary practices for mediating internal social reorganization, and as a means of mitigating the impacts of the historic period.

Oneota Mounds: Previous Research

Comprehensive efforts to either document or explain the presence and meaning of Oneota mound ceremonialism are relatively lacking. Kreisa's (1999) work represents the most comprehensive effort to study and interpret the larger pattern of Oneota mound use and construction. His overview found that the evidence for mounds occurred on each of the tradition's "temporal peripheries," primarily in

Colin M. Betts, *Luther College; Dale R. Henning, National Museum of Natural History, Smithsonian Institution*

The Wisconsin Archeologist, 2016, 97(2):101–119

Iowa and Wisconsin. The most common explanations invoked to explain the occurrence of this taxonomically anomalous element at the earliest peripheral sites have sought their origins in either the processes of Oneota emergence or the resulting cultural interactions that immediately followed it (Betts 2010:98–99). The former considers Oneota mounds to be transient vestiges of the emergence of the Oneota pattern out of an incipient Woodland base, while the latter views Oneota cultural materials in earthen mounds as the product of cultural exchanges between contemporaneous Woodland and Oneota groups. Within these general categories, Kreisa (1999) and Benn (1989) are among the few who have attempted to provide cultural explanations rooted in the nature of mound function and the specific cultural context.

Kreisa (1999:6) suggests that the mortuary elements of mound ceremonialism were retained by emergent Oneota groups to serve as an "integrative link between kin units and the larger social whole," during the initial development of the Oneota mode of production. The subsequent replacement of tumuli by house floor or cemetery interments co-occurred with shifts in residence and descent patterns that were part of a larger "re-negotiation of social roles and statuses within Oneota society" after ca. A.D. 1300 (Kreisa 1999:6). Benn (1989:253) also viewed the presence of Oneota mounds as being associated with the expansion of the Oneota mode of production. However, he interpreted the mounds as the appropriation of Woodland mortuary practices by inherently expansive Oneota groups as a means of "winning the minds of potential new members from other cultures."

At the other end of the temporal spectrum (A.D. 1600–1725), explanations have focused largely on mound construction as a response to the upheavals associated with the contact period. Kreisa (1999) proposed that this later stage of mound construction was employed as an integrative mechanism following historic period shifts in residence and descent patterns stemming from European contact. More recently, Betts (2010) has linked the occurrence of mound ceremonialism in early historic contexts in western Iowa to its use as an integral part of an early revitalization movement intended to spiritually and socially mitigate the impacts of the contact period.

While undoubtedly providing valuable contributions to our understanding of the continued presence of mound ceremonialism after the emergence of the Oneota Tradition, the research noted above is inherently incomplete. On the one hand, recent work has shown Kreisa's observation to be fundamentally correct that Oneota mound use and construction occurred primarily in a temporally peripheral manner. It also revealed the fact that mound ceremonialism was stubbornly persistent throughout the Oneota cultural continuity in the La Crosse region (Betts 2010). Further, as detailed below, a consideration of this topic utilizing additional data, the reinterpretation of extant data, and a more inclusive consideration of the evidence for mound use and construction finds a much broader temporal, spatial, and cultural scope than previously acknowledged, and by extension, reveals more details about the use of this ritual practice among Oneota groups.

Late Prehistoric Mound Ceremonialism

Throughout the Woodland period, mounds served as a ritual means of achieving a multitude of pragmatic and religious objectives that extended beyond the interment of the dead. Understanding those roles is essential for providing insight into the means by which they would have been incorporated into Upper Mississippian tradition religious and social practices. Of particular interest for the current paper are the various ways in which the communal participation in mound ceremonialism served to define and reinforce the social relationships between the participants. At the intragroup level, mound construction employed socialized labor and collective mortuary rites to foster social solidarity among seasonally mobile kin groups who did not co-reside throughout the year (Benn 1979:69; Mallam 1976:38). On a broader scale, as material symbols of this collective identity, mounds served to both demarcate territories and create sacred landscapes. At the same time that mounds served to differentiate groups, mound ceremonialism also played an important role in the establishment and maintenance of intergroup alliances and as a means of negotiating access to resources (Benn 1979, 1988:2; Benn et al. 1993; Charles 1995; Charles and Buikstra 1983; Hall 1997; Mallam 1976:38–39; Rosebrough 2010).

Prior to presenting data illustrating the temporal and spatial scope of Oneota mounds, it is necessary to consider the nature of mound ceremonialism and its relationship to the available archaeological evidence. Following Betts' (2010) earlier consideration of Oneota mound ceremonialism, the current paper employs a broad definition that includes the evidence for both primary mound construction and the secondary use of mounds through "intrusive" burials. This usage draws heavily on Robert Hall's extensive consideration of the role of mounds in the larger context of ritual activities in native North America, and his observation that mounds represent the material product of a larger corpus of ritual activities and religious objectives. The

larger ritual purposes of this practice were designed to realize a broader array of both spiritual and secular goals that extended beyond the disposition of the dead. Hall (1997:57) argues that mound ceremonialism served fundamentally as "a World Renewal ritual... with ritual identification of the dead reincarnated by adoption with the earth re-created during the course of mound construction." This ritual process also served the largely secular function of creating and maintaining social bonds within and between Late Woodland societies. The decline of mound ceremonialism at the end of the Woodland tradition may have occurred when the separate, but related, Calumet, Spirit Adoption, and Sun Dance rituals supplanted many of its associated functions. Throughout the Midwest,

> [t]he dissociation of mound construction from World Renewal ritual could have led to the replacement of mound construction by cemetery burial for the general population and in time to the emergence of the Sun Dance and Calumet ceremony from elements previously associated with burial mound ceremonialism (Hall 1997:167).

Within this broader understanding of the symbolic meaning and sociocultural function of the mounds, it is important to recognize that well after the time of their initial construction, mounds remained potent symbols, and hence important vehicles for achieving equivalent religious and spiritual ends. Further, we should not make the mistake of assuming that intrusive burials are inherently distinct from primary mound interments. Detailed studies of the internal structure of Woodland mounds suggest that mound construction was a protracted process, with repeated visits and ritual activities occurring well after the initial stages of mound construction (Benn et al. 1993; Mallam and Bettis 1979). As such, the apparent temporal break associated with intrusive burials does not necessarily equate to an attendant ritual or symbolic discontinuity.

Oneota and Oneota-Related Mounds

The following section provides an overview of the spatial, temporal, and cultural dimensions of mound ceremonialism among Oneota groups, as well as from a variety of temporally and spatially proximate contexts. These non-Oneota groups are also considered because, just as Oneota mound ceremonialism cannot be understood from the perspective of an individual region, neither can it be understood without consideration of the larger sociopolitical environment in which

it occurred. Given the central role that mound ceremonialism played in the creation and maintenance of ties between groups, it would be unrealistic to expect that this behavior would not extend beyond the strict confines of the Oneota cultural taxon. The following discussion starts with a concise review of the contexts with well-documented mounds, and is organized temporally and geographically; summaries of the evidence from each site are presented in Table 1.

Grand River Phase (A.D. 1150–1350), Eastern Wisconsin

Evidence for early Oneota mound construction is found at the Grand River phase Walker-Hooper site (47GL65), located in the Fox River passageway in eastern Wisconsin (Overstreet 1997) (Figure 1). Mound excavations at the site revealed multiple flexed and extended Oneota burials in a large, communal mound structure (Gibbon 1972; Jeske 1927) Debate exists about whether this mound was accretional in nature, or was a single construction episode as interpreted by the original excavators (Foley Winkler 2011; Overstreet 1995).

The Langford Phase (A.D. 1100–1400), Northeast Illinois

The Upper Mississippian Langford phase components occur in a cluster of occupations located along the Illinois River in northeastern Illinois (Berres 2001; Emerson 1999, 2012; Jeske 2000, 2003). The Langford phase is in part defined by the presence of Oneota-like motifs on grit-tempered vessels, and is considered to be the result of an in-situ cultural development from the preceding Woodland Des Plaines Complex (Emerson 1999, 2012; Emerson and Brown 1992). Four Langford phase sites in northeastern Illinois contain substantial evidence for mound ceremonialism (Figure 1). This practice appears to have involved two different forms of mound construction. The Gentleman Farm (11LS2) and Oakwood Mound (11WI1) sites contain large accretional communal mounds; in contrast, those from the Robinson Reserve (11CK2) and Wild Rose (11CK35) sites are "small simple mounds containing relatively few individuals associated with habitation sites" (Jeske 2003:167).

Red Wing Region (A.D. 1150–1400), Eastern Minnesota

The Red Wing region spans approximately 100 square miles at the confluences of the Cannon, Vermillion, and Trimbelle Rivers with the Mississippi. Here were more than 2,000 mounds, earthworks and villages, large and small, occupied from the Late Woodland through Oneota periods. A new series of AMS

TABLE 1. AGE AND CHARACTERISTICS OF SITES MENTIONED IN THE TEXT.

Site	Age	Mound/Interment Form	Burials
Grand River Phase			
Walker Hooper (47GL65)	A.D. 1150–1350	accretional/submound pit	multiple flexed and extended
Langford Phase			
Gentleman Farm (11LS2)	A.D. 1100–1400	accretional/submound pit	multiple semi-flexed
Oakwood Mound (11WI1)	A.D. 1100–1400	small simple mound	multiple scattered, flexed, extended
Robinson Reserve (11CK2)	A.D. 1100–1400	accretional/submound pit	flexed
Wild Rose Mounds (11CK25)	A.D. 1100–1400	small simple mound	multiple flexed, semi-flexed, bundle
Red Wing Region			
Mero (47PI2)	A.D. 1150–1400	n.a.	multiple flexed
Double (47PI81)	A.D. 1150–1400	n.a.	none
Camden Style			
Dwire Farm (21LY1)	A.D. 1250–1350	n.a.	multiple
Mitchell Mounds (39DV2)	A.D. 1250–1350	submound pit	multiple flexed, extended
Rushford Mound (21FL9)	A.D. 1250–1350	submound pit	multiple flexed
La Crosse Region			
Bird Bluff (47LC158)	A.D. 1200–1625	n.a.	n.a.
Younger (47LC142)	A.D. 1200–1625	small simple mound/ intrusive?	single extended
Pertzsch (47LC73)	A.D. 1400–1625	intrusive pit	single extended
Hogback (13AM86)	A.D. 1500–1625	intrusive pit	multiple extended
New Galena (13AM108)	A.D. 1500–1625	intrusive pit	single extended
Lane Farm Mounds (13AM104)	A.D. 1500–1625	intrusive pit	single extended
Hartley Fort (13AM103)	A.D. 1500–1625	submound pit	multiple extended
John Henry Mound (13WH105)	A.D. 1625–1685	submound pit	none
Grant Village (13AM210)	A.D. 1400–1685		
Bradbury Phase			
Cooper (21ML16)	A.D. 1675–1700	submound pit	multiple semiflexed & bundle
Chariton Locality			
Old Fort (23SA104)	A.D. 1400–1725		
Northwest Iowa			
Blood Run (13LO2)	A.D. 1650–1714	submound pit	single & multiple extended
Gillette Grove (13CY2)	A.D. 1650–1714	n.a.	n.a.
Harriman (13CY1)	A.D. 1650–1714	n.a.	n.a.
Milford (13DK1)	A.D. 1650–1714	n.a.	n.a.
Minnesota			
Riehl (21FL8)	A.D. 1100–1700	intrusive	n.a.
High Island (21SB1)	A.D. 1100–1700	intrusive	extended
Howard Lake (21AN1)	A.D. 1100–1700	intrusive	extended
Femco (21WL1)	A.D. 1100–1700	intrusive	multiple extended

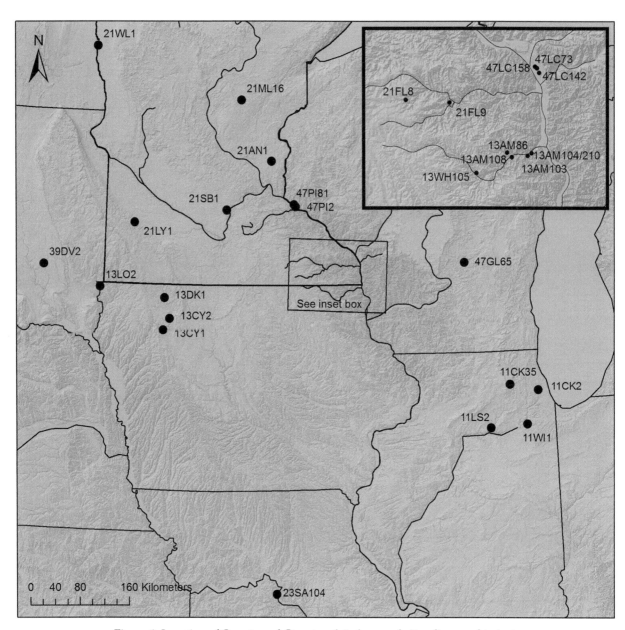

Figure 1. Location of Oneota and Oneota-related mound sites discussed in text.

dates reveals that the Oneota tradition persisted here from A.D. 1150 to 1400 (Schirmer 2016). The contexts of these dates confirm that the Bartron, Silvernale, and Link ceramic types have longer time spans than formerly believed, and that these three types were simultaneously produced for more than a century. Schirmer identified two sequential Oneota phases, Bartron (A.D. 1150–1300) and Spring Creek (A.D. 1300–1400), and suggested that both Silvernale and Link pottery types dated ca. A.D. 1190–1240, through much of the Bartron phase. Many regional villages and mounds were occupied and constructed by Late Woodland groups that were apparently ancestral to the subsequent Oneota

groups. The Late Woodland period is generally dated from A.D. 800; very likely, the ceramic identifiers of Late Woodland persisted well into the beginning of the Bartron phase. Two sites within this area, Mero (47PI2) and Double (47PI81), provide convincing evidence for Oneota authorship of mounds (Figure 1). This evidence includes shell-tempered ceramics contained within mound fill, Oneota vessels associated with primary burials, and radiocarbon assays from mound contexts, suggesting that Oneota mound construction was part of a corpus of practices directly traceable to the Late Woodland forebears. The close association of Oneota villages with mound groups at multiple sites in

the Red Wing area suggests that mound construction comprised a central part of early Oneota cultural practices (Dobbs 1984; Maxwell 1950; Penman and Sullivan 1995; Shirmer personal communication 2016). Oneota people had vacated the Red Wing region by A.D. 1400.

The Camden Style (A.D. 1250–1350), Minnesota and South Dakota

Holley and Michlovic (2013) propose a general category of Oneota-like ceramics, the "Camden Style," named after a vessel recovered from a mound at the Camden (21LY1), or Dwire Farm, site in southwestern Minnesota (Figure 1). Based on characteristics shared between this vessel and comparable vessels from other sites in the general vicinity of the Camden type site, they propose a general style that links ceramics from several sites thought to date from roughly A.D. 1250 to 1350. Camden Style pottery is defined by the authors as small to miniature shell-tempered vessels with thumb impressed or pinched shoulders, lip impressions, sharp shoulder profiles, and alternating triangle decorations, which they suggest are a blend of Oneota and Middle Missouri influences originating in southwest Minnesota. The three Camden Style vessels were all recovered from primary mound contexts. The presence of Camden Style vessels at the Dwire Farm in southwest Minnesota, in the Mitchell Mound 1 in the James River valley, South Dakota, and in the Rushford Mound group in southeastern Minnesota not only offers a relative time for their interment (ca. A.D. 1300), but suggests strong traditional ceremonial and religious links shared by the occupants of these disparate locations. Seven shell-tempered bodysherds from the Correctionville Oneota sites (13WD6, 13WD7) also exhibit "pinched-up" shoulder margins (Henning n.d.). Three recent AMS dates from 13WD6, A.D. 1300–1350, suggest contemporaneity with the Camden style.

The Camden site is the location of a mound excavated in 1934 in Lyon County, Minnesota (Chamberlain 1936, 1942), and subsequently reported by Griffin (1945) and Arzigian and Stevenson (2003). The unique shell-tempered vessel (Figure 2b), identified by Griffin as the Camden "Vase," was recovered in the right hand of one of several burials interred in a submound pit. This small vessel (approximately one-fourth of the rim and upper shoulder is missing) is ca. 8.3 cm in height and 12.5 cm in maximum diameter. We believe that it originally had two opposing loop or narrow strap handles decorated with deeply slashed vertical lines, and four evenly-spaced horizontal slots, all cut through the upper rim when the vessel walls were still moist. A single trailed line encircles the neck; the shoulder is decorated with a series of trailed lines in alternating triangles. The outer margin is decorated with finger and nail impressions that suggest that the moist clay was "pinched up."

Another Camden Style vessel was recovered from burial Mound 1, very near the Mitchell Initial Middle Missouri tradition village site (39DV2) in southwestern South Dakota (Figure 1). This mound and several others in the group were excavated in 1938 by E. E. Meleen, whose notes and maps, along with many of the artifacts recovered, clearly suggest that the extended remains of an "elderly" individual and associated vessel were originally placed on or near the floor when Mound 1 was constructed, and were not intrusive (Archived Document 1938; Meleen 1968). Meleen suggested either that the mound was the result of joint mound construction by Initial Middle Missouri (Mill Creek) and early Oneota groups or that Oneota people built the mound after the Mitchell village was abandoned. Meleen's notes suggest that Oneota people were responsible for the burial of the "elderly" individual with the tiny vessel, and were present and participated in some or all of Mound 1 construction. While a few small Oneota sites are recorded along the James River, none are recorded near the Mitchell mound group (Alex 1981).

Figure 2. Photographs of Camden Style vessels: (a) Mitchell Mound 1 (39DV2); (b) the Camden Mound (21LY1).

The shell-tempered Mitchell vessel is tiny and symmetrical, measuring 4.3 cm in height, 3.3 cm minimal diameter at the orifice and 7.0 cm maximum diameter (Figure 2a). It has two opposed strap handles decorated with three parallel, vertical deep slashed lines. The exterior surface is smoothed; decoration is applied to the flattened shoulder with characteristic Oneota trailed lines. Decoration consists of four opposing chevrons with tool impressions along the upper lines, and four opposing equilateral crosses within the open spaces between chevrons. Two unique characteristics link this vessel to the Camden "vase". On the rim and above the crosses on the shoulder, there are four horizontal slots (8.7 to 11.3 mm long, and 2 to 2.4 mm in height) that were cut through the moist rim wall ca. 6.2 mm below the lip, and once again we find deep finger impressions that pinched up the moist clay around the shoulder margin.

The Rushford Mound group (21FL9), located in the lower Root River valley near Rushford, Minnesota, represents the third mound site that has yielded Camden Style ceramics (Figure 1). Excavation of four of the six mounds on the site (all presumed Oneota on the basis of comparable construction methods and burial arrangements) yielded two burials associated with shell-tempered vessels in primary, non-intrusive contexts (Arzigian and Stevenson 2003:377–378; Wedel 1959; Wilford 1941). Wilford (1941) initially assigned these vessels to the Oneota tradition largely on the basis of general vessel form and the presence of shell temper. Mildred Wedel (1959:108–109) took exception to this assignment, offering that a combination of formal and decorative characteristics set the two vessels apart from the ceramics commonly associated with Oneota occupations in the La Crosse region. She argued instead that the vessels were more similar to those from the Grand River phase in Wisconsin (McKern 1945), and the Mitchell and Camden vessels illustrated by Griffin (1945) (Wedel 1959:108–109). Overall she felt they fit better within the Middle Mississippian Tradition (Wedel 1959:109). Reconsideration of these vessels after more than a half century of additional Oneota research provides both support for some of Wedel's assertions and greater clarity to the likely Oneota-associated cultural affiliation of the vessels assignable to the Camden Style (Holley and Michlovic 2013).

Rushford Mound 1 was a small (3–4.5 m diameter, .5 m high) conical structure covered with rock slabs. The single burial, an infant with a small vessel (Figure 3a) between its legs, was placed in a sub-mound pit beneath four closely spaced rock slabs that formed a rough diamond shape (Arzigian and Stevenson 2003:377). Mildred Wedel noted that the (now repatriated) Mound 1 vessel:

has a medium sized cylindrical neck that merges into a gently sloping shoulder area. The shoulder is sharply angled. The base is narrowly rounded. The lip surface has small consecutive angled impressions or excisions on it. Around the [outer] lip is a series of vertical lugs, and at the base of the neck are two encircling lines. On the shoulder area are irregularly drawn triangular-shaped hachured (sic) zones that so abut each other than an area of almost solid decoration results. It is not a precisely executed motif, however. Around the equator of the jar is a series of "pinched up" ridges. On the base are two pairs of parallel lines that cross each other at right angles. At this intersection several concentric circles are carelessly drawn. (Wedel 1959:108–109) (parens added).

We should add here that, while it has no handles, this vessel has two opposed circular holes that were punched through the neck when it was moist (Figure 3a). The unusual trailing on the base of the vessel is illustrated in Figure 4.

a

b

CM

Figure 3. Photographs of ceramic vessels from Rushford Mounds (21FL9): (a) Mound 1; (b) Mound 3.

Mound 3 was conical, 4.5 to 7 m in diameter and .75 to 1m high and was covered with dolomite slabs. A single submound pit contained an extended adolescent male covered with flat rocks; a small, shell-tempered mortuary vessel (Figure 3b) was placed at the left shoulder (Arzigian and Stevenson 2003:378). Mildred Wedel describes the (repatriated) vessel as:

> a medium mouthed, flaring rimmed jar with an angled shoulder, two loop handles, and on the shoulder four unit designs of trailed lines involving a large chevron with verticals filling the triangular area below it. The base is rounding but not broadly so (Wedel 1959:109).

This second vessel is obviously not of the Camden Style. However, it bears some early Oneota characteristics in the simplicity of the quadrant motif applied to the angled shoulder, and the loop handles. It is quite possibly contemporaneous with the Camden Style vessel from Mound 1.

The La Crosse Region (A.D. 1450–1685), Southwest Wisconsin, Southeast Minnesota, and Northeast Iowa

The La Crosse Region is defined by a cluster of Oneota occupations in three geographically distinct localities: the La Crosse terrace in southwestern Wisconsin, the Root River in southeastern Minnesota, and the Upper Iowa River valley in northeastern Iowa (Sasso 1993:325) (Figure 1). Oneota occupations in the region make up a cultural continuity (Boszhardt 1994, 1998) that may date ca. A.D. 1200–1685. On the La Crosse terrace the Bird Bluff Mound (47LC158), Younger (47LC142), and Pertzsch (47LC73) sites contain evidence for reuse of extant Woodland mounds by Oneota groups ca. A.D. 1200–1625 (Penman and Sullivan 1995:139–140). Both the Bird Bluff Mound and the Younger sites had Oneota ceramics within the mound fill, while the Pertzsch Mound contained an extended burial directly associated with an Oneota vessel (Boszhardt et al. 1984; Gallagher et al. 1982:25–26).

The Upper Iowa locality contains an Oneota cultural sequence that extended into the early historic period and has been linked to the Ioway tribe (Betts 2015; Mott 1938; Wedel 1959). Woodland mounds at the Hogback (13AM86), New Galena (13AM108), and Lane Farm (13AM104) sites contained intrusive Oneota burial pits (Wedel 1959). The mounds at the Hartley Fort (13AM103) and John Henry (13WH105) sites were clearly constructed by Oneota Tradition people (Benn and Bettis 1977; Betts 2003, 2010; McKusick 1973; Tiffany 1982). The superimposition of mound outlines over mid-fourteenth century Oneota longhouses at the Grant Village site (13AM210) may be additional indications of Oneota mound construction (Betts 2010; McKusick 1973). In their entirety, the radiocarbon assays and temporally diagnostic ceramics from these sites indicate the presence of Oneota mound construction and use from approximately A.D. 1450 to 1685 (Betts 2010:100). In summary, the nature of mound

5 cm

Figure 4. Base of vessel from 21FL9, Mound 1.

ceremonialism included several forms, ranging from mound reuse (in the form of intrusive pits) to primary mound construction with extended, primary burials, as well as the construction of mounds lacking a clear mortuary component.

The Bradbury Phase (A.D. 1675–1700), Central Minnesota

The Bradbury phase is defined as the protohistoric archaeological manifestation of the Mdewakanton Dakota, based on 17 mound and village sites along the three lakes of the Rum River outlet of Lake Mille Lacs (Arzigian and Stevenson 2003; Birk and Johnson 1992; Lothson 1972). Burials are found in both mounds and village sites. Contact period European artifacts have been found on four Bradbury phase sites; the presence of cuprous tinklers and the lack of gun parts suggest a date from ca. 1675 to 1700 (Betts 2015; Mazrim and Esarey 2007). The phase is defined in part on the co-occurrence of the local grit-tempered Sandy Lake ceramics with the shell-tempered ceramics commonly referred to as either Oneota or Ogechie—the taxonomic differentiation between the latter two is unclear (Ready 1979). Regardless of name, the strong similarities between the Ogechie/Oneota ceramics from the Bradbury phase components and those from the La Crosse region indicate that they were either made by Ioway women or directly copied by local potters using an Ioway model.

The Cooper mounds (21ML16) and associated Cooper village (21ML9) provide crucial details about the nature of Bradbury phase mortuary practices and mound ceremonialism (Figure 1). Mound 1 contained the remains of both primary and secondary inhumations along with a variety of Ogechie/Oneota ceramics and European trade items (Arzigian and Stevenson 2003:437–439; Aufderheide et al. 1994; Birk and Johnson 1992; Lothson 1972; Streiff 1994a, 1994b) (Figure 5a). Burials and burial pits were also located in the associated village; most had grave inclusions, including traditional stone tools and Sandy Lake and Ogechie pottery, but no European trade items. A pipestone disk pipe was found with one of the village burials, further evidence of interaction between the Dakota and Ioway (Arzigian and Stevenson 2003:437).

The Chariton Locality (A.D. 1350–1725), North Central Missouri

The Chariton locality is defined by a large complex of Oneota sites around the confluence of the Chariton and Missouri Rivers in north central Missouri. Within this locality, near the immense (ca. 120 ha) Utz Oneota site (23SA2) (Bray 1991; Chapman 1980; Henning 1970; O'Brien and Wood 1998; Yelton 1998), is the Old Fort

Figure 5. Photographs of Oneota vessels: (a) the Cooper Mound (21ML16); (b) Femco Mound (21ML1).

(23SA104), a large (4–6 acres) enclosure of earthen embankments and ditches constructed by Oneota inhabitants (Wood 1973) (Figure 1). Four mounds were reported from inside the enclosure. Gerard Fowke (1910), citing West (1882), states that the mounds were previously opened by a Mr. Middleton of Kansas City, who found decayed human bones, broken pottery, and flakes. Fowke suggested that the remains of multiple individuals were found in the mounds, possibly in the form of collective or communal burial (Fowke 1910:86).

The pottery was described as the same as that found in nearby fields, doubtless the Utz Oneota site, a village occupied by the Missouria tribe when they were first contacted by Europeans (Bray 1991; Chapman 1959, 1980; Chapman and Chapman 1964; Chapman et al. 1985; Henning 1970; West 1882; Wood 1973; Yelton 1998). Wood (1973) and Leaf (1976) attributed the Old Fort and the four central mounds to Oneota construction. No historic trade materials have been

reported, suggesting that the interments were made before European trade began. This leaves us with a broad range of possible dates for Oneota mound construction in this locality, from ca. A.D. 1350 into the contact period, perhaps as late as A.D. 1725 (Henning 1970; Yelton 1998).

Northwest Iowa Region (A.D. 1650–1714)

Evidence for Oneota mound construction in the Northwest Iowa region is temporally restricted to the early historic period. The most clear cut and compelling example of Oneota mound construction is found on Blood Run (13LO2), located on both sides of the Big Sioux River in northwestern Iowa and southeast South Dakota (Figure 1). The Blood Run site is immense, comprised of at least five discrete mound and village units, likely associated with Omaha/Ponca, Ioway/Oto and (far fewer) Arikara occupations (Alex 2000; Henning 1982, 1985, 1998a, 1998b; Henning and Thiessen, eds. 2004). Initial accounts of the site in the nineteenth century recorded at least 275 mounds; many of these have subsequently been destroyed by cultivation, curiosity-seekers, and gravel mining (Thomas 1894). Unfortunately, few records of any kind offer information about what was found in the mounds (Henning 2011). The 11 mounds at Blood Run that have been even minimally reported upon offer evidence of Oneota mound construction during the early contact period, ca. A.D. 1650–1714 (Betts 2010; Benn 1988; Harvey 1979; Henning and Schermer 2004; Lueck et al. 1995; Schermer 2004; Schermer, et al. 1998; Starr 1887, 1893, 1895). The available evidence includes mound construction, and associations with extended, primary burials, as well as one example of a mound with no evidence of a mortuary component (Benn 1988; Harvey 1979). Of the 11 documented mounds, nine had early contact period European objects (glass beads, copper or brass bracelets, beads, earrings, a small serpent, and iron bracelets) included in the mound fill or in direct association with burials (Henning 2011). A unique characteristic of this site is that the mounds are closely integrated with village occupations. The Pettigrew map of "The Silent City" offers an excellent record of this integration shortly before the stones outlining house edges were removed for cultivation (Pettigrew 1889; see enhanced copy in Henning and Schermer 2004:406–407).

In addition to Blood Run, three Okoboji phase village sites, Gillett Grove (13CY2), Harriman, or Bur Oak, (13CY1) and Milford (13DK1) also exhibit likely evidence for Oneota mound construction immediately adjacent to or within the villages (Alex 2000; Anderson 1994; Doershuk and Resnick 2008; Henning 1998b; Keyes 1921, 1926; Spargo 1984; Tiffany and Anderson 1993) (Figure 1). Each of these sites is

primarily defined by their historic occupation components dating from ca. 1675 to shortly after 1700, and they offer close cultural similarities to the Orr phase (Betts 1998, 2010, 2015:136; Henning 1961, 1970). As a whole, the Okoboji phase sites are thought to be the result of the movement of the Ioway from the La Crosse region, specifically the Upper Iowa locality ca. 1650, to avoid disease and the increasing depredations of eastern tribes (Betts 2006, 2015; Green 1993; Henning and Thiessen 2004; Wedel 1981, 1986). Unlike Blood Run, the evidence for Oneota mound construction at these sites is circumstantial, and is based on the close association of the village and mound components, and their inclusion within a larger cultural continuity with a deep legacy of Oneota mound construction and use.

Minnesota

Arzigian and Stevenson (2003) list several mounds and mound groups in Minnesota that have been tentatively assigned to Oneota construction or provide evidence for intrusive Oneota burials (Figure 1). Wilford's excavations of two of the six mounds in the Riehl group (21FL8) produced one burial and a projectile point "of the Oneota type" (Wilford et al. 1969:2). An extended burial associated with an Oneota vessel was encountered just below the surface on the High Island Mound (21SB1), an extended primary burial was intruded into the Howard Lake mound (21AN1), and some primary burials accompanied by an Oneota vessel (Figure 5b) were probably intruded into the Femco mound (21WL1) (Arzigian and Stevenson 2003). Vessel morphology and decoration of the Femco vessel suggest that it was decades later than the Camden Style jars. Unfortunately, no precise temporal data are available, and the mounds cannot confidently be dated more precisely than to the Oneota tradition as a whole. However, minimally, these mounds provide additional evidence for the widespread persistence of mound ceremonialism.

Discussion

We believe that the preceding data offer the most complete perspective to date on Oneota and Oneota-related mound construction and use, and underscore the fact that it was a temporally and spatially widespread phenomenon through the late prehistoric and early historic periods. Consistent with previous considerations of the topic, the bulk of the evidence for Oneota and Oneota-associated mound ceremonialism, whether in the form of mound construction or reuse, occurs primarily at the temporal margins of the Oneota

tradition. Although the preponderance of evidence is found in these early and late periods, evidence from the La Crosse region indicates that mound ceremonialism continued to be a consistent, albeit minor, aspect of lifeways in that region throughout the late Developmental and Classic Horizons (Betts 2010:100). Mound construction and use during each of these periods is linked by more than just contemporaneity; trends in the form of the mounds and the interments also exist relative to their temporal distribution. Notably, the earliest period shows the greatest degree of variability with respect to the nature of mound construction and interments—including construction of both discrete and accretional mounds, and the occurrence of primary and secondary burials. Those from the later periods are much more homogenous and include a

greater number of intrusive burial pits; the majority of the burials, when they occur, are primary and extended, often of a single individual (Table 1). Specific consideration of each context provides important details about the function and meaning of mound ceremonialism in each setting.

The first primary expression of Oneota mound ceremonialism occurs in a large arc extending from northeastern Illinois to southeastern South Dakota and dates from ca. A.D. 1100 to 1400, with the suggestions of a more focused and intensive occurrence ca. A.D. 1250–1350 (Figure 6). These early Oneota mounds cannot be viewed simply as vestiges of the preceding Woodland period. In particular, the mounds associated with Camden Style ceramics indicate an expansion of mound ceremonialism in novel contexts rather than

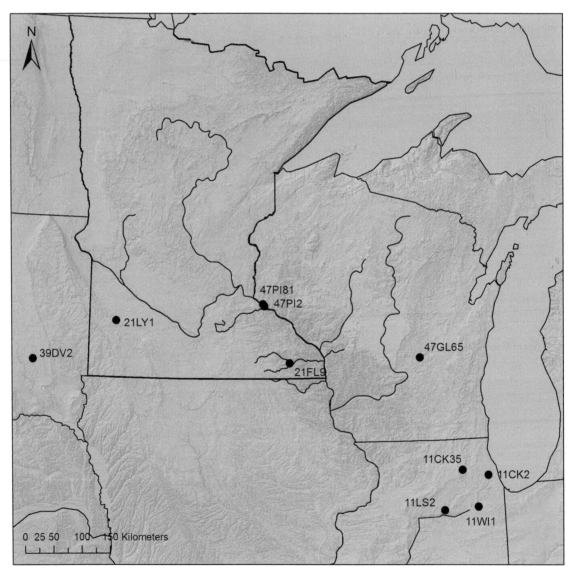

Figure 6. Location of early period (ca. A.D. 1100–1400) mound sites.

simply the conservative retention of an existing trait. Further, a great deal of variability underlies the general shared presence of mound ceremonialism at this time. A wide spectrum of mound forms are encountered during this time period, ranging from smaller, discrete interments with one or a few individuals to large accretional mounds with multiple interments; the presence of both accretional and discrete mounds in the Langford phase serves as an important reminder that different mound structures are not inherently a reflection of larger cultural differences. Explaining these characteristics, as well as the widespread decline of Oneota mound ceremonialism ca. A.D. 1350, requires a consideration of both the nature and function of mound ceremonialism, as well as the larger cultural context in which it occurred.

The cultural dynamics behind the early phase of Oneota mounds are tied to the wide-scale cultural changes that occurred after ca. A.D. 1100—notably the development of sedentary, tribal social polities as well as the attendant increase in the intensity of intergroup interaction. The degree of heterogeneity in mound form can be seen as rooted both in different traditions of mound construction, as well as in the specific processes involved in the development of social complexity. In the case of the latter, Kreisa's (1999) argument that mound ceremonialism would have served as an important nexus for the negotiation of the myriad changes in social structure that accompanied this development provides a valuable perspective. Although the long-term trajectory of the transition to complex social organization across the Upper Midwest is generally comparable, this apparent homogeneity in outcome likely obscures a greater degree of heterogeneity in the specific social mechanisms by which it was achieved. The degree of variability seen in the presence, form, and distribution of the mounds and their included burials during this time is likely a reflection of the contested and situational nature of this process across time, space, and culture. At the most basic level, the diversity in communal and individual burials implies a tension between the emphases on egalitarianism and an emerging ranked social identity (Benn et al. 1993:68; Benn and Green 2000:442).

Just as important for understanding the persistence and even the expansion of mound ceremonialism during this time is its role in the creation and maintenance of social networks to facilitate the passage of people, ideas, and materials across the Upper Midwest. In this role, the effectiveness of this process was based on the fact that it drew on a deeply rooted element of cultural practice—albeit within a new cultural context. As such it would have represented a culturally familiar and ritually appropriate means

of facilitating trade, prior to the widespread use of the Calumet pipe, as previously proposed by Hall (1997). The appearance of the Calumet Ceremony and the predominant shift to non-mound burial practices after ca. A.D. 1400 are directly tied to the decline in Oneota mound ceremonialism at this same time. Not coincidentally, the general decline in Oneota mound ceremonialism co-occurs with the initial appearance of disk pipe forms in the Upper Midwest by A.D. 1300, and likely represents the ascendancy of the Calumet ceremony for establishing trade and ceremonial contacts. Disk pipes were not restricted to Oneota recipients; they have been recovered in Late Mississippian mound and burial sites in the lower Mississippi Valley, and Gulf Coast states to the Atlantic coast (Brown 1989). Hall argues that across the midcontinent

> [t]he dissociation of mound construction from World Renewal ritual could have led to the replacement of mound construction by cemetery burial for the general population and in time to the emergence of the Sun Dance and Calumet ceremony from elements previously associated with burial mound ceremonialism (Hall 1997:167).

Likewise, the widespread shift to cemetery and house floor interment after this time was likely due both to this ritual transition, as well as to the larger transformation in the social and residential structure of Oneota societies after ca. A.D. 1300. Kreisa (1999) proposed that part of this shift was associated with a trend towards individual identity over that of the corporate group. Alternately, with the advent of greater sedentism and year-round co-residence among Oneota groups, the use of mound ceremonialism as a form of socialized labor to foster social cohesion declined in importance, likely being replaced, in part, by clan ceremonialism and agricultural activities.

The second well-defined occurrence of mound ceremonialism occurs in the late Classic and early Historic horizons, ca. A.D. 1600–1725 (Figure 7). This is best demonstrated in northeast and northwest Iowa, as well as in the Bradbury phase in Minnesota. Although lacking concrete temporal data, it may be that the Old Fort mounds in Missouri are also part of this same phenomenon. If these mounds are part of this same trajectory, they could be from the earlier stage just prior to the introduction of historic trade goods. As noted above, and by Betts (2010), the evidence for mound ceremonialism in northeast and northwest Iowa displays much more homogeneity than the earlier period—largely subsumed by discrete mounds constructed in a single event that may include primary extended burials. This manifestation can be seen as the

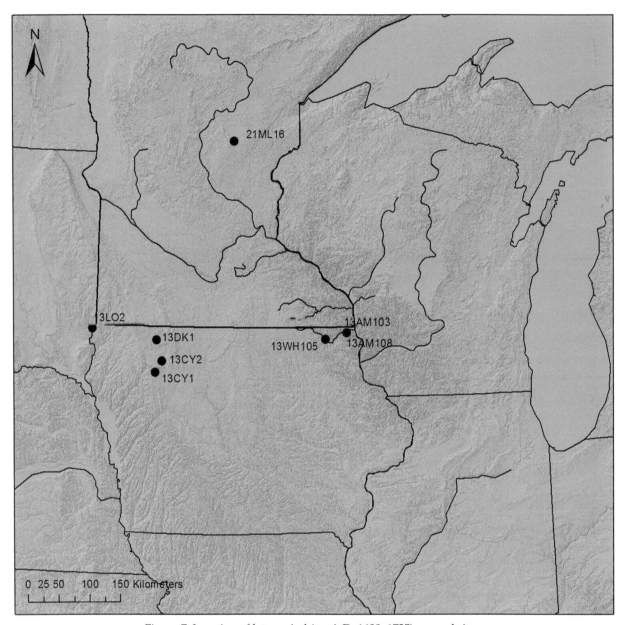

Figure 7. Location of late period (ca. A.D. 1600–1725) mound sites.

specific expression of a single cultural continuity that follows the movement of the Red Wing and La Crosse region Oneota peoples, likely the nascent Ioway tribe, from the Mississippi Valley to villages in northwest Iowa. The predominance of primary burials during this later period can be explained in part due to the greater degree of sedentism and residential stability associated with the Oneota tradition. However, the relative degree of homogeneity of mound construction during this time stands in somewhat marked contrast to that of the earlier Late Woodland period. As such, the nearly exclusive presence of individual extended burials, rather than communal or multiple burials,

in a manner similar to that seen more commonly in cemeteries or house floors is likely a reflection of the continued use of elements of mound ceremonialism in a novel social setting. Only small differences in the nature of mound ceremonialism, such as the inclusion of the bison skull in one of the Blood Run mounds, or the presence of elaborate prepared soil layers, provides hints to the changing or multi-ethnic nature of the mounds in this area. The ultimate expression of this phenomenon in the Bradbury phase, as well as in the multi-ethnic Blood Run site, is indicative of the geographic and cultural variability, and evidence for a brief expansion outside of this cultural continuity.

Neither the Bradbury phase mound nor the Cooper village burial patterns compare closely to the procedures often employed by the Orr phase Oneota occupants in the Root and Upper Iowa localities. While disarticulated secondary inhumations, bundle, and semiflexed individuals are present in the Bradbury phase, Orr phase interments were often extended, sometimes defleshed and re-articulated (Henning and Peterson 1965), and only rarely secondary, bundle, or flexed (Bray 1961; Wedel 1959), suggesting important differences in the manner in which mortuary practices were integrated within the larger process of forging and sustaining sociopolitical bonds.

This resurgence of mound ceremonialism has previously been interpreted as an early revitalization movement employed to cope with the challenges presented by the historic era. In this context, it is thought to have been employed as a means of addressing the forces of European contact—particularly the population loss and attendant political reorganization that followed on its wake. The centrality of world renewal and spirit regeneration to mound ceremonialism would have represented a logically consistent means of addressing the spiritual dimensions of depopulation and facilitating a demographic revitalization (Betts 2010). As in the earlier manifestation of this phenomenon, however, the role of this behavior in organizing external social relationships cannot be ignored. Benn (1989) was the first to suggest that the Blood Run mounds, in particular, likely served in this capacity in the context of the multi-ethnic nature of the site occupations. Similarly, the presence of mounds among the Mdewakanton may indicate their use as a means of facilitating intergroup interactions. The Ioway were very important in the Midwest–Plains exchange system through the early contact period; often, members of the tribe established temporary residence with trading partners of other tribes (Henning 2003; Mott 1938; Wedel 1986). The trade items found in Bradbury phase sites were likely brought to the Mdewakanton Dakota through down-the-line exchange initiated by the Ioway, a few decades before French traders made contact with them (Birk and Johnson 1992:232–233; Lothson 1972:21). We believe that a comparable residence-exchange relationship functioned here. In this manner it is possible that mound ceremonialism served its earlier role in the establishment of trade relations.

Summary

The preceding overview of mound ceremonialism among Late Prehistoric groups in the Upper Midwest reveals substantial evidence for its continued practice well after the appearance of the Upper Mississippian period. As such, it can no longer be viewed as solely culturally anomalous or marginal—but rather as a durable part of Late Prehistoric life ways. The detailed consideration of the temporal, spatial, and formal variation in this phenomenon provides important insights for understanding the roles that it played in the creation and maintenance of internal and external social networks. As such, we believe that this research reinforces the perspective that Oneota mound ceremonialism was a dynamic process intimately associated with the cultural and social processes that defined the Oneota tradition, rather than simply the static survival from a previous cultural period.

Acknowledgments

Upon completion of any research endeavor, one always owes someone. And, we do. We submitted our first draft to three good friends, each of whom reviewed it from his own informed perspective. David W. Benn, Bear Creek Archaeology, Ronald C. Schirmer, Department of Anthropology, Minnesota State University–Mankato, and Lance Foster, Tribal Historic Preservation Officer, Iowa Tribe of Kansas and Nebraska, all promptly made useful, sometimes very necessary, comments. Bruce Koenen and Pat Emerson from the Office of the State Archaeologist, Minnesota Historical Society, graciously provided records and photographs relevant to our Oneota mounds research. Katie Lamie, Repository Manager, South Dakota Archaeological Research Center, sent copies of Meleen's all-important Mitchell Mound 1 field notes and made the pottery vessel available for photography and research. George Holley, Department of Anthropology and Earth Science, Minnesota State University–Moorhead, provided the photo and responded quickly and helpfully to a barrage of questions about the Camden "vase" and the intricacies of western Minnesota prehistory. Finally, we have been frankly amazed at the rapidity and thoroughness of editorial review and processing offered by Constance Arzigian and Katherine Stevenson upon submission of our manuscript. They have made the whole process a real delight. And, finally, we want to state that any errors, omissions, or inconsistencies, which remain despite the best efforts of all of those noted above, are entirely the fault of the authors.

References Cited

Alex, Lynn M.

2000 *Iowa's Archaeological Past.* University of Iowa Press, Iowa City.

Alex, Robert A.

1981 Village Sites off the Missouri River. In *The Future of South Dakota's Past*, edited by Larry J. Zimmerman and Lucille C. Stewart, pp. 39–45. Special Publication No. 2. South Dakota Archaeological Society.

Anderson, Duane C.

1994 *Stone, Glass, and Metal Artifacts from the Milford Site (13DK1): An Early 18th Century Oneota Component in Northwest Iowa.* Research Papers 19(5). Office of the State Archaeologist, University of Iowa, Iowa City.

Archived Document No. 16

1938 *E.E. Meleen Collection. Volume 39DV2, Mitchell Site and Mounds.* South Dakota State Historical Society, Archival and Manuscript Collection Summary, Archaeological Research Center, Rapid City, South Dakota.

Arzigian, Constance M., and Katherine P. Stevenson

2003 *Minnesota Indian Mounds and Burial Sites: A Synthesis of Prehistoric and Early Historic Archaeological Data.* Publication No. 1. The Minnesota Office of the State Archaeologist, St. Paul.

Aufderheide, Arthur, Elden Johnson, and Odin Langsjoen

1994 Health, Demography, and Archaeology of Mille Lacs Native American Mortuary Populations. Memoir 28. *Plains Anthropologist* 39(140):251–375.

Benn, David W.

1989 Hawks, Serpents, and Bird-men: Emergence of the Oneota Mode of Production. *Plains Anthropologist* 34(125):233–260.

1979 Some Trends and Traditions in Woodland Cultures of the Quad-State Region in the Upper Mississippi River Basin. *The Wisconsin Archeologist* 60(1):47–82.

1988 Mound Salvage Excavations at Blood Run. *Iowa Archeological Society Newsletter* 38(2)126:1–3.

Benn, David W., E. Arthur Bettis III, and R. Clark Mallam

1993 Cultural Transformations in the Keller and Bluff Top Mounds. *Plains Anthropologist* 38(145):53–73.

Benn, David W., and E. Arthur Bettis III

1977 *Salvage Excavations at the John Henry Mound (13WH105) Winneshiek County, Iowa.* Research Papers 2(14). Office of the State Archaeologist, Iowa City.

Benn, David W., and William Green

2000 Late Woodland Cultures in Iowa. In *Late Woodland Societies: Tradition and Transformation across the Midcontinent*, edited by Thomas E. Emerson, Dale L. McElrath, and Andrew C. Fortier, pp. 429–496. University of Nebraska Press, Lincoln.

Berres, Thomas E.

2001 *Power and Gender in Oneota Culture: A Study of a Late Prehistoric People.* Northern Illinois University Press, Dekalb.

Betts, Colin M.

1998 The Oneota Orr Phase: Space, Time, and Ethnicity. *The Wisconsin Archeologist* 79(2):227–237.

2003 Oneota Mound Construction: Evidence from the John Henry Mound (13WH105). *Newsletter of the Iowa Archeological Society* 53(2):6–7.

2006 Pots and Pox: The Identification of Protohistoric Epidemics in the Upper Mississippi Valley. *American Antiquity* 71(2):233–259.

2010 Oneota Mound Construction: An Early Revitalization Movement. *Plains Anthropologist* 55(214):97–110.

2015 A Twenty-First Century Perspective on Oneota Cultural Affiliations. In *Oneota Historical Connections: Working Together in Iowa*, edited by Shirley J. Schermer, William Green, Larry J. Zimmerman, Linda Forman, and Robin M. Lillie, pp. 133–142. Report 24. Office of the State Archaeologist, University of Iowa, Iowa City.

Birk, Douglas A., and Elden Johnson

1992 The Mdewakanton Dakota and Initial French Contact. In *Calumet and Fleur-de-Lys: Archaeology of Indian and French Contact in the Midcontinent*, edited by John A. Walthall and Thomas E. Emerson, pp. 203–240. Smithsonian Institution Press, Washington, D.C.

Boszhardt, Robert F.

1994 Oneota Group Continuity at La Crosse: The Brice Prairie, Pammel Creek and Valley View Phases. *The Wisconsin Archeologist* 75(3–4): 173–236.

1998 Oneota Horizons: A La Crosse Perspective. *The Wisconsin Archeologist* 79(2):196–226.

Boszhardt, Robert F., James P. Gallagher, Thomas Bailey, Robert F. Sasso, and Katherine Stevenson

1984 *Archaeological Investigations at the Mouth of Sand Lake Coulee: The 1982 Season.* Report of Investigations Number 8. Mississippi Valley Archaeology Center, University of Wisconsin–La Crosse.

Bray, Robert T.

1961 The Flynn Cemetery: An Orr Focus Oneota Burial Site in Allamakee County. *Journal of the Iowa Archeological Society* 10(4):15–25.

1991 The Utz Site: An Oneota Village in Central Missouri. *The Missouri Archaeologist* 52.

Brown, Ian W.

1989 The Calumet Ceremony in the Southeast and Its Archaeological Manifestations. *American Antiquity* 54:311–331.

Chapman, Carl H.
1959 The Little Osage and Missouri Indian Village Sites, ca. 1727–1777 A.D. *The Missouri Archaeologist* 21(1):1–67.
1980 *The Archaeology of Missouri, II.* University of Missouri Press, Columbia.

Chapman, Carl H., Leonard W. Blake, Robert T. Bray, T. M. Hamilton, Andrea A. Hunter, Deborah M. Pearsall, James H. Purdue, Eric E. Voigt, Robert P. Wiegers, and Jeffrey K. Yelton
1985 *Osage and Missouri Indian Life Cultural Change: 1675–1825.* Final Performance Report on National Endowment for the Humanities Research Grant RS-20296. On file, Division of American Archaeology, University of Missouri–Columbia.

Chapman, Carl H., and Eleanor F. Chapman
1964 *Indians and Archaeology of Missouri.* Missouri Handbook No. 6. University of Missouri Press, Columbia.

Chamberlain, George
1936 The Story of the Camden Vase: Made at a Time When the Sioux Indians Were Mound Builders. *Club Dial (Contemporary Club, White Plains, N.Y.)* 9(6):15–16, 37–38.
1942 The Story of the Camden Vase. *The Minnesota Archaeologist* 8(4):182–183.

Charles, Douglas K.
1995 Diachronic Regional Social Dynamics: Mortuary Sites in the Illinois Valley/American Bottom Region. In *Regional Approaches to Mortuary Analysis,* edited by Lane Beck, pp. 77–99. Plenum, New York.

Charles, Douglas K., and Jane E. Buikstra
1983 Archaic Mortuary Sites in the Central Mississippi Drainage: Distribution, Structure, and Behavioral Implications. In *Archaic Hunters and Gatherers in the American Midwest,* edited by James L. Phillips and James A. Brown, pp. 117–145. Academic Press, New York.

Doershuk, John F., and Kayla D. Resnick
2008 Gillett Grove: A 17th-Century Oneota Site in Northwest Iowa. *Iowa Archeological Society Newsletter* 58(3):4–5.

Dobbs, Clark A.
1984 Oneota Origins and Development: The Radiocarbon Evidence. In *Oneota Studies,* edited by Guy E. Gibbon, pp. 91–106. Publications in Anthropology No. 1. University of Minnesota, Minneapolis.

Emerson, Thomas E.
1999 The Langford Tradition and the Process of Tribalization on the Middle Mississippian Borders. *Midcontinental Journal of Archaeology* 24(1):3–55.

2012 Cahokia Interaction and Ethnogenesis in the Northern Midcontinent. In *The Oxford Handbook of North American Archaeology,* edited by Timothy R. Pauketat, pp. 398–409. University of Oxford Press, Oxford and New York.

Emerson, Thomas E., and James A. Brown
1992 The Late Prehistory and Protohistory of Illinois. In *Calumet and Fleur-de-Lys: Archaeology of Indian and French Contact in the Midcontinent,* edited by John A. Walthall and Thomas E. Emerson, pp. 203–240. Smithsonian Institution Press, Washington, D.C.

Foley Winkler, Kathleen
2011 *Oneota and Langford Mortuary Practices from Eastern Wisconsin and Northeast Illinois,* Vol. 1 Ph.D. dissertation, Department of Anthropology, University of Wisconsin–Milwaukee. Proquest, Ann Arbor, Michigan.

Fowke, Gerhard
1910 *Antiquities of Central and Southeastern Missouri.* Bulletin 37. Bureau of American Ethnology, Washington, D.C.

Gallagher, James P., Roland L. Rodell, and Katherine P. Stevenson
1982 *The 1980–1982 La Crosse Area Archaeological Survey.* Reports of Investigations Number 2. Mississippi Valley Archaeology Center, University of Wisconsin–La Crosse.

Gibbon, Guy E.
1972 The Walker Hooper Site: A Grand River Phase Oneota Site in Green Lake County. *The Wisconsin Archeologist* 53(4):149–290.

Green, William
1993 Examining Protohistoric Depopulation in the Upper Midwest. *The Wisconsin Archeologist* 74(1–4):290–323.

Griffin, James B.
1945 An Unusual Oneota Vessel from Minnesota. *American Antiquity* 11:120–121.

Hall, Robert
1997 *An Archaeology of the Soul: North American Indian Belief and Ritual.* University of Illinois Press, Urbana.

Harvey, Amy E.
1979 *Oneota Culture in Northwestern Iowa.* Report 12. Office of the State Archaeologist, University of Iowa, Iowa City.

Henning, Dale R.
1961 Oneota Ceramics in Iowa. *Journal of the Iowa Archeological Society* 11(2):3–64.
1970 Development and Interrelationships of the Oneota Culture in the Lower Missouri River Valley. *The Missouri Archaeologist* 32:1–180.
1982 *Evaluative Investigations of Three Landmark Sites in Northwest Iowa.* Luther College Archaeological Research Center, Decorah, Iowa.

1985   Blood Run Excavations - 1985. *Iowa Archeological Society Newsletter* 35(3)115:1–2.

1998a The Oneota Tradition. In *Archaeology of the Great Plains*, W. Raymond Wood, editor, pp. 345–414. University Press of Kansas, Lawrence.

1998b Oneota: The Western Manifestations. *The Wisconsin Archeologist* 79(2):238–247.

2003   The Archeology and History of Ioway/Oto Exchange Patterns, 1650–1700. *Journal of the Iowa Archeological Society* 50:199–221.

2011   What Might We Learn from the Mounds on Blood Run? *Newsletter of the Iowa Archeological Society* 61(2):8–10.

n.d. Analysis of Artifacts from the Correctionville Villages. Manuscript in personal files.

Henning, Dale R., and Martin Q. Peterson

1965   Rearticulated Burials from the Upper Iowa River Valley. *Journal of the Iowa Archeological Society* 13:1–16.

Henning, Dale R., and Shirley J. Schermer

2004   Blood Run Archaeological Investigations. In *Central Siouans in the Northeastern Plains: Oneota Archaeology and the Blood Run Site*. Dale R. Henning and Thomas D. Thiessen, editors. *Plains Anthropologist Memoir* 36:399–434.

Henning, Dale R., and Thomas D. Thiessen, editors

2004   Central Siouans in the Northeastern Plains: Oneota Archaeology and the Blood Run Site. *Plains Anthropologist Memoir* 36:339–591.

Henning, Dale R., and Thomas D. Thiessen

2004   Regional Prehistory. In *Central Siouans in the Northeastern Plains: Oneota Archaeology and the Blood Run Site*. Dale R. Henning and Thomas D. Thiessen, editors. *Plains Anthropologist Memoir* 36:381–398.

Holley, George R., and Michael G. Michlovic

2013   The Camden Style: A Glimpse into Late Prehistoric Mortuary Patterns in the Prairies of Minnesota and South Dakota. Paper presented at the 71st Annual Plains Anthropological Conference, Loveland, Colorado.

Jeske, John A.

1927   The Grand River Mound Group and Camp Site. *Bulletin of the Public Museum of the City of Milwaukee* 3(2).

Jeske, Robert J.

2000   The Washington Irving Site: Langford Tradition Adaptation in Northern Illinois. In *Mounds, Modoc, and Mesoamerica: Papers in Honor of Melvin L. Fowler*, edited by S. R. Ahler, pp. 265–294. Scientific Papers 28. Illinois State Museum, Springfield.

2003   Langford and Fisher Ceramic Traditions: Moiety, Ethnicity or Power Relations in the Upper Midwest? In *A Deep-Time Perspective: Studies in Symbols, Meaning, and the Archaeological Record: Papers in Honor of Robert L. Hall*, edited by J. D. Richards and M. L. Fowler. *The Wisconsin Archeologist* 84(1–2):165–180.

Keyes, Charles R.

1921   Notes, Milford site, July 13, 1921. Spirit Lake Region. Field Notes. Book R, Keyes Collection. On file, Office of the State Archaeologist, The University of Iowa, Iowa City.

1926   Field Notes of July 7–14, 1926. On file, Office of the State Archaeologist, The University of Iowa, Iowa City.

Kreisa, Paul K.

1999   Oneota Mounds. Paper presented at the 64th Annual Meeting of the Society for American Archaeology, Chicago.

Leaf, Gary R.

1976   The Function of the Old Fort in Central Missouri Oneota Subsistence and Settlement Systems. *Plains Anthropologist* 21:93–110.

Lueck, Edward J., R. Peter Winham, L. Adrian Hannus, and Lynnette Rossum.

1995   The Map, of the Map, of the Map, of the Map: Tracking the Blood Run Archaeological Site. *Journal of the Iowa Archeological Society* 42:21–43.

Lothson, Gordon A.

1972   Burial Mounds of the Mille Lacs Lake Area Unpublished Master's thesis, Department of Anthropology, University of Minnesota, Minneapolis.

Mallam, R. Clark

1976   *The Iowa Effigy Mound Manifestation: An Interpretive Model*. Report No. 9. Office of the State Archaeologist, University of Iowa, Iowa City.

Mallam, R. Clark, and E. Arthur Bettis III

1979   *Mound Investigations in Garnavillo Township, Clayton County, Iowa*. Research Papers 4(2). Office of the State Archaeologist, University of Iowa, Iowa City.

Maxwell, Moreau S.

1950   A Change in the Interpretation of Wisconsin's Prehistory. *Wisconsin Magazine of History* 33:427–443.

Mazrim, Robert, and Duane Esarey

2007   Rethinking the Dawn of History: The Schedule, Signature, and Agency of European Goods in Protohistoric Illinois. *Midcontinental Journal of Archaeology* 32:145–200.

McKern, Will C.

1945   Preliminary Report on the Upper Mississippi Phase in Wisconsin. *Bulletin of the Public Museum of the City of Milwaukee* 16(3):109–285.

McKusick, Marshall

1973   *The Grant Oneota Village*. Report No. 4. Office of the State Archaeologist, University of Iowa, Iowa City.

Meleen, Elmer E.
  1968   A Preliminary Report of the Mitchell Indian Village
          Site and Burial Mounds on Firesteel Creek Mitchell,
          Davison County, South Dakota. Reprinted. Columbia,
          Missouri. Originally published 1938, Archaeological
          Studies, Circular No. II, Part I. University of South
          Dakota Museum, Vermillion.

Mott, Mildred
  1938   The Relation of Historic Indian Tribes to
          Archaeological Manifestations in Iowa. Iowa Journal of
          History and Politics 36(3):227–314.

O'Brien, Michael J., and W. Raymond Wood
  1998   The Prehistory of Missouri. University of Missouri
          Press.

Overstreet, David F.
  1995   The Eastern Wisconsin Oneota Regional
          Continuity. In Oneota Archaeology: Past, Present, and
          Future, edited by William Green, pp. 33–64. Report
          20. Office of the State Archaeologist, University of
          Iowa, Iowa City.
  1997   Oneota Prehistory and History. The Wisconsin
          Archeologist 78(1&2):250–296.

Penman, John T., and Norman C. Sullivan
  1995   Late Prehistoric Mortuary Practices in the Upper
          Mississippi Valley. The Minnesota Archaeologist
          54:130–141.

Pettigrew, Frederick W.
  1889   The Silent City. Pettigrew map curated by
          Siouxland Heritage Museums, Sioux Falls, South
          Dakota.

Ready, Timothy
  1979   Ogechie Series. In A Handbook of Minnesota
          Prehistoric Ceramics, edited by Scott F. Anfinson,
          pp. 143–148. Occasional Publications in Minnesota
          Anthropology No. 5. Minnesota Archaeological
          Society, Fort Snelling.

Rosebrough, Amy L.
  2010   Every Family a Nation: A Deconstruction and
          Reconstruction of the Effigy Mound "Culture" of
          the Western Great Lakes of North America. Ph.d.
          dissertation, Department of Anthropology,
          University of Wisconsin–Madison. Proquest, Ann
          Arbor, Michigan.

Sasso, Robert F.
  1993   La Crosse Region Oneota Adaptations: Changing
          Late Prehistoric Subsistence and Settlement Patterns
          in the Upper Mississippi Valley. The Wisconsin
          Archeologist 74(1–4):324–369.

Schermer, Shirley J.
  2004   Human Osteology. In Dhegihan and Chiwere
          Siouans in the Plains: Historical and Archaeological
          Perspectives, edited by Dale R. Henning and
          Thomas D. Thiessen, pp. 435–524. Memoir 36. Plains
          Anthropologist 49(192) part 2.

Schermer, Shirley J., Linda Forman, Robin M. Lillie, Jill
  Robinson, and Larry Zimmerman
  1998   NAGPRA Inventory and Consultation: Human
          Remains and Funerary Objects in the Charles R. Keyes
          Collection. Research Papers 23(1). Office of the State
          Archaeologist, University of Iowa, Iowa City.

Schirmer, Ronald C.
  2016   Radiocarbon Dating Early Oneota Sites in
          Southern Minnesota. Research Report, Department
          of Anthropology, Minnesota State University,
          Mankato.

Spargo, Lise
  1984   The Milford Site (13DK1), an Oneota Component
          in Dickinson County, Iowa. Manuscript on file. Office
          of the State Archaeologist, University of Iowa, Iowa
          City.

Starr, Frederick
  1887   Mounds and Lodge Circles in Iowa. American
          Antiquarian 9:361–363.
  1893   Mound Explorations in Northwestern Iowa.
          Proceedings of the Davenport Academy of Natural
          Sciences 5(1885–1889):110–112.
  1895   Summary of the Archaeology of Iowa. Proceedings
          of the Davenport Academy of Natural Sciences
          6(1897):98–100.

Streiff, Jan
  1994a   Cooper Mound No. 2 (21ML16). In Health,
          Demography, and Archaeology of Mille Lacs Native
          American Mortuary Populations, by Arthur C.
          Aufderheide, Elden Johnson and Odin Langsjoen.
          Memoir 28. Plains Anthropologist 39(149):313–315.
  1994b   Cooper Mound No. 3 (21ML16). In Health,
          Demography, and Archaeology of Mille Lacs Native
          American Mortuary Populations, by Arthur C.
          Aufderheide, Elden Johnson and Odin Langsjoen.
          Memoir 28. Plains Anthropologist 39(149):315–317.

Thomas, Cyrus
  1894   Report on the Mounds Explorations of the Bureau
          of Ethnology. 12th Annual Report of the Bureau
          of Ethnology 1890–91, pp. 3–742. Smithsonian
          Institution, Washington, D.C.

Tiffany, Joseph T.
  1982   Hartley Fort Ceramics. Proceedings of the Iowa
          Academy of Science 89:133–150.

Tiffany, Joseph A., and Duane C. Anderson
  1993   The Milford Site (13DK1): A Postcontact Village in
          Northwest Iowa. In Prehistory and Human Ecology
          of the Western Prairies and Northern Plains, edited
          by Joseph A. Tiffany, pp. 283–306. Memoir 27. Plains
          Anthropologist 38(145).

Wedel, Mildred M.
  1959   Oneota Sites on the Upper Iowa River. The
          Missouri Archaeologist 21(2–4).

1981   The Ioway, Oto, and Omaha Indians in 1700.
        Journal of the Iowa Archeological Society 28:1–13.

1986   Peering at the Ioway Indians through the Mist of
        Time: 1650–Circa 1700. *Journal of the Iowa Archeological
        Society* 23:1–74.

West, E.P.

1882   Archaeological Exploration of the Missouri River.
        Kansas City Review of Science and Industry 7:290–93.

Wilford, Lloyd A.

1941   A Tentative Classification of the Prehistoric
        Cultures of Minnesota. *American Antiquity* (6):231–
        249.

Wilford, Lloyd A., Elden Johnson, and Joan Vicinus

1969   *Burial Mounds of Central Minnesota.* Minnesota
        Prehistoric Archaeology Series No 1. Minnesota
        Historical Society, St. Paul.

Wood, W. Raymond

1973   Culture Sequence at the Old Fort, Saline County,
        Missouri. *American Antiquity* 38:101–11.

Yelton, Jeffery A.

1998   A Different View of Oneota Taxonomy and
        Origins in the Lower Missouri Valley. *The Wisconsin
        Archeologist* 79(2):268–283.

Recognition for Wisconsin Archeologists in 2016

Compiled by Constance Arzigian

The Wisconsin Archeologist is pleased to acknowledge the work of four archaeologists who were recognized by regional professional organizations in 2016 for their contributions:

- **Alice Kehoe**, 2016 Distinguished Service Award by the Plains Anthropological Conference

- **David F. Overstreet**, 2016 Distinguished Career Award from the Midwest Archaeological Conference

- **James L. Theler**, 2016 Distinguished Career Award from the Midwest Archaeological Conference

- **Dan Wendt**, Increase A. Lapham Award from The Wisconsin Archeological Society

Alice Kehoe, Emeritus Professor at Marquette Univrsity, was honored with the 2016 Distinguished Service Award by the Plains Anthropological Conference. "The award, for 'research, teaching, and scholarship,' recognizes her 'enduring work in Anthropology and Archaeology' and, not on the plaque, her persistence, in sisterhood with several other women of her generation, in breaking the opposition to women working professionally" (*Central States Anthropological Society Bulletin* 51(2):8).

David F. Overstreet, received the 2016 Distinguished Service Award from the Midwest Archaeological Conference (MAC) for his long and varied career. He served as a professor at the University of Wisconsin–Waukesha, Marquette University, and College of the Menominee Nation, as well as a contract archaeologist, founding and serving as CEO of Great Lakes Archaeological Research Center, Inc., where many of today's active archaeologists have gained invaluable experience. Research has included Early Paleoindian archaeology in Wisconsin, definition of the Eastern Oneota Regional Continuity, and the Wolf River Complex and associated garden bed sites on the Menominee Indian Reservation. In "retirement" Dave continues to work with the Menominee Nation, serves as a mentor to former students, and on University of Wisconsin–Milwaukee PhD advising committees. (Adapted from John D. Richards and Patricia B. Richards, nomination letter to MAC Board of Directors 2016.)

David Overstreet (left) receiving award from Robert Jeske, President of MAC, at the 2016 Midwest Archaeological Conference in Iowa City.

Constance Arzigian, University of Wisconsin–La Crosse

The Wisconsin Archeologist, 2016, 97(2):121–122

James L. Theler received the 2016 Distinguished Service Award from MAC for his legacy as a teacher, mentor, and steward of archaeology and science at the University of Wisconsin–La Crosse, and for his scholary contributions to the prehistory of the Upper Midwest. His research has focused on faunal analysis for prehistoric diet and subsistence behavior, and reconstruction of past environments. He is one of only a few experts on the identificatoin and analysis of land snails, and has contributed his expertise to many archaeological and environmental studies. His works have appeared both in professional journals, and, with colleague Robert "Ernie" Boszhardt, a 2003 book *Twelve Millennia: Archaeology of the Upper Mississippi River Valley*, that presents archaeological research to the general public. Now "retired" and an emeritus professor, Jim continues his research and publications on regional studies of land snails and interpretations of faunal remains from archaeological sites. He remains active in working with students and colleagues. (Adapted from Matthew G. Hill and Joseph A. Tiffany, nomination letter to MAC Board of Directors 2016.)

Dan Wendt received the Increase A. Lapham Award in 2016 for a long and diverse record of archaeological research contributions. Dan's professional career was spent as a chemical engineer, and his avocational archaeology studies are based on rigorous scientific observation and testing that reflect this background. He first published in 1985 on Paleoindian localities, then with the Institute for Minnesota Archaeology in the 1980s on Oneota site resources in the Red Wing locality. By the early 2000s he had initiated a long-term archaeological survey of various counties in northwest Wisconsin and identified hundreds of sites in the region, preparing detailed reports of results. He is an expert flintknapper and has added over 2,400 specimens to the Minnesota Historical Society lithic comparative collection, with identification key and photomicrographs. Research on Knife Lake Siltstone led to the identification of a series of workshops. In "retirement" he continues to work with professional and avocational archaeologists and students, providing his unique contributions. (Adapted from Robert "Ernie" Boszhardt letter to the Wisconsin Archeological Society Awards Committee.)

James L. Theler (left) receiving award from Robert Jeske, President of MAC, at the 2016 Midwest Archaeological Conference, Iowa City.

Dan Wendt (right) receiving Lapham award from Kurt Sampson, President of the Wisconsin Archaeological Society, at the spring meeting, May 21, 2016, at Lake Emily, Wisconsin.